REINVENTING CH

Reinventing China
A Generation and Its Films

Paul Clark

The Chinese University Press

Reinventing China: A Generation and Its Films
By Paul J. A. Clark

© **The Chinese University of Hong Kong**, 2005

ISBN 962–996–230–6

THE CHINESE UNIVERSITY PRESS
The Chinese University of Hong Kong
SHA TIN, N.T., HONG KONG
Fax: +852 2603 6692
    +852 2603 7355
E-mail: cup@cuhk.edu.hk
Web-site: www.chineseupress.com

Printed in Hong Kong

Illustrations are reproduced with the kind permission of
the respective producers and directors.
Cover photo: Gong Li in *Judou*, courtesy of the
China Film Corporation.

Contents

—⁓⁓—

Acknowledgments

—⚊—

The idea for this book came as I was standing waist-deep in the Pacific Ocean at the quiet end of Waikiki Beach in December 1985. I turned to Chen Kaige and Zhang Yimou and remarked: "I should write my next book about you and your classmates." The long journey from there to here has been made a joy by the kindness of many people. First I thank the ten filmmakers portrayed here for generously sharing their stories over many years. As the notes show, other Chinese filmmakers have also contributed much to the project. Chris Berry has been a fine friend and inspiration through his own work on Chinese film. Bonnie McDougall read the earliest version of the manuscript and has always offered encouragement. As an old friend, Tony Rayns continues to share his enthusiasm for Chinese cinema.

Wu Tianming, Luo Xueying, John Ching, He Jianjun, Ni Zhen, Xie Fei, Chen Huaikai, Donald Richie and Sharon Yamamoto are among those to offer help and advice. Teachers and mentors have in their various ways over the years made this book possible. They include Keith Sinclair, Nicholas Tarling, Michael Bassett, John King Fairbank, Patrick Hanan, Mary Bitterman and Bryce Harland. My colleague Zhou Xuelin read an earlier draft and made insightful comments. Colleagues at the East-West Center in Honolulu and at The University of Auckland offered support and tolerated my distraction. A Wang Fellowship in Chinese Studies funded an early period of the research. Esther Tsang has been an ideal editor. Paul Yee and Jeff Lau lived at different stages with the project and offered warm understanding. The errors in what follows are mine alone. All of the above have tried, directly or otherwise, to make this a better book and I thank them.

Introduction

—ɯ—

In the 1980s a new group of Chinese filmmakers burst into international cinema with a series of unprecedented films of great color and strength. Chen Kaige's *The Yellow Earth* announced the arrival of major new talent from a country whose films were mostly unknown and always dismissed as propaganda. When Zhang Yimou won the top prize at the 1988 Berlin International Film Festival for his debut feature *Red Sorghum*, the film world sat up and took notice. This book offers a history of these films and their makers. Their importance lay not just in the world-wide acclaim but in the unusual ways in which these filmmakers re-examined their own histories and that of their culture and nation. They in effect set out to reinvent China.

China in the 1980s underwent a remarkable transformation. The dull and frequently disastrous days of Maoist excess, still alive in people's memories of the Cultural Revolution (1966–76), gave way to a more diverse and, for some, more unpredictable time. The Cultural Revolution had been a powerful experience for almost all Chinese, even those unscathed by political campaigns of criticism. Millions of young people had been sent out of the cities to less developed parts of the country. Some spent years in this rural exile; others managed to find ways to return to urban homes, though not to resume their interrupted educations. The empty rhetoric of the official media had turned many Chinese into hearty skeptics, liable to discount anything that aspired to the status of art or entertainment. More exciting were the new entertainments and ideas being imported from abroad, as China's leaders promoted economic reform and further "opening up" to the world.

The combination of political bankruptcy of the last ten years of Mao

Zedong's rule with the new ideas and opportunities arising in the new, reform era produced a major shift in cultural production. Much of the new fiction, poetry and essays had roots in underground writings that had circulated in the late Cultural Revolution among young intellectuals, often newly returned from the countryside. The new era gave these thinking young Chinese the means to publish their new works. The bombast of the Cultural Revolution made inevitable a push to reassess how the excesses of those years had had so much currency. Was it Mao's fault or were there deeper cultural wells for those events that needed to be acknowledged, so that they might not happen again? At the same time, the obsessions with the legacy of the Cultural Revolution rapidly lost importance, as the new opportunities and ideas helped reshape the cultural landscape. But an opening to the rest of the world also raised issues of national character and identity. The new-style literature and art, along with the availability of translations of foreign works and ways of interpreting the world, reflected an effort to redefine notions of China, its society and its cultural inheritance.

Films were slow to become part of this new cultural endeavor. Most films in the early 1980s were based on scripts written some years before, when new fiction picked at the wounds of the Cultural Revolution, often telling maudlin stories of sacrifice and suffering. Real change in films had to wait until a new generation of filmmakers, shaped by Cultural Revolution experiences, seized opportunities in the studios to present striking new images of their cultural and historical legacies. This book tells the story of these young men and women and their remarkable achievement in the 1980s and subsequently to reinvent China.

In any country film is a vital component of popular culture. Even in North Korea, feature films provide some color in otherwise difficult lives as well as conveying the views of the Pyongyang leadership. Taleban-governed Afghanistan was perhaps the one place on earth where film had no place in popular culture, though the penetration of the video-cassette player probably undermined that assumption. As an art as well as an industry, film lends itself to analysis from aesthetic, social and political perspectives. In China, from the Communist Party victory in 1949 until the twenty-fold increase in television ownership in the 1980s, films were a major means of creating a mass, socialist culture directed from Beijing.

In nationalizing the film studios and redirecting filmmakers after 1949 to a new aesthetic, the cultural authorities largely rejected the earlier achievements of Chinese film artists. Films arrived on Chinese soil at about the same time as they reached, say, Cincinnati, and since then most films shown in China have been imported, even at times when Communist China appeared closed off from the rest of the world. Despite market domination by Hollywood, in the 1930s and 1940s politically progressive artists in the Shanghai studios produced works of great artistic invention and social relevance. The Communist authorities approved of the social commitment evident in these films, while requiring artists (starting in the 1950s) to reach a much wider, national audiences with films endorsing the new regime.

The results of this re-orientation were mixed. Many of the filmmakers had worked in Shanghai before 1949 and tried to preserve the qualities of earlier films, only to be condemned for bourgeois thinking. The new political demands generally encouraged simplification of plot, characters and artistry. Most stories had clear beginnings and rose to a climax before a satisfying denouement in which good (in any modern story, Communist good) triumphed. Protagonists were obviously good or bad, although at some points in the three decades after 1949 certain characters could start out apparently bad or uncertain and be converted to goodness. Cinematic flourishes like flashbacks were rare, for fear mass audiences, unfamiliar with the medium, might be confused. Themes and messages were conveyed chiefly through dialogue, rather than by images and mood. Films made in the mid-1970s, at the end of the Cultural Revolution, took these qualities to extremes, epitomized by one film featuring a deaf and dumb soldier assigned to be a telephone operator who eventually learns to communicate (somewhat vital for her career) under the care of the Communist Party. Although filmmakers returning to activity in the early 1980s revived the industry and began to find less false screen voices, Chinese film art, like much of art and literature by the end of the Cultural Revolution, had reached something close to exhaustion.

Meanwhile Chinese society and economic organization were changing rapidly. During the Cultural Revolution years many Chinese at all levels in society, realizing the limitations imposed by the existing system, began to recognize the need for change. In this respect the Cultural Revolution marked a sea change in modern Chinese history as significant as the war against Japan. After 1978 Deng Xiaoping promulgated economic reform, including greater involvement in world trade and increased private production and consumption in the rural and urban sectors. The results were spectacular. Ordinary urban Chinese by the 1980s had begun to eat more food in wider variety. Consumer goods like television sets, tape recorders and cameras allowed people to take advantage of broadening choices in recreation. Many younger artists and writers engaged in a "cultural fever" (*wenhua re*) in which discussions covered such matters as the relationships between modern art and Chinese tradition, the true nature of that tradition, and the disjunctions between Marxist principles and ancient Chinese philosophies. A cultural "search for roots" encouraged interest in tribal and non-Han Chinese traditions.

The films coming out of the studios changed also. Starting in 1984, a series of new films emerged that bore limited resemblance to the simplifications and absolute clarity typical of earlier works. The new films were often dense, obscure examinations of life on the margins of Chinese society that relied on images and music to carry their themes and impacts and challenged their audiences to think. For the first time in seventy years of Chinese filmmaking, foreign critics and film-goers began to take an interest in films and film artists from that country.

A distinctive group of young artists were responsible for the new films. Most had been unable to complete their high-school educations during the Cultural Revolution, being sent instead to communes and factories, often far from their homes. Enrolment about ten years later in 1978 at the Beijing Film Academy, then China's only film school, was an opportunity to return to the cities and to gain the artistic means to express their thinking about their experience and society. The films they made after graduation in 1982 were unprecedented, creating a "New Wave" in Chinese cinema. The group and their films were so distinctive that they were almost immediately identified as a new, distinctive generation of artists. A broad calculation back to the 1920s produced the novel idea that this was the "fifth generation of Chinese filmmakers."[1]

This book examines the histories of this generation of artists and discusses their films with two purposes: to better appreciate some extraordinary works of invention and artistry and in order to gain a broader understanding of the nature of change in China in the second half of the twentieth century. The study is divided into three parts. In the first, the stories of ten filmmakers prior to entering film school in 1978 are told in the form of a shared or group biography. They include directors like Chen Kaige and Zhang Yimou, who won international praise for their work. But they also include Liu Miaomiao, the youngest member of the group, who remained relatively unknown even in China. This mix of the famous and the obscure derives from our purpose to construct a history of the broad dynamics of Chinese cultural change: the mix should enrich understanding. In the middle section of the book, the students' crucial four years together at film school are outlined. The third part discusses the work of each of the filmmakers until the 1990s. It makes no special claims to the utility of an auteurist approach, but simply chooses to view developments through the continuing histories of these individuals. This part ends by introducing other members of this generation, who did not attend film school with them, and outlines their impact on older filmmakers.

The histories presented here come to an end in the 1990s. By the turn of the twenty-first century, globalization and the growth of the market meant Chinese had even more choices in entertainment, employment and even life-style. The obsessions with history and the Cultural Revolution that had shaped the 1980s now seemed distinctly old-fashioned. Artists needed to change with the times and the fifth-generation filmmakers now formed the core artistic personnel in the industry. Rising commercial pressures, and the near bankruptcy of the state-owned studios, caused most of the filmmakers to adjust their work to the new requirements to satisfy a broader domestic audience less inclined to bother watching Chinese-made films. Some directors, like Zhang Yimou and Chen Kaige, managed to find production support from abroad to continue in the special vein they had explored since film school. Others made careers in television production. All the fifth generation, despite their different paths in the 1990s, could look back on an extraordinary window of time that produced some remarkable films. This book seeks to open that window.

Part One

FLASHBACKS:
The Cultural Revolution Generation

—〰—

The Beijing Film Academy's class of '82 consisted of more than 150 graduates in five departments: acting, art direction, cinematography, directing and sound recording. In addition, there were other men and women active in the film industry whose age, experience and outlooks qualified them as members of the fifth generation. Childhoods in the relatively optimistic though politically-charged 1950s and early 1960s were generally happy times. For several of these future filmmakers, lives of relative privilege were spent with caring parents, some of whom had public profiles. After 1966 this comfort came to an end. Several saw their parents taken away for interrogation or punishment for alleged misdeeds, often allegedly committed before their children had been born. Schooling stopped or was highly disrupted. Self-education became a habit for several of these teenagers.

After 1968 the seminal experience in shaping this generation of artists took place: being sent to the countryside "to learn from the peasants." Rural exile and efforts to escape their assignments forged a determination that lay at the heart of their future achievements. Many had managed to shift back to urban homes by the mid-1970s, as the Cultural Revolution came to an end with the death of Mao Zedong in September 1976 and the arrest of his widow and her associates the following month. The restoration of nationwide university entrance examinations in 1978 offered the Cultural Revolution generation a chance to regain formal education. The Beijing Film Academy's class of '82 were no exception.

What follows is the outline of a collective biography, based on the recollections of ten classmates who entered the academy in the fall of 1978. These ten stories cannot adequately represent the full range of fifth-generation personal histories. Eight of the students represented here entered the directing department. Three of the ten are women: a higher proportion than the number of women in the academy class or active in the film studios. Some of the subjects were the most prominent members of their group, who gained an international reputation for their films. Others were little known, or charitably, in the 1980s had yet to make their mark.

In alphabetical order, the ten persons whose stories make up this generational biography are:

Chen Kaige: born in Beijing in 1952, director of *The Yellow Earth* (1984), *Farewell, My Concubine* (1993), *The Emperor and the Assassin* (1998), among other films.

Hu Mei: female, born in Beijing in 1957, director of *Army Nurse* (1986), *Far from War* (1988) and television historical serials.

Jiang Haiyang: born in Shanghai in 1955, director of *The Anonymous Phonecall* (1988), among other films and television dramas.

Liu Miaomiao: female, born in Ningxia, northwest China in 1962 and the youngest member of the class of '82. Director of *The Sound of Hoofbeats* (1990) and *Innocent Babbler* (1992), among other films and television works.

Peng Xiaolian: female, born in Shanghai in 1953, director of *Three Women* (1988), among other films. Later graduate of New York University film school and maker of documentaries.

Tian Zhuangzhuang: born in Beijing in 1952, director of *Horse Thief* (1986) and *The Blue Kite* (1992), among other films. Producer at the Beijing Film Studio.

Wu Ziniu: born in Sichuan province in 1953, director of *Evening Bell* (1988), and *The Nanjing Massacre* (1995), among other works.

Zhang Jianya: born in Shanghai in 1951, director of *Ice River* (1986), *San Mao Joins the Army* (1992) and *Crash Landing* (1999), among others. Producer at the Shanghai Film Studio.

Zhang Li: born in Beidaihe, north China in 1957, cinematographer and one-time husband of Liu Miaomiao.

Zhang Yimou: born in Xi'an in 1950, cinematographer of *The Yellow Earth* (1984), director of *Red Sorghum* (1987), *Judou* (1989), *Raise the Red Lantern* (1992), *The Road Home* (2000), *Hero* (2001), and *House of Flying Daggers* (2004), among other films.

A collective biography is possible because these ten classmates shared a lot of experiences growing up in Mao's China. Nine of the ten were "educated youths" (*zhishi qingnian*), sent to the countryside, factories or the army when their high schooling ended in 1968. This experience lies at the heart of the group's artistic achievements after graduation from film school in 1982. Rustication forced these young men and women to examine critically the political and social system that had curtailed their formal education and sent them to often remote places to labor in fields or workshops.

Details in these personal stories have a special eloquence. The dates many of these people recall mark the important events of these years. Hu Mei remembers exactly the day she was driven as a child past Tian'anmen Square and saw Red Guards massing to see Chairman Mao. Wu Ziniu committed to memory the date he was sent to a semi-militarized unit on a huge commune to haul boatloads of fertilizer up a river. Tian Zhuangzhuang, like several others, can cite the day he was accepted into the Chinese Communist Party. Zhang Yimou can identify the winter day when he bought his first still camera. Just about all these filmmakers recall with special clarity the day they received official notification of acceptance into the Beijing Film Academy.

The ten people presented here all had interesting stories to tell and a willingness to relate them over a period, mostly from 1985 to 1992, in Beijing, Shanghai, Xi'an, Fuzhou, Hong Kong, Honolulu and New York. I have heard many more histories of this group of filmmakers, but these are the ones told with the greatest vividness and even urgency.[1]

There is an ancient Chinese cultural habit of recording and compiling histories, which are used to provide lessons for the present. An inclination to moralistic teleology may have lasted longer in Chinese views of history than in those of other societies, for the German teleologies of Marx and Engels have reinforced this tendency. In grouping the stories of these ten lives before entering film school in 1978, I have tried to avoid foreshadowing the subsequent, sometimes remarkable, careers of any of these three women and seven men.

These ten stories form part of the mythology of a group that turned these histories into a significant cultural phenomenon. The films that these ten people, their classmates and others from their generation went on to produce were a major component in the reinvention of contemporary Chinese culture in a brief moment in the 1980s. Bloodshed on the night of 3–4 June 1989, mostly of a younger generation with very different histories, brought some of this effort (at least in its public manifestations) to a close. Subsequent economic growth and rampant consumerism changed China more obviously than any film or army tank. The following collective biography helps explain a cultural phenomenon that had deep roots.[2]

1. Children of Mao

The seventeen years between the founding of the People's Republic in 1949 and 1966 came to be remembered (or reconstructed by those who had no direct experience of these years) as a sharp contrast with China during the ten years of the Cultural Revolution and the era of economic reform that followed to the turn of the millennium. This period came to be regarded as a "golden age" when idealism and service characterized public life. The picture of the 1950s and early 1960s that emerges from an examination of the lives of several members of the Beijing Film Academy class of '82 is less idealized. Many future classmates came from somewhat privileged backgrounds, with parents who were filmmakers, teachers, public servants or artists. But in Mao's China privilege also carried risks, as parents became targets of criticism even in the political campaigns of the 1950s, long before the difficulties of 1966.

Two of the more privileged members of the class of '82 were Chen Kaige, future director of *Farewell, My Concubine*, and Hu Mei, one of several accomplished women directors from the group. Hu Mei's father, Hu Defeng, was a celebrated conductor of the People's Liberation Army Central Orchestra. Her mother was also a musician. As a twelve-year-old Hu Defeng had made a dangerous 1,000 kilometer journey through Japanese lines and Nationalist blockade from Shandong to the wartime Communist headquarters in Yan'an. There he became attached to the Eighth Route Army, serving an apprenticeship of sorts as one of the "little red devils."[3] Hu excelled in his studies and was identified as potential officer material. At the Resistance University in Yan'an he was trained for a career in the cultural and propaganda wing of the armed forces. Hu's daughter, the youngest of three children, started piano lessons at an early age and seemed to do well at school too. Western classical music from the stereo record-player or piano (unheard of luxuries for most Chinese at the time) would fill the family apartments in the army barracks at Xiaoxitian, coincidentally near the then campus of the Beijing Film Academy. Her father had some involvement in films through his music. In 1964, for example, he was one of two conductors of the ambitious soundtrack music for *Heroic Sons and Daughters* (*Yingxiong ernü*), a feature film set in the Korean War.[4]

Chen Kaige's parents were directly involved in the film industry. Chen Huaikai, his father, became a film director in 1950. From a carpenter's family in Fujian province in southeast China, Chen senior arrived in Beijing soon after the city's liberation by the Red Army. He was given an assistant director's position at the newly established Beijing Film Studio and a teaching job in the acting department of the film academy. Like most of his generation of Chinese filmmakers, Chen Huaikai crossed the divide between the stage and screen. While studying in the 1940s at the National Drama Academy in Nanjing as a scholarship student, he had met Liu Yanchi, eight years his junior and the daughter of a wealthy construction firm proprietor. Through her participation in patriotic resistance movements among students, Liu Yanchi had been invited to join the Communist Party. She did so in 1946, a fact that stood the family in good stead twenty years later. Chen Huaikai had been encouraged at the drama academy to join the Nationalists. But, after several brushes with the police, who accused him of being a Communist, Chen left the drama academy, where he had become a teacher, and eventually joined the Communist side towards the end of the 1940s civil war. He served as head of a drama troupe in north China. Chen and Liu were married after their move to Beijing. Kaige, their first child, was born in August 1952.[5]

While his father was making a name for himself as a director, particularly of historical dramas and Chinese opera adaptations, and his mother worked as a script editor and consultant, first at the Ministry of Culture's Film Bureau and later at the Beijing Film Studio, Chen Kaige was at school. Like his primary school that had been attached to the Beijing Normal University (teachers college), his junior middle school had a relatively privileged student body. The sons and daughters of government cadres and intellectuals made up a disproportionate number of the students. Several of his schoolmates were offspring of his parents' filmmaking colleagues.

One such boy was Tian Zhuangzhuang, the future director of *The Blue Kite*. One of Tian Zhuangzhuang's first memories of films was sitting in the dark in an auditorium at the Film Bureau in Beijing. His father was a deputy head in the bureau, a section of the Ministry of Culture charged with supervising and censoring film production and distribution. Zhuangzhuang was seven or eight at the time and found it hard to follow the long, two-part Soviet film his father and other colleagues were watching. It was summer time and the room was hot and stuffy. Zhuangzhuang felt dizzy and restless. Eventually he vomited violently over the big stuffed armchair he had been squirming in. For many years after that Tian Zhuangzhuang disliked going to the movies: his stomach never felt right in the dark in front of the bright screen.[6]

Tian's parents were well-known film actors who had been associated with the Communist Party, first in the underground organization among film and theatre people in Shanghai and then in the Communist Party wartime headquarters in Yan'an. Tian Fang had met Yu Lan, an actress from northeast China, in Yan'an in 1938, soon after his arrival there during the Anti-Japanese War. Yu Lan had made her way to Yan'an after finishing high school in Tianjin, southwest of Beijing. Both Tian Fang and Yu Lan started their Yan'an years at the War of Resistance Military and Political University there, the training ground for civilian and army cadres. Quickly proving his leadership qualities, Tian was invited to join the Communist Party. He moved on to serve as head of the stage directing section of the Lu Xun Art Academy Experimental Drama Troupe. Yu Lan, who became a Party member in 1939, joined the troupe in 1940.

Tian Zhuangzhuang's parents began their film careers during the civil war in the northeast after Japan's defeat in 1945. Tian Fang became a leader of the Northeast Film Studio, the first Communist Party-run studio. His duties took him to Xingshan in the extreme north of Heilongjiang province, hard by the Soviet Union. The studio had withdrawn there from Changchun in the central northeast at the start of hostilities between the Nationalist and Red Armies. Meanwhile Yu Lan became a film actress, as well as participating in rural land reform in the region. She had a leading role in *White-Coated Fighter* (*Baiyi zhanshi*), one of the first features made at the studio upon its return to Changchun. Soon after that film's completion, Tian and Yu moved to Beijing: Tian to a career as administrator at the Beijing Film Studio and in the Film Bureau, and Yu to more film acting. Tian Fang continued to act occasionally. Yu Lan in 1951 spent time at the war front in Korea, following the Party direction for artists to experience the lives of workers, peasants, and soldiers. She returned to join a special three-year class at the Central Drama Academy. Their second son, Zhuangzhuang, was born in April 1952.

His was a comfortable childhood, illuminated occasionally by the reflected glory of his parents' achievements. In 1961, for example, his mother won the best actress award at the Moscow International Film Festival for her performance as the long-suffering mother of *A Revolutionary Family* (*Geming jiating*), a film set in the pre-Liberation period.

But eminent parents, even those with long-standing association with the Communist Party, could be a liability. Peng Xiaolian, a directing classmate of Chen Kaige and Tian Zhuangzhuang, had reason to regret her father's past connections. Peng's parents were patricians of the Chinese Communist revolution. Her father, Peng Boshan, served as head of the Party's Shanghai Propaganda Bureau after 1949. This was an important post: Shanghai was the most cosmopolitan city in China. In the Party's eyes, the city's writers, artists and filmmakers were most in need of political guidance and reform to serve the new, socialist order. Peng Boshan's job was to direct this cultural transformation. Peng had first joined the outlawed Red Army in his native Hunan almost twenty years earlier. Later Peng Boshan fled to Shanghai, where the International Settlement offered leftist rebels and criminal elements some sanctuary beyond the reach of the Nationalist government. He became involved with the Communist-front League of Left-Wing Writers. His mentor among the leftist writers was Hu Feng, a disciple of Lu Xun (1881–1936), China's pre-eminent writer of the twentieth century. Lu Xun had been instrumental in creating a new-style, modern Chinese literature in the May Fourth (or New Culture) Movement after 1915. Participation in student protests in 1936–37 against Japanese invasion landed Peng Boshan in a Guomindang (Nationalist) jail. Upon his release, Peng Boshan returned to the hills, joining the New Fourth Army, the Red Army's main force south of the Yangzi River. His education and Communist credentials enabled him to rise to the responsibility of Political Commander of the 24th Army Division.[7]

By the time Peng Boshan marched back into Shanghai and became head of propaganda work in the city, he had married and started a family. His wife, Zhu Weiming, worked as a translator of Russian novels and film scripts. The Pengs' fourth daughter (their fifth child) was born in June 1953 in Shanghai. Peng Xiaolian ("Little Lotus") arrived as the youngest in a happy family of considerable privilege. The Pengs lived in a special compound for high cadres, where the size and relative luxury of the living arrangements set them apart from most other Shanghai residents.

Xiaolian was barely three years old when this world ended. In 1955 her father fell victim in the officially-sponsored campaign of public condemnation directed against the writer Hu Feng. Peng Boshan spent almost a year in prison in the city and then at the end of 1956 was transferred to the countryside in Shanghai county, where a little over two years passed. Worse was to follow: in 1958 Peng Boshan was sent 2,500 kilometers away to the wastes of northwestern Qinghai province, China's Gulag. Xiaolian's childhood was spent without her father, except for his twice yearly visits from Qinghai.

The kind of exile to which Peng Boshan was subjected could have a positive side. Liu Miaomiao, the youngest member of the Beijing Film Academy's class of '82, grew up in the Ningxia Muslim Autonomous Region, a province north of Qinghai. But her school there had been of exceptional quality, thanks to the presence of several teachers from the eastern seaboard. This northwestern province has been notorious for centuries as a destination for internal exile in China. Political opponents and awkward imperial relatives were traditionally sent to the remote northwest. After 1949 the Communist Party regime also found Ningxia and neighboring provinces a useful dumping ground for critics. Many intellectuals who had spoken up in 1956 in response to Chairman Mao's call for "a hundred flowers" to bloom were sent to the underdeveloped towns of Ningxia for being too frank in their public criticisms. Two of Liu Miaomiao's teachers of Chinese literature were graduates of Wuhan University and of Fudan University in Shanghai, among the top Chinese universities. The man who taught her geography had studied at Beijing Normal University and her math teacher had similar qualifications. This was an extraordinary calibre of teacher for so remote a location.[8]

Liu Miaomiao was born in September 1962 in Yinchuan, the capital of Ningxia, a place, as she described it later, "with no grass and no trees." Her father, a Muslim, was a local administrator. Miaomiao's mother was a Han Chinese who had grown up in the northwest. During the War of Resistance to Japan she had been a performer in a travelling propaganda troupe. She later studied law and was appointed a member of the provincial supreme court in Ningxia. Miaomiao herself was the seventh child in a family of eight, and was born when her father was already fifty-one years old. He died in 1971 when his youngest daughter was nine. Headship of the Liu family nominally passed to Liu Miaomiao's eldest brother, who was more than thirty years older than Miaomiao. He was the head of Guyuan county, which formed the southern tongue of Ningxia as it thrust into neighboring Gansu province, along the line of the ancient Silk Road through northwest China.

In Guyuan Liu Miaomiao proved a precocious student, and at eleven advanced to middle school. In her four years there she made a name for herself in the school cultural team, performing songs and dances for her classmates in praise of the wise leadership in Beijing. English classes promised to be a special treat. Liu Miaomiao sat in the front row and solemnly intoned: "I am a worker." After only three weeks, the education authorities replaced English with an Agricultural Knowledge course. In Ningxia opportunities to speak English in the early 1970s were rare at best, but the need for agricultural improvement was great, and the agricultural course catered to the late Cultural Revolution emphasis on practical education. Liu Miaomiao's two English teachers included an elderly, rather sickly scholar who had worked for the State Council, China's cabinet: once he had even interpreted for premier Zhou Enlai. After junior high school, Liu completed one year of senior high before setting off for film school in 1978.

These lives of relative privilege, even when a parent became a political target, were not shared by Zhang Yimou, the most widely known of the fifth-generation filmmakers. Before his emergence on world screens, Zhang had spent most of his life labelled the son of an "anti-revolutionary" political pariah. Zhang's father had been an officer in the Nationalist army before 1949. Zhang senior's brothers had encouraged him to join them in the fight against the Japanese. The three brothers were all graduates of the Huangpu Military Academy, training ground of the Nationalist army's officer corps. Many leaders of the Communists' Red Army had also been trained at Huangpu, near Guangzhou in the south. In the late 1940s, however, the split between the Nationalists and Communists became full-scale civil war. After the People's Liberation Army's victory in 1949, the Communist Party determined that several kinds of people should not enjoy the privileges of citizenship in "the new society." Intent upon creating a social revolution to match their military victory and political revolution, Mao and his comrades separated big landlords, crime bosses, and other representatives of "the old society" as beyond the pale. There were eight such groups, and the lowest was the eighth category.[9]

As a former officer in the Nationalist Army, Zhang Yimou's father did not necessarily belong in this lowest category. The fact that his oldest brother had fled to Taiwan in late 1948 with the Nationalist government, however, earned Zhang's father special dishonor. His other brother had been killed in the 1947 Nationalist attack on Yan'an, the Communist Party wartime headquarters. The family later learned that he had apparently been assassinated by Nationalist thugs when he expressed an interest in leaving Chiang Kai-shek's army, and heading for Yan'an. But this show of interest in the Communist side by one brother apparently did not outweigh the stigma of the brother in Taiwan. Zhang Yimou's father was labelled "historically anti-revolutionary," a clumsy turn of phrase which implied a hereditary streak in an individual's political attitudes. The label prevented Zhang senior from finding regular work in Xi'an and obtaining all the other social services that having a regular workplace provided.

Zhang Yimou's mother became virtually the sole support of her family. Zhang Yimou was born in November 1950, the first in a family of three sons. Their mother was a trained physician and worked as a dermatologist at the Xi'an Medical College, while their father made some earnings from odd jobs. Zhang Yimou grew up as something of an outsider. He found comfort in the somewhat solitary pursuit of drawing. At the Beidajie (North Street) primary school he was at least permitted to don the red scarf of a Young Pioneer, like his classmates.

Other members of the Beijing Film Academy class of '82 had rather more settled childhoods, prior to start of the Cultural Revolution in 1966. Zhang Li, a future cinematography student and Liu Miaomiao's future husband, grew up in Changsha, the capital of Hunan province where Mao Zedong had also been schooled. Zhang Li had been born in north China. His mother, a graduate of a Tianjin music conservatory, taught music (piano and voice) at the seaside town of Beidaihe. Zhang Li, her second son, was born in this summer retreat for high government and Party officials in April 1957 (on Shakespeare's birthday, Zhang Li later found out). His father taught structural engineering at the Tangshan Railway Academy, a major center in China's post-1949 transport industry.[10]

The railway took the family south, first to Shijiazhuang, an important railway junction 250 kilometers south of Beijing, and then, when Zhang Li was five, to Changsha. For northerners from the bright, dry plains, this misty city must have seemed particularly unfamiliar. In a culture where dietary conservatism has survived revolution and national reintegration, the fiery cuisine of Hunan, like the city itself, took some getting used to. The Zhangs preferred wheat products: noodles and bread. People in Changsha ate rice. But the five-year-old Zhang Li found it easy to adapt to this new place. He started school at the primary school associated with the Changsha Railway Academy, his father's new work unit. His mother taught music, geography, and natural science at the academy's high school. She had not taught geography before and knew nothing about it, so Zhang's father would coach her on the following day's lesson the night before at the family table. Her young son would listen, knowing that this would help him in his own geography classes.

Zhang Jianya was a directing classmate of Chen Kaige, Tian

Zhuangzhuang and Zhang Yimou. Born in Shanghai in May 1951, his father was a pharmacologist and administrator. In 1973, soon after China was admitted to the United Nations, Zhang senior worked in Geneva and in Britain for the World Health Organization. Zhang's mother was a librarian. Having a member of the family overseas in the 1970s was exceptional, although it could be an embarassment, if questions were raised about "bourgeois pollution" from abroad.[11]

Zhang Jianya had his first contact with film in his fourth year at elementary school. He was "discovered" as a member of the Shanghai Children's Palace amateur drama troupe. In an educational film, he played a ten-year-old who helps an old man. The old man was played by Shen Yang, one of China's most renowned pre-Liberation actors, who had starred in the 1948 realist classic, *Lights for Ten Thousand Homes* (*Wanjia denghuo*). When he lent on Zhang Jianya's arm during the filming, he was already blind from the cancer that wracked his body. The film went on to win selection as the favorite science documentary in the first "Hundred Flowers" popularity poll conducted by *Popular Cinema* (*Dazhong dianying*), China's biggest film magazine.

Another son of Shanghai in the directing class was Jiang Haiyang. His father, Jiang Jun, had started his acting career in Shanghai in the mid-1930s. Jiang Jun was associated with the Film Group of the League of Left-Wing Writers, headed by the playwright Xia Yan. A Shanghai actress who moved in the same circles as Jiang Jun, went by the stage name Lan Ping. When she became Mao Zedong's wife in Yan'an, Mao gave her the name Jiang Qing.[12]

Jiang Jun considered himself primarily a stage actor and so he appeared only rarely in films. In 1951, four years before his son's birth, he had appeared in *Shangrao Concentration Camp* (*Shangrao jizhongying*), playing a pre-Liberation leftist intellectual. When Jiang Haiyang was a small child, his father made his second film in a story about left-wing Shanghai artists of his youth. The film, *Nie Er* (1959) was a reverential biography of the composer of the song whose tune became the Chinese national anthem after 1949. Zheng Junli, one of the most accomplished figures in the pre-1949 Shanghai cinema, was the director. Another pre-1949 favorite, the actor Zhao Dan, under layers of pancake makeup, played the youthful hero. Jiang Jun appeared as the leader of the Communist underground responsible for Nie Er's patriotic, anti-Japanese participation in Party front activities between 1930 and his death in Japan in 1935 at age twenty-three.

The father of Wu Ziniu, a future member of the directing class, was a teacher of educational psychology. Wu Tingtan had grown up in the household of a large landholder, and, like Zhang Yimou's father and uncles, had briefly attended a Nationalist military academy. Wu Ziniu's mother was also from a wealthy background. Before moving to Leshan in Sichuan province, Wu Tingtan had taught psychology at Hubei University in central China. Wu Ziniu, his second child and only son, was born in November 1953, shortly after the move westwards to Sichuan. Later, the birth of a second daughter completed the family.[13]

Under a regime which judges class as having a determining force in people's behavior, psychology was a somewhat risky line of work. In 1957 the Party's personnel file on Wu Tingtan had listed him as a Rightist. The 1957 Anti-Rightist campaign had been inspired by the outpouring of criticisms of the system, chiefly from intellectuals like Wu, in response to Mao Zedong's call in 1956 to "let a hundred flowers bloom, a hundred schools of thought contend." Most schools of thought proved unacceptable to Mao. Labelled "poisonous weeds," they were figuratively closed down, when tens of thousands of critics, bold or otherwise, were labelled Rightists. As in other campaigns, institutions and work units were pressed to fill quotas of "bad elements." Many such victims were demoted, sacked, prevented from publication, or even assigned to places far from their homes or imprisoned. Some Rightists were rehabilitated after a few years. Others had to wait until the late 1970s to have their names officially cleared. One of Wu Tingtan's nephews was condemned as opposing the Party, but Wu himself was never publicly declared a "Rightist." The label was added to his personnel file as an internal Party matter.

From these sketches of the family backgrounds and childhoods of several future Beijing Film Academy graduates, we can see that even for young children politics was a not unfamiliar element in their lives. Growing up in Mao's China in the 1950s and early 1960s, political campaigns, such as the Hundred Flowers liberalization and the consequent Anti-Rightist backlash, were not just public events. They could have sometimes devastating private reverberations. But nothing had prepared most families for the upheavals of 1966.

2. The Start of the Cultural Revolution

By the late spring of 1966 Chairman Mao had become restless. His last piece of political theatre in the 1950s, the so-called Great Leap Forward in

1958 had proved a disaster. Instead of a successful lunge to modernization through mass mobilization of productive capacity, China suffered a grave slump in agricultural production. Peasants spent time making backyard steel of no value, while planting and maintenance of irrigation works and crops suffered in the rush for greater productivity. A famine followed over the four years from 1959 to 1962. Some estimates put the loss of life from starvation at over thirty million.[14] Even Mao Zedong could not brazen out the consequences and took a back seat in the early 1960s to other Party leaders as they sorted out the mess. But Mao smarted at the humiliation of second-tier leadership. Moreover, he was convinced that a decade and a half since the establishment of his regime had not affected a sufficient revolution in the attitudes of his bureaucracy and Party colleagues. By the mid-1960s Mao determined that the time had come to reassert his authority, aided by the ambitions of insurgent leaders who saw opportunities in a regime shake-up. Among these insurgents were the future Gang of Four: Mao's wife Jiang Qing, Zhang Chunqiao, Yao Wenyuan and Wang Hongwen.

In the late spring 1966, Chairman Mao called upon the youth of China to rise up. In response, high school and college students throughout the nation formed groups to attack aspects of the "old culture," such as temples, antique collectors, and classical books. Initially such groups were led by the sons and daughters of Party and state officials. Unlike children who enjoyed the proper revolutionary class backgrounds (i.e. workers, peasants, or soldiers), these students often felt themselves handicapped by their parents' privileged class origins and positions. Their parents may have been leading officials in the socialist state, but they often had backgrounds that lacked proper proletarian purity. The attack on the "four olds" in 1966 offered an opportunity for these children of cadres to prove separately their own political dedication. Children of poor and lower-middle peasants had parents who were presumed to have suffered under the yoke of landlord oppression. Worker parents' experience, either in so-called "semi-colonial" servitude in factories and workshops before 1949 or in humdrum employment in Mao's factories since, also earned their children political standing. In 1966, the children of cadres started out as the most furious attackers of elements of the "old society," even if such elements sometimes included their own parents or grandparents. Soon, however, the older orthodoxy reasserted itself, and the classmates of poor peasants, soldiers, and workers gained control of the Red Guard factions.

For the future Beijing Film Academy classmates, themselves products of the seventeen years of Mao's revolution, these were heady times. Some of these youths felt exhilarated by the opportunity to assert their loyalty to Chairman Mao and to make mischief in a change from usual dull routines. Most felt threatened, for they or their families were vulnerable to accusations of privilege.

For Zhang Yimou, the rise of the Red Guards, in whichever groups' hands, meant further alienation from his schoolmates. When regular classes ended in 1966 Zhang was in the second year of junior high. Like many of his age, he never went on to graduate from senior high school. Red Guard revolutionary purity prevented five sorts of children from joining the activists. Fifteen-year-old Zhang belonged to the third group: anti-revolutionary elements. The other groups included former landlords, rich peasants, and "bad elements" (a catch-all category that included former criminals and the like). More than twenty years later, he remembered being called a "son of a dog" (*gou zaizi*) by Red Guards, on account of his father's background.

Another condemned group were the children of Rightists, that is, intellectuals who had had the temerity in 1956 to answer Mao's Hundred Flowers call for public criticism of the system and had then been caught in the reaction when the critics proved too embarrassing for the Party. Peng Xiaolian had grown up with an absent father, exiled to labor camp in remote Qinghai province. When the Cultural Revolution began, twelve-year-old Peng Xiaolian was finishing her elementary schooling. She entered junior high school in the autumn of 1967, in the midst of the disruption on campus and in the streets. Periods of physical labor in the countryside and on the Shanghai docks with her classmates helped toughen Xiaolian. At school she flung herself into revolutionary enthusiasm, as if to prove her loyalty to Chairman Mao despite her father's offence. But the pressure on the family owing to her father's past continued, in part due to Peng Boshan's first wife's friendship with Jiang Qing in Shanghai in the 1930s. Peng Boshan was a potential source of embarrassment to Chairman Mao's wife. Zealous university Red Guards beat up Peng Boshan in Zhengzhou, when he transferred trains once on his way back to Qinghai after a visit to his family in Shanghai. Peng Boshan died in his Qinghai exile in 1968. His family did not learn of his death until three months later. When the notification arrived, Xiaolian's mother was not at home. She had been arrested by Red Guards in March 1968 and taken away. Xiaolian's oldest sister represented the family in making the sad journey to Qinghai to collect her father's remains.

Peng Xiaolian's brother was jailed for six months in July 1967, just as his youngest sister was finishing primary school. His crime in 1967 had been keeping a manuscript of his father's unpublished novel, *War and the People* (*Zhanzheng yu renmin*). Later her brother was sent to Gansu province in the northwest, where he spent more than a year in detention. Peng Boshan was officially rehabilitated in 1980, twelve years after his death. Only in 1981 was his son allowed to return to live in Shanghai. In the same summer of 1967 Peng Xiaolian's mother had been taken away for questioning for several days. When her mother returned from detention Xiaolian took down the obligatory portrait of Mao that hung in a central spot in their cramped apartment. She remembered years later the sting of her ears after her mother boxed them in anger at finding the portrait gone.

Wu Ziniu's father was also a target for Red Guards. Wu was twelve years old when the police came for his father in the summer of 1966. So-called "educational authorities" were a particular object of youthful Red Guard scorn, and Wu was a leader of the Leshan Teachers' Training College and until 1964 a faculty member of the Sichuan Provincial Education Academy, west China's pre-eminent teachers' college. At a mass rally in a city stadium and in front of his family, Wu Tingtan was forced to crouch in the "jet-plane" position (arms spread-eagled and body bowed over). Red Guards and older Maoists spat out accusations and were joined in a chorused roar from the assembled students and staff of his own and other colleges.

Professor Wu survived the experience, but his three children found it hard to take. They had always thought of their father, Wu Ziniu later recalled, as a man respected for his learning and moral character. Suddenly, his former students and colleagues were denouncing him as a bad element. Wu Ziniu's older sister, a rather pure and innocent person according to her brother, suffered most. Wu and she were particularly close: his sister used to meet him everyday near his elementary school gate and take him home. When her classmates started joining the Red Guards, his sister found herself assigned to the "black five categories" (*heiwulei*) of bad elements. She was sixteen at the time of the stadium rally. The pain of these denunciations of her father apparently affected her mental stability. In March 1970, a day after her younger sister was sent to the countryside, Wu's older sister had a nervous breakdown. She was hospitalized for six months in a mental institution and never fully recovered.[15] Wu Tingtan's detention eased somewhat after 1968: instead of only being allowed to see his family every month or so, he could now see them every week. His wife, however, was sent down to the countryside at about this time, so family reunions became even more difficult.

In Shanghai, Jiang Haiyang's family also faced disruption. His father, now deputy head of the People's Art Theatre, the most prestigious acting group in Shanghai, was in a vulnerable position in a movement that placed great emphasis on rooting out what Cultural Revolution insurgents regarded as conservative (in the jargon of the day, "reactionary and counter-revolutionary") authority figures in the performing arts. Jiang Jun's position was compounded by his pre-1949 acquaintance with Jiang Qing, the leading stalwart in the revolution in the arts in 1966. Mao's wife was intent on rewriting the history of pre-war leftist cultural activities in Shanghai and her own part in them. Jiang Jun was publicly criticized in wall posters as a small-time supporter of the so-called "black line in literature and art," associated with Jiang Qing's rivals. The elderly actor was taken away from his family and confined in a make-shift jail with similar offenders and was later sent, along with his wife, to a May Seventh Cadre School, which were rural retraining camps for unapproved intellectuals.

At the start of the Cultural Revolution Hu Mei's father's professional association with Western (and "bourgeois") music as army symphony conductor became a liability. This was despite some key works in the Cultural Revolution cannon (including two ballets and a symphony) relying on this performing art. In 1966 her father was arrested as a counter-revolutionary. The family was not permitted to see him for almost a year. They were eventually allowed to take food to him in his prison in the Western Hills about ten kilometers beyond the northwestern outskirts of Beijing city. Hu Mei's mother hid messages in the food, so that their statements to the interrogators about their pasts would be consistent. Their young daughter saw the guards beat her father in the "cow shed," as these often makeshift prisons were called. Hu Mei was also obliged to attend mass criticism sessions against her father.

The trauma of this for a ten-year-old is easy to imagine. It was worse, however, because of the disjunction between what Hu Mei knew of her father's Yan'an past and his accusers' charges. In the Cultural Revolution which claimed direct descent from the Yan'an revolutionary tradition, Hu Defeng was being accused of counter-revolutionary crimes. This startling turn of events was even more difficult for his daughter to understand, for some of his accusers had been welcome visitors to the family home. Even the family servant, a mark of the status the family enjoyed before 1966, was obliged to voice criticism of her erstwhile employers.

After the arrest of her father, Hu Mei, her brothers and two cousins were sent to stay with their maternal grandmother in the eastern suburbs of Beijing. The widowed grandmother had been married to the former secretary of Qi Baishi (1863–1957), China's pre-eminent twentieth-century painter. The secretary had become the director of the Qi Baishi memorial museum, but died of a heart attack soon after Red Guards had interrogated him on his alleged backwardness in being associated with a painter of shrimps and crabs in the old style. On a bright November morning in 1966 Hu Mei sat in the back of a car with her family on her way to her grandfather's funeral. As they were driven through the center of the city, the ten-year-old gazed out intrigued at the hordes of young people, each clutching a small, red plastic-covered book. Her mother explained that they were Red Guards, some of whom had walked for hundreds of kilometers, assembling in Tian'anmen Square. That afternoon Chairman Mao would appear on the rostrum for his eighth review of the youth who served as the shock troops of his attack on his own party.

Two other future classmates also saw their parents repudiated by the new Cultural Revolution authorities. The parents of Tian Zhuangzhuang and Chen Kaige, who all worked in the film world, were also criticized for alleged shortcomings. Tian Fang, by then head of the Beijing Film Studio, was condemned for his long association with Zhou Yang, the chief propagandist since the 1950s for Mao Zedong's policies on art and literature. In 1966 Tian Fang represented the cultural establishment that Jiang Qing and her allies wanted to replace. Yu Lan came under fire by association and also, her son argued years later, because she was a star. Tian Fang and Yu Lan were arrested in the autumn of 1966. Chen Huaikai's past as a student at a Nationalist-run drama school was resurrected as a mark against his revolutionary purity. He was arrested and confined to a "cow shed." His son, Kaige was not permitted to become a Red Guard at his school or in the neighborhood in the Xinjiekou district in Beijing. Kaige was even obliged to participate in mass criticism meetings called to denounce his father and other leading staff of the Beijing Film Studio. It was an experience his son never forgot: father-son relationships occur with striking regularity in his films.

Zhang Yimou had spent a childhood on the wrong side of the political tracks, so the coming of the Cultural Revolution in the spring of 1966 had less impact on his view of his place in the world. He spent a lot of time painting and drawing, for which he had developed a real talent, and reading as much as he could at a time when many books ended up in Red Guard confiscations. He also had plenty of spare time to work on his basketball skills. That year his father had been taken away to confinement in a "cow shed." Zhang's mother was able to visit her husband, but she insisted that the three boys not see their father in that condition.

Reading was a past-time many of the future film-school classmates took up in these years. Schooling itself, at both primary and secondary levels, became a somewhat haphazard affair, with frequent rallies and disruptions, including exercises designed to prove the students' revolutionary fervor. The world of books offered an escape from the pressures of the present and had the added frisson of risk at a time when most Western and many Chinese books were being condemned. Jiang Haiyang, for example, became a bookworm, borrowing books from a neighbor, who had been able to keep her husband's collection of foreign and Chinese literature intact despite the depredations of Red Guards. The latter made occasional raids on targeted households seeking evidence, like books, of "bourgeois thinking." Like Haiyang's father, the neighbor's husband had been confined by the authorities. Jiang Haiyang escaped into the world of Balzac, Byron, and Mikhail Lermontov in translation. In private expression of his confusion at what had happened to his family and his world, Jiang also wrote his own poems. Likewise thirteen-year-old Chen Kaige in Beijing was trying to fill his days after classes ended in his second and last year at No. 4 Boys High School. For the next two years he read a great deal and honed his basketball skills. He took an interest in historical writing and classical novels set in times far removed from his own. The *Historical Records* (*Shiji*), a moralistic text from the second century B.C., and *The Dream of the Red Chamber* (*Honglou meng*), an eighteenth-century novel of the decline of a great and prosperous family, were Chen's particular favorites. He also spent time learning how to cook.

Reading could have risks. At Peng Xiaolian's home in Shanghai the bookcases had been sealed by Red Guards with glued strips of paper forming crosses on the glass doors. A sister applied hot towels to the strips and carefully peeled them off. One of the first novels Peng Xiaolian read was *Tracks in the Snowy Forest* (*Linhai xueyuan*), a picaresque novel from 1956.[16] Peng began working her way through her parents' collection of foreign novels in translation, in much the same way as her future classmate

Chen Kaige was doing in Beijing. Lermontov, Turgenev, *The Scarlet and the Black*, all of Balzac (which she didn't really like at the time), and Romain Rolland offered escape into other worlds. She sampled Kafka's *The Trial*, but finding she did not understand it, decided not to read the modernist writers on the shelves. Only later, after the arrest of the Gang of Four when the bookshelves could be openly unsealed, did she try Kafka's novella again. The parallels with China of the Cultural Revolution were striking.

Tian Zhuangzhuang also discovered the pleasures of foreign novels in translation: he found Tolstoy particularly enjoyable. He also read the classic Chinese novel, *Dream of the Red Chamber*. Music, on records his father had brought back from trips to the Soviet Union, also appealed, especially Tchaikovsky and other Russian romantics. There were also records of old-style Chinese opera that the teenager learnt to enjoy, notably *Liang Shanbo and Zhu Yingtai* (*Liang Shanbo yu Zhu Yingtai*, a.k.a. "The Butterfly Lovers") which had been made into China's first color film in the mid-1950s.

The disruptions of 1966–67, when youthful Red Guards commandeered much of public life in China's cities, also offered the young unprecedented freedoms. The absence of parents in many cases and the denunciation of teachers removed normal restraints on behavior. Hu Mei, aged ten, heard that students at the No. 4 Girls' Middle School had beaten the principal in a latrine. The beating was so severe that half the principal's hair and face was reduced to a pulp. She later died from the experience.

A happier freedom was the opportunity to travel in a society that had severely controlled most journeys. Red Guards were notorious for intimidating train crews into letting them travel free, as promulgators of Mao Zedong Thought to "establish ties" (*chuanlian*) with similar groups, in imitation of the Communist Long March of the 1930s. In the summer of 1966 Tian Zhuangzhuang's brother, five years his senior, took the fourteen-year-old on a long train journey south to Shanghai and Hunan, Mao's native province. The brothers undertook a more arduous trip in the winter of 1966–67 to Yan'an, where their recently arrested parents had almost thirty years earlier forged their commitment to the Communist cause. The Tian brothers, with several friends, made the 1,800 kilometer journey on foot. Upon his return to Beijing, he and his brother found odd jobs in factories and communes around Beijing.

Growing up in Changsha, the future cinematographer Zhang Li was well placed to undertake political pilgrimages to sacred sites of the Communist revolution. He and his classmates made the 130-kilometer roundtrip to Shaoshan, birthplace of Chairman Mao, fourteen times, the first in 1964. His father used his railway connections to obtain a free pass for the ten-year-old at the start of the Cultural Revolution, entrusting him into the care of railway staff he knew. Like the older Red Guards who were flocking to Beijing, Zhang Li hoped to see Chairman Mao on one of his appearances before hundreds of thousands massed in Tian'anmen Square. He never saw Mao, but he did see the Chairman's wife on 30 September 1967. Two months earlier Zhang had gone to Beijing to live for a year. His mother's older sister taught at the No. 27 Middle School in the northern part of the center of the city. Schooling and public life were in such disorder that a ten-year-old could move to Beijing and attend high school without bureaucratic barriers. School did not amount to more than three classes each day. The only problem was the boy's lack of a Beijing household registration. His aunt had to make her allocation of grain, cotton, oil, and other rationed goods stretch to include her young nephew's needs. On the eve of the 1967 National Day celebrations, Zhang Li and some new Beijing friends had crept into Tian'anmen Square from the Beijing Hotel, east of the square. In the shadows of the ancient gate where Mao would stand to survey the Red Guards, the boys saw Jiang Qing and Kang Sheng (a top Party leader and head of China's secret police) inspecting the floats for the next day's parade.

Wu Ziniu was another aspirant Red Guard who made the pilgrimage to the capital, but without success. At the gates of Beijing—in this case the railway station at Fengtai, southwest of the city proper—the thirteen-year-old boy travelling alone was turned back. Only true "Red elements" were permitted to tread the streets of the capital: "black elements" or the off-spring of the "fifth category" (*diwu lei*) like the teacher's son could not sully the chairman's precincts. There were notices to this effect in the hostels where Red Guards and others like Wu Ziniu stayed on their travels. At this time, Wu had a mere ten *yuan* (about US$2) in his pocket. But, instead of returning to Sichuan, he journeyed south to Shanghai.

Beijing youngsters often stayed home. At her new school in Chaoyang district, among classmates from less privileged backgrounds than at her previous school, Hu Mei flung herself into classroom work and political activities. She was anxious to prove her worth, and, by extension, that of her father. In this troubled atmosphere the students spent only about half their time at class work. At any one time, one grade would be in a commune or factory for two months, supposedly learning a proletarian world outlook from contact with workers and peasants. The other grades stayed at school. Hu Mei probably learned more about ordinary people not from this organized "going to the people" but from her informal contact with some of her schoolmates. The army, having taken away her father, paid her and her brothers a monthly nine *yuan* allowance. At a time when a university student, for example, would have only a couple of *yuan* left each month after dormitory and food expenses, nine *yuan* was rather generous for an eleven-year-old. In contrast, some of Hu Mei's friends in Chaoyang had to work hard for a living. Out of friendship and an urge to show her closeness to worker and peasant classmates, she joined them. Sometimes she skipped what classes there were to help her friends deliver the coal brickettes that were the main source of cooking and heating fuel in Beijing. Years later Hu Mei recalled with apparent nostalgia these days of labor with school friends.

Hu Mei had continued living at her grandmother's home in Chaoyang district. The place became rather crowded when, in addition to the three Hu children, two cousins were sent by an uncle in Taiyuan in Shanxi province, in order to avoid the armed fighting among Red Guard and other "rebel" factions there. Things got a little less cramped when Hu Mei's two older brothers (the younger was a year older than her) joined the stream of educated youths to communes and farms. Hu Mei, like a lot of her contemporaries, had by now found that the best way to survive in society was to be an "activist" (*jiji fenzi*) to ensure leadership approval, while hiding her real emotions. The way she grew up taught Hu Mei the importance, for a woman and for a Chinese citizen, of adopting an outward persona which might not truly reflect her real feelings. At thirteen, in her first year of middle school, she threw herself into the productive labor that was a large part of the curriculum. At a flour mill in the district, Hu Mei and her classmates helped load and carry forty-five *jin* (22.5 kilo) bags of wheat flour. Hu Mei was the only schoolgirl who tried carrying two bags at a time, balanced at the ends of a bamboo shoulder pole. She noticed how a lot of other students were dropping out of school, bored by classroom and labor routines. In contrast, Hu saw school as a chance to succeed where her parents had failed.

Hu Mei did well at high school in music, singing, and dancing. She had never liked piano practice much, although she recalled gazing wistfully through the windows of their old apartment at the family piano one Spring Festival when her brother and she visited their confined mother. She danced the parts of the heroine and the company commander in school productions of the ballet *The Red Detachment of Women* (*Hongse niangzijun*), one of Jiang Qing's "model performances" (*yangbanxi*) designated as models for a new kind of revolutionary art and literature. This display of enthusiasm, however, did not prevent her from on occasion singing popular, unofficial songs (chiefly Soviet songs remembered from the years before the model performances became the orthodoxy) with a giggling group of friends during the anonymity of power cuts.

The coming of the Cultural Revolution disrupted life for all the future members of the Beijing Film Academy class of '82. For many, lives of relative privilege and comfort were replaced by fear and loss. For all, the old routines and assumptions about the rightness of the political picture were brought into question. By 1969 the People's Liberation Army had stepped in to restore order to urban workplaces and universities. China settled into a period of relative quiet. But for many urban teenagers a new life, far away and with no guarantee of an eventual return home, was just beginning.

3. Sent-Down Youths

The seminal Cultural Revolution experience for the future members of the Beijing Film Academy class of '82 was not the trauma of parents being arrested or teachers being beaten. It was going "down to the villages and up the mountains" (*shangshan xiaxiang*) to live as peasants, soldiers or workers after 1968. Wrenched from the familiarity of home and hometown, young people found themselves in exile with no firm forecast of ever returning to the cities or resuming their education. This experience was crucial in shaping the attitudes of a generation of Chinese, who went on in the 1980s to reinvent contemporary Chinese culture, including films.

The transfer of urban dwellers to the less-developed parts of China had been government policy since the 1950s. It was inspired in part by an urge to move China's industrial and productive centers away from the eastern seaboard and the supposed range of Taiwan and American missiles or bombers. But such colonization of the western regions of China had a long history, dating back to military settlements on the central Asian frontier in the first millennium A.D. Mao's call for young people to go out into society and put down roots in the countryside or in factories and mines had modern rationales, both practical and theoretical. Moving the kinds of young people who had been Red Guards away from their homes would help restore social order in the cities. It would also ensure that a new generation was exposed to a version of the rustication experienced by early Chinese Communists in Yan'an days and before. Close to seventeen million young people were rusticated in the late 1960s and early 1970s.[17]

In 1968 Zhang Yimou joined the stream of urban high school students heading for the countryside. His parents had also been sent to labor in the country as punishment for their alleged transgressions.[18] His younger brother, almost five years his junior, remained in Xi'an, because his ear condition required regular attention and medication. With only his baby brother and a grandmother in her eighties left at home, his hearing deteriorated rapidly. By 1970 he was deaf. Working at a people's commune in Guanzhong, fifty kilometers northwest of Xi'an, offered Zhang Yimou a chance to prove his value to the community and his commitment to the revolutionary cause. The sweat on his back might help wash away the stain of his father's background. Eventually it became clear that some of the "sent-down youths," through good performance at work and political study, could win transfer to more attractive, urban factory jobs. Several times the peasants in Guanzhong recommended Zhang Yimou for transfer, but each time the examination of his background brought up his father's past and no factory dared take him on.

Almost twenty years later Wu Ziniu recalled the exact day, 17 January 1969, when he was sent to the countryside on a semi-permanent basis. The fifteen-year-old boy was among the first wave in Sichuan to be transferred from the cities. His assignment was harsher than most, especially for a teenager of his relatively slight build. Wu Ziniu joined more than 700 high-schoolers assigned to an enormous commune, Angu People's Commune, about one hundred kilometers from his Leshan hometown. For the next two and half years, his working life resembled that of a soldier's. His living arrangements, however, had a semblance of family life. He and four other educated youths were assigned to a production team, the smallest element in the commune organization. They were billeted with peasant families. The couple who took Wu Ziniu in were in their seventies. They had never had a son and treated Wu as a substitute.

Work was tough and included the usual labor in the fields, hauling and spreading human and animal waste, constructing and clearing irrigation waterways and general labor. For a day's work the youths earned

six *fen* (Chinese cents), about one American cent. There was a way to earn
more. The commune would give a month off to youths who hauled barges
loaded with fertilizer the two-day distance to the county seat.[19] Wu served
as a boat-hauler on the Dadu river that wound through mountainous
southern Sichuan and flowed into the Yangzi river. Mao Zedong's Red
Army had fought one of the most famous battles of the Long March at the
Dadu river. On the eve of the Cultural Revolution in the early 1960s, the
exploits of this victory had been included in inspirational ballet and song
in the historical dance-drama *The East is Red* (*Dongfang hong*). In its 1965
filmed version, with chorus, orchestra, and cast of hundreds, *The East is
Red* became compulsory viewing for the Chinese population. Wu Ziniu
and his classmates could sing the songs and knew the Dadu crossing
sequence by heart. But in real life, the exploitation of Wu Ziniu and his
companions on the Dadu, thirty-five years after the Long March, was
closer to serfdom. In the spare time he gained by hauling the boats, Wu
Ziniu lost himself in a world of books brought from his father's library.
His reading included *The Scarlet and the Black* and other novels in
translation.[20] He swapped the books with other educated youths.

Wu Ziniu hoped to escape by joining the People's Liberation Army or
becoming a factory worker. In 1971 he tried to join the army. Although he
was not yet the required eighteen-years-old, he altered his year of birth
back a year. He passed the physical, but his political background check
revealed Nationalist military connections in his family as well as his
father's case. His application was set aside.[21] New policies stated that after
two years in the countryside, educated youths could be transferred to
university or to factories. His dream was to return to a setting like the
campus of his childhood. By 1971 there were signs that classes would start
again at some colleges for worker-peasant-soldier students. But his family's
political disgrace worked against Wu's chances. His four companions were
the first to leave the production team to return to the city; only Wu Ziniu
was left.

More than twenty years later, some former sent-down youths recalled
some of their experiences in those years with nostalgia, even pleasure. Tian
Zhuangzhuang, then seventeen, moved to the countryside in 1969. He
went with his older brother's classmates to the far northwest border of Jilin
province in the northeast. Zhenlai county lay in the marshy country in the
strip of territory between Heilongjiang province and the Inner Mongolian
Autonomous Region. Assigned to the Datun People's Commune on the
provincial border, Tian found himself in a land of lakes, forests and rolling

plains. Forestry and pig raising were the main occupations, but it was horseback riding to which Tian took an instant liking. Unlike many educated youths in less welcoming places, Tian actually enjoyed living in Datun, as he reported to friends in Beijing on a Lunar New Year visit home in early 1970. On this trip he made the equivalent of a month's salary for a factory worker by selling a 25-kilo sack of wheat he had carried down from the northeast.

Meanwhile Tian Zhuangzhuang's brother had been sent on to a commune in Shanxi province, west of Beijing. His skill at basketball gained him enlistment in the People's Liberation Army. Soon his unit transferred to Hebei province, to a camp in Dingxing county, a few hours by train south of Beijing. He played basketball for the 38th Army. At this point personal connections came into play, as so often in all areas of Chinese life.[22] Chen Dejun, the deputy division commander and a hero from the War of Resistance to Japan, saw Tian Zhuangzhuang's brother playing on the courts at a tournament and learned that he was the son of the actress Yu Lan. Chen had met Yu Lan during the war and summoned her son to his presence. Asking how his family was, Chen learned that younger brother Zhuangzhuang was still in the northeast. Commander Chen felt that the brothers should not be split up, seeing their parents were under detention. He made arrangements for Zhuangzhuang to come south and join the army.

Tian Zhuangzhuang was reluctant to leave the grassland and forests of Jilin. His friends were there and the peace and relative freedom of Datun was much more appealing than the discipline of life in the army. Finally, after eleven telegrams from his brother urging him to come, Zhuang-zhuang relented and headed south. He was assigned to a propaganda team that gave performances on military themes. He tried his hand at writing plays and even comic dialogues (*xiangsheng*, "crosstalks"), a favorite entertainment that survived during the Cultural Revolution and provided opportunity for highly circumspect satire. In the third of his five years in the army, Zhuangzhuang became a photo-journalist at the 38th Army headquarters in Baoding city.

In 1971 Tian Zhuangzhuang made his first application to join the Communist Party. He was unsuccessful, on account of his family "problem." But in the early 1970s Party ranks were being replenished and expanded, particularly by members of the military. Eventually, on 28 March 1973 Zhuangzhuang became a member of the Chinese Communist Party. In China such dates are as well remembered as birthdays.[23]

In 1968 Chen Kaige and his classmates did not wait to be assigned to somewhere remote. They volunteered to go to the southwest. There in the Dai Autonomous Region of Yunnan province, near the Vietnam and Laos borders, state farms had been experimenting since the 1950s with growing rubber trees in commercial plantations. Chen Kaige arrived in the tropical lushness of Xishuangbanna in June 1968. There was excitement among the group, for the place had an exotic appeal known to them from films set in these national minority regions. Far from dry, dusty Beijing, the youths felt also that the constraints of school, political organizations, and parents were distant. Despite the harshness of life and discipline in the state farm, Xishuangbanna offered a new feeling of freedom. Most of the extra-provincial sent-down youths in Yunnan came from Beijing, Shanghai and Sichuan province.[24]

After two years tapping rubber trees, Chen Kaige joined the People's Liberation Army. The army provided a way out of rustication for many such urban youth, as it had for Tian Zhuangzhuang. In Kaige's case recruitment was local, because of his height (an inheritance from his mother's Shandong province ancestors). The local army commander wanted him to play basketball. When the army unit's request to enlist Kaige reached headquarters in Beijing, it was denied. His father's Nationalist background was apparently cited as reason for rejection. Down in Yunnan, however, Kaige's skills on the basketball court made him too valuable to lose. His unit commanders quietly ignored Beijing's decision.

Chen Kaige was stationed in an army unit near Kunming, the provincial capital, for five years. The army offered a relatively easy way into the Communist Party: Kaige joined the Party in 1974. Meanwhile in Beijing his father had begun to work again at the reopened Beijing Film Studio. In 1974–75 Chen Huaikai was one of three directors of *Haixia*, a story of militia women on the south China coast. Upon its completion in 1975, *Haixia* came under attack from Jiang Qing for its alleged failure to follow Cultural Revolution artistic policy.[25]

As some young people were making their way back to the cities, others were heading for the countryside in a second wave around 1972–74. Zhang Li graduated from high school in Changsha in January 1974. As the only child at home (his older brother still lived in the north with relatives), he could have stayed with his family. Instead, he wanted to join his schoolmates that spring in moving to Pingjiang county, over one hundred kilometers northeast of Changsha. Compared to most "educated youths," Zhang and his eleven friends were lucky. Although there was not much wealth in Pingjiang, there was plenty of grain to eat. Here, at least, the educated youths were not a big burden on the peasants. The twelve teenagers built their own housing, as was standard practice. Through the three years that Zhang Li spent as a peasant in Pingjiang some harmonious relationships were established. Even in the 1980s, when his and most Chinese farmers' lives had changed considerably, Zhang and some of the people from Pingjiang exchanged letters and saw each other on occasion.

Others had a less pleasant time in country exile. Peng Xiaolian left Shanghai in March 1969 with a large group of Shanghai students. Her two years at No. 51 High School had been largely spent in laboring on communes, in factories, and in army camps. Now came the real thing. Xiaolian and the other Shanghai students arrived in Fengxin county on the northeastern, hilly fringe of the central river basin of Jiangxi province, about 600 kilometers west of Shanghai. There they were assigned to the Zha Village People's Commune.

The fourteen members of Peng Xiaolian's group lived in a converted storehouse, in the walls of which they cut out holes for windows. Peng would lie awake on the smelly grasses they gathered from the hills in the summer to ward off mosquitoes, listening to the rats gnawing on wood in the dark corners of their hut. Soon the students were scavenging for extra rations. Their official allocation included one kilo of oil per person per year and meat three times a year: at Spring Festival (the lunar New Year), the Dragon Boat Festival in the summer, and the Mid-Autumn Festival. The rest of the time the students caught snakes to eat. Xiaolian also tried cat and yellow weasel. At the end of the agricultural year the work points earned by the students and commune members were added up. For the students, the cost of their state-supplied grain and oil rations were deducted, so that each student generally got about eight *yuan* (less than US$3) for the year's labor.[26] Much of these wages went on lamp oil, for there was no electricity in the district. The youths stole vegetables and hens from the villagers, episodes that also provided welcome adventure in otherwise dull lives.

If relations with the local peasants were not warm, arguments between the students themselves hardly made for solidarity. When they had first arrived in Zha Village, the fourteen students in Peng Xiaolian's party had been divided into three groups for assignment to work with the commune's production teams. About half of the fourteen shared a common background as offspring of former capitalists, fallen Party cadres, and other parents subject to reform through labor. This did not prevent the three groups from fighting over the work points they received in the production teams. Some of the Shanghai students accused others of bribing the production team leaders to receive more points than they deserved. Accusations of stealing and of opening other people's letters from home sometimes flew about the students' hut. After a time, some students were transferred to places closer to Shanghai, others used back-door connections to secure better paid, though more dangerous, work in the small coal mines in the Jiangxi hill country, and some took up jobs as untrained teachers in rural schools. They could visit their families back in Shanghai once every year or two.

In the summer of 1972 Peng Xiaolian fell ill. The rivers in Zha Village were swollen by summer rains, so the peasants carried the highly feverish young woman in an old bamboo chair to the commune clinic. The "barefoot doctor" there, who had only elementary medical training, was alarmed at what he saw. Xiaolian was put on a long-distance bus and bumped her delirious way to a hospital in Nanchang, the provincial capital, where the doctors diagnosed hepatitis A. Xiaolian remained in the hospital for three weeks and then took the train back home to Shanghai. There she lay on her bed for two straight months, barely moving. As she recovered, her brother returned from Gansu province in the northwest, also with hepatitis. When she went back to Zha Village in January 1974, Xiaolian was the only one left of the fourteen students who had moved into the converted storehouse five years earlier. She lived alone until May 1975, cooking for herself, and reading translated Balzac and Stendhal novels she had managed to bring back from Shanghai. Apart from an invitation to a meal to celebrate the lunar New Year in a peasant's home, Xiaolian led a solitary existence once work in the fields was over. The opportunity, arranged through a Shanghai friend, to work for two months at the Jiangxi Iron and Steel Works in Xinyu, a major city 100 kilometers southwest of Fengxin, came as a welcome relief from farm work and loneliness.

Some young people did not join the exodus from the cities. Zhang Jianya in Shanghai graduated from junior high school in 1968, just as he turned seventeen. He was rather older than usual because of the Cultural Revolution disruption, but he was unable to go on to senior high school and complete his secondary education. The reason was not his ability but the timing. The year of his graduation marked the last year of regular university education for almost five years. Completing high schooling had less purpose now that colleges had dispersed their students and staff.

Zhang Jianya was lucky. Because his older brother had been recently dispatched to the countryside, he was allowed to remain with his parents in Shanghai, as a common practice to provide for the elderly urban population. He was assigned to the Jing'an district housing administration in the former French Concession, where he worked as a carpenter for the next seven years. He often went to the grand homes that had housed expatriates and wealthy Chinese before 1949: now they were crumbling, providing shelter for several families where once a single family and servants had held sway. Under the guidance of older craftsmen, Zhang learned the special qualities of different kinds of wood, how to hang a door and how to plane a window frame. Slowly his skill increased. He was even able to help friends, when he could get his hands on the materials, with home repairs or making a baby carriage. Frustrated by the termination of his formal schooling, Zhang found a certain satisfaction in gaining a skill and learning to work with his hands. Shaping wood into practical items offered some modest reward. Had it not been for his brother, he could, after all, have been stuck more than 3,000 kilometers away in Xinjiang instead.

When Jiang Haiyang graduated from senior high school in Shanghai, he too should have been sent to a commune or state farm away from the city, like other educated youths. But by 1972 political mobilization had eased somewhat, and Jiang Haiyang was able to remain in Shanghai and study at one of the tertiary technical schools which had begun to reopen to provide specialist personnel to industry. He enrolled, after an examination, in the Shanghai Metallurgical Middle-level Training School. Machine design, principally of steel presses, became his focus of study. He did well, and after two years was asked to stay on at the institute as an instructor. He had also apparently succeeded in overcoming the political embarrassment of his parents' recent dispatch to a rural May Seventh Cadre School for reform through labor. Jiang Haiyang was even regarded as potential cadre material, based on his performance as deputy chairman of the metallurgical institute's student association.

Two future fifth-generation directors were too young to be part of the sent-down youth phenomenon. Hu Mei had been only nine when the Cultural Revolution began. When she finished high schooling in 1974, the expected avenue to a university education was not available, although in that year some universities reopened for the first time in over six years. The small numbers of students were politically approved, so-called worker-peasant-soldier students. The army offered an alternative for seventeen-year-old Hu Mei. Coming from a musical family and having endured piano lessons for a few years before her parents were taken away, she succeeded in passing auditions for the People's Liberation Army Song and Dance Troupe. The irony of the disgraced Hu Defeng's daughter joining the army was not lost on Hu Mei, as she started her new life in an all-woman troupe. Later, after becoming a film director, Hu Mei looked back on the separation of the sexes that she had encountered first at high school and then in the army as rather old-fashioned and conservative (she used the word "feudal"). As earlier at school, in the army dance troupe: "I had two faces: one was pretty and revolutionary, but the other was worried that people would find out about my parents. I played two roles."

Liu Miaomiao in Ningxia was born in 1962. A precocious student, she advanced to junior high school at age eleven. Along the lines of Hu Mei's more professional experience in the army, young Miaomiao joined the school cultural team, performing songs and dances in praise of the wise leadership in Beijing.

Most sent-down youth took a different view of China's leaders, though they dared not voice it except among trusted friends. The years of exile from the cities, often in arduous conditions, scarred a generation. Many resented the interruption to their education and life plans. The more thoughtful began to question the wisdom of a political and cultural system that had led to China's youth being wasted in harsh, unskilled toil. This questioning laid the foundation for the revitalization of Chinese culture, including its films, in the 1980s.

4. Return to the Cities

Within years of the great wave of young people being sent down to the countryside, the armed forces or large state factories, the tide began to turn. By the early 1970s, a trickle of youths began to return to the cities, usually to menial jobs, but in some cases to further education in newly reopened and purged institutions of higher learning. After the drama of the fall in September 1971 of Marshal Lin Biao, Mao's chosen successor and alleged would-be assassin, public life in China began to calm down. A generalized dullness in most peoples' lives was punctuated by hysterical rhetoric in the media. In 1972 adaptations of the first of the eight "model performances," consisting of five modern-style Peking operas, two ballets and a symphony, began to appear on China's movie screens. Two years later the first new feature films were released. Predictable and wooden as they may have been, their appearance signalled a further relaxation in public discourse. In this new atmosphere, many sent-down youths and others who had not completed their schooling were able to start new careers or at least return to city life.

Zhang Yimou, destined to become the most well-known of his generation of filmmakers, succeeded in his third year of rustication in Shaanxi province to get a transfer to a factory in 1971. His basketball skills outweighed finally his family background. "I got to the cotton mill because I was good at basketball, just like getting to college in the U.S. on a sports scholarship."[27]

The No. 8 Cotton Mill was on the outskirts of Xianyang, a city of 100,000 people twenty-five kilometers northwest of Xi'an. Zhang Yimou was to spend the next seven years of his life there. As an unskilled newcomer with no personal connections, Zhang started in the worst jobs in the factory, in one of the teams that made desultory efforts to keep the place clean. Promotion to a relatively good position, such as the machinery repair teams, seemed far off. But within his first year, Zhang became a maintenance man in the mill. After three years, however, his artistic skills were recognized and he joined the art studio in the factory, working on textile designs as well as drawing propaganda pictures in chalk on blackboards around the factory. He became a skilled calligrapher for this purpose.

Zhang found solace outside the mill. Xianyang was close enough to Xi'an for him to visit home occasionally to see his two younger brothers. A friendship had developed between himself and Xiao Hua, a high school classmate from Xi'an who had been in Zhang's commune. She was later transferred to a factory about twenty kilometers west of Xianyang. Zhang saw her once every two weeks, when she would come and wash and cook for him.[28] They had been the two best artists in their high school class. For several years Xiao Hua's parents refused their daughter permission to bring her boyfriend to their home and opposed all thought of marriage. When Xiao Hua's older sister gave birth to a baby, Zhang Yimou wanted to share the joy. He splurged some of his limited savings on a chicken for the family, but was not permitted to present it to the new mother. All he could do was fling it over the wall into the Xiao family courtyard.[29] The political embarrassment of his father's background extended to all parts of Zhang's life. In the mid-1970s Xiao Hua entered college as a worker-peasant-soldier student, when universities only admitted students who could obtain this label. Zhang did not qualify for this educational advancement.[30]

Zhang Yimou sought escape also in his discovery of photography. Perhaps in creating images on film he could create a world in which he was master rather than victim. He was unable to save all but a few cents each month from his low wage of thirty *yuan* (about US$8) as a cotton mill laborer. Zhang's solution to the problem of getting his own camera was simple, if startling. He sold his own blood. Selling may be too strong a term, for the Party regarded the *yuan* the hospital gave him for donating blood as a reward for volunteering a social duty. Slowly, half-liter by half-liter, Zhang Yimou accumulated enough money to buy a camera. He had his heart set on a Seagull, made in Shanghai, that cost an enormous 180 *yuan*. The Seagull gave him a means to capture images of the world as he saw it, not as teachers or mill Party committee members told him it should be. Almost fourteen years later Zhang remembered the exact day that he bought his Seagull: 24 December 1974. That night he joined the night shift as usual, then, abandoning sleep, he went out the next day and took a roll of shots of a fresh snowfall around the city.

For the next four years Zhang Yimou devoted much of his spare time to becoming a photographer. Rather than buy books with savings that could be used on film and materials, he borrowed books and copied them into note books. He later estimated that he had written out almost 200,000 characters from these photography texts, the equivalent of a good-sized book. The illustrations and diagrams he drew himself. His subjects were frequently from nature: ancient trees, hills, and the Wei river that flowed by Xianyang. At a time when lofty photos of idealized workers, soldiers, and peasants filled the media, Zhang deliberately avoided overtly political subjects.

Without equipment or access to a darkroom, Zhang Yimou made do with the facilities at hand. The porcelain trough of one of the squat lavatories in his factory dormitory served as an effective place to wash the chemicals which he could secure for developing films. Zhang would wait until the three other young men with whom he shared a room were asleep before starting on his photo work. From his enamel wash-basin he stretched out the developed film, then hung it among the socks, shirts and underclothes strung across the cramped room. Such make-shift methods produced creditable results: several of his photographic studies were selected for local amateur exhibitions. Among his future cinematography classmates, Zhang Yimou had more skill than most with chemicals, timing, and temperature.

Having failed acceptance into the army, in late 1971 Wu Ziniu settled for second best, enrolling in the Leshan District Mao Zedong Thought Literature and Art School. He had some experience in this field. At high school in 1968 Wu had participated in the Mao Zedong Thought Literature and Art Troupe and had learned to play the accordion. The way Wu Ziniu managed to enter the Leshan arts school in 1971 suggests how ineffective Mao's attempt at revolutionary transformation had been. It was accomplished through personal connections of the kind for which the Red Guards had criticized people like his parents. One day an urgent telegram came for Wu Ziniu, announcing that his father was ill. It was a ruse by his father to enable Wu to obtain leave from his semi-militarized unit and return to Leshan. In the city Wu Tingtan took his son to meet the head of the Literature and Art School, who happened to be a former student of his. Wu junior was administered a simple entrance examination that included singing a song. At Angu he had played the *erhu*, the two-stringed Chinese violin, as well as the piano accordion in the propaganda troupe organized among the sent-down youths as a means of educating the peasants and to occupy youthful spare-time. Wu was admitted on a probationary basis.

After four months he was allowed to stay on as a regular student. Wu studied writing and performance at the school. Sometimes he wrote song lyrics. A four-act play about two sisters, one in the countryside and the other remaining in the city, was well received by the classmates to whom he showed the script. But his teachers felt it was not politically acceptable and banned it from being performed.

Having completed the eighteen-month course at this local, low-level Literature and Art School, Wu Ziniu was assigned to a travelling drama troupe.[31] He had developed his talent as an actor, although the two-dimensional characters of the officially endorsed dramas of the time did not offer much challenge even to the incompetent. Wu spent six months with the travelling players, performing, writing what he later described as "bad poems," playing the *erhu* and other instruments, and also directing for mostly peasant audiences in the environs of Leshan. By about this time in mid-1973, he later recalled, he had already resolved to make his mark in filmmaking, where his audiences would be unlimited. An actor could only express other people's ideas: he would be a director.

Wu later transferred to a "spoken drama troupe" (*huaju tuan*) attached to the Leshan Prefectural Song and Dance Ensemble (*wengong tuan*). Before Cultural Revolution reorganization and a "cleansing of the ranks," the ensemble had been Leshan city's official theatre troupe. By 1974 the revolutionary model operas gave way to a more mixed repertoire, which added some older material and some nationally approved and standardized spoken dramas. In the drama troupe Wu Ziniu performed large and small roles. He proved a versatile member of the troupe, on the stage or with the orchestra, even playing second violin in Western-style pieces. He also helped with painting sets. Although he was not allowed to direct anything, he did assist in guiding rehearsals of one-act plays. Wu Ziniu's life was certainly better than the three years he had spent on the commune. There was still a degree of glamor attached to being a performer even in those rather drab years.

But Wu Ziniu felt he was cut out for greater things. In 1972 his younger sister had managed to get back from the countryside by winning a place at a school of public health. In 1977 some university entrance exams were reinstated. His father was full of encouragement. Wu applied to take the exams, but his work unit would not allow him to participate. A drunken argument with a violinist well connected in the drama troupe led to him being sent to the countryside for six months as punishment. Instead of working in the fields, as in his previous time in the countryside, he served in the Qianwei county cultural troupe, 100 kilometers from Leshan city: arranging performances to commemorate public occasions, and organizing a reading room and club for elderly and young commune members. He also took time to formally complete high school level studies in Chinese, history and geography.[32]

The next year Wu Ziniu prepared for the nationwide university entrance exams, coached for several months by a professor from Southwest Jiaotong University, who had been a classmate of his father.[33] Examinations for art schools were held before the tests for regular universities. In May in the provincial capital Chengdu, on the last day of the exams, he tried out for a place in the Central Drama Academy in Beijing. But the acting department had an age limit of twenty-two and Wu Ziniu was twenty-four in reality, and according to his previously altered household registration card, he was already twenty-five. He applied for three regular universities, the maximum number allowed: if he could not enter Peking University's Chinese or history departments, then the Chinese department at Sichuan University in Chengdu would do nicely. With competition fierce for the first degree classes in universities for ten years, students of Wu's generation felt an extra burden preparing for the exams. For most candidates, this would be their first and last chance to go to college. Wu Ziniu spent a month studying mathematics and other subjects with the professor. Exam prep devoured all his waking moments. For a time he was sleeping only two hours a day, such was the drive to make a better future for himself.

Zhang Jianya, Wu Ziniu's future classmate, was also active in the theatre by the mid-1970s. He had other skills, beyond the carpentry he had worked at since leaving school. Even at high school he had been active in the art propaganda team, performing songs and skits for schoolmates to spread the Cultural Revolution message. This ability to act, sing, and even dance led to his selection as a member of the Shanghai City Workers Cultural Palace drama troupe in 1973, an amateur group that rehearsed and performed in the evenings. The plays were usually dramatizations of current public political concerns: "capitalist roaders" within the ranks of the Communist Party, Legalist reformers competing with Confucian philosophers a millennium earlier, or the international solidarity of the proletariat. In addition there was a steady stream of dramatized songs in praise of the Communist Party and Chairman Mao to learn and perform at factories and on temporary stages around the city.

In 1975 the Shanghai Film Studio was looking for worker-peasant-soldier performers to replenish its acting ranks. Many of its actors had been dispersed during the five years after 1966 when, as at all the other studios in China, no new feature films were produced. Production had resumed in Shanghai in 1970 with celluloid versions of the "model performances." By 1974 the depleted studio staff had begun to make new fiction films: these so-called "model films" needed new actors to play their parts.[34] Zhang Jianya was not a real worker in terms of family background, but his years as a carpenter was considered close enough. Real workers or peasants with artistic talent were harder to find and train. Zhang left the amateur stage of the Shanghai Workers Cultural Palace and joined the Shanghai Film Studio Actors' Troupe. Film production was still at a low ebb, so opportunities to act in front of a camera were hard to come by.[35] Actors' troupes were established at most film studios to provide a training ground for performers and a stage outlet for their skills. For the next three years Zhang Jianya worked in the troupe, rehearsing and on occasion actually performing plays in public.

In January 1976, premier Zhou Enlai, the leader generally attributed with moderating the excesses of Mao, died. Public reaction was slow to build, but on 5 April citizens of Beijing demonstrated spontaneously in

Tian'anmen Square in Premier Zhou's memory and in favor of political liberalization. April 5 was the date of the traditional Qingming Festival, the time to remember ancestors and sweep their graves. The immediate reaction from the Jiang Qing faction to the popular remembrance of Zhou in Beijing and throughout the country was to intensify their cultural and political narrowness. The demonstrations provided Jiang and her allies the excuse for direct criticism of vice-premier Deng Xiaoping. Deng had been purged at the start of the Cultural Revolution and rehabilitated in 1974, under the protection of Zhou Enlai. Purged again in April 1975, he withdrew to a hot spring resort outside Guangzhou under the patronage of a local political chief. Meanwhile, in film studios and other cultural organizations, scripts were adjusted to reflect the new official line. Deng Xiaoping was the focus of attack in plays, films, and other media for the period through the huge Tangshan earthquake in late July, Mao's death in September, and the arrest in October of the leaders who became known as the Gang of Four.

Zhang Jianya appeared in a feature film for the first time in this eventful year. He took a minor role in a typical anti-Deng tract, *Rejoicing in Cold Creek Commune* (*Huanteng de Xiaolianghe*). The so-called "two-line struggle" dominates the story, expounded largely through highly uncinematic, lengthy political meetings and dialogue. Zhang Jianya played a country tradesman, Yao Mengtian, a role for which he could draw on his years as a carpenter. As his homonymous name ("Wants to dream of fields") suggests, Zhang's character is one of the "capitalist roaders," on the wrong side of the "two-line struggle." At about this time Zhang became friends with Zhang Yu, the actress who would become his wife. She had been appearing in Shanghai films for four years already.[36]

During his four years as a Shanghai Film Studio actor, Zhang had only one other opportunity to appear on screen in a speaking part. His role in *The Camel Bell in the Desert* (*Shamo tuoling*) in 1978 was not much bigger than his carpenter part. Again, the film reflected current policies, in this case the rehabilitation of intellectuals after the anti-intellectualism of the Cultural Revolution years. A professor of geology, with some help from the People's Liberation Army and a Uygur minority camel driver, foils in turn local bandits and a Soviet spy while prospecting in the remote borderlands of Xinjiang province in 1952. The prospects for finding minerals seem grim until a telegram arrives from premier Zhou Enlai praising Li Siguang, the father of modern Chinese geology. Inspired by the concern of the Party, Professor Zhu and his team eventually succeed in their task, at the same time exposing the spy in their midst. Zhang Jianya played Young Li, one of the geology students. In his two credited screen appearances Zhang Jianya thus played on both sides: in a Gang of Four excoriation of Deng Xiaoping and in a paean to Deng's political mentor.

In Shanghai in the 1970s Jiang Haiyang, the metallurgist, also dreamed of stardom. In 1975 he took the entrance examination and auditions for the Shanghai Drama Academy. His father's reputation and current circumstances may have worked against him, however, and he was not accepted. Unlike Zhang Jianya, he was also unsuccessful in his application to join the Shanghai Film Studio Actors' Troupe. Nevertheless, his actor father's name and connections encouraged several of the studio's directors to make unofficial use of Jiang in their films. Jiang Haiyang was not acknowledged in the films' credits because his work unit remained the metallurgical school.

In *The Unforgettable Battle* (*Nanwang de zhandou*) Jiang played a small part as a soldier in a fight over grain supplies in a recently liberated east China city in 1949. Made in 1976, the film was a collectively scripted salvo in that year's battle between the Cultural Revolution faction and the pragmatists associated with Deng Xiaoping. One of the three directors of this film cast Jiang Haiyang in another minor role in another film started in 1976 and only completed in 1978. *Special Task* (*Teshu renwu*, a.k.a. *Qianqiu ye*, literally "A Thousand Year Enterprise") also had a military setting, in this case among a band of Communist guerrillas on Hainan island towards the end of the war with Japan. Modified to reflect the enormous political changes between its initial scripting and completion, the story played down the problem of treachery within the Chinese ranks and played up the military action. As with all Chinese films before 1986, the film's dialogue was dubbed in the studio upon completion in 1978. Jiang Haiyang's part was dubbed by Zhang Jianya. Apart from the problem of his non-film work unit, in neither of these films was Jiang's role big enough to be listed in the credits in the official published filmography.[37] Jiang also played a small role in an uncompleted film, *The Glorious Festival* (*Shengda de jieri*) by the well-known Shanghai director Xie Jin. His recently rehabilitated father also acted in this film, which was overtaken by the changing political climate and shelved. Discouraged at his failure to get larger parts, Jiang Haiyang returned to full-time work at the metallurgical school, and resigned himself to studying for the national technical university entrance examinations, scheduled for July 1978.

The kinds of connections which Jiang Haiyang used in Shanghai continued to lubricate the workings of Chinese society during the Cultural Revolution. In Hunan Zhang Li moved back to Changsha after two years on the commune in Pingjiang. The father of one of the sent-down youths in the commune was the head of the Hunan Cultural Bureau. He arranged for his own son and one other teenager in Pingjiang to help fill a newly created quota of jobs at the Hunan Film Studio. As Zhang Li noted years later, this job was heaven-sent.[38]

The city he returned to in December 1976 was beginning to change: Mao was dead and the Gang of Four (including his widow) had been arrested three months earlier. The excesses of the Cultural Revolution were now ascribed to these four disgraced political leaders. The peasants in Pingjiang had been confused by this change. People in Changsha, Zhang discovered, were delighted. Moreover, Hua Guofeng, the man who had ordered the arrest of Jiang Qing and her three associates, was from Hunan. As the appointed successor of that greater Hunanese, Chairman Hua even began to brush his hair back off his forehead, to help heighten the similarities between himself and the late Mao.

Zhang Li enrolled in a study class at the Hunan Film Studio. The studio had been established five years earlier and had produced its first films in 1972: these were newsreels, documentaries, and educational films. Permission to start feature film production came in December 1977 and the first feature film was completed in 1980. At the same time the studio name was changed to the Xiaoxiang Film Studio.[39]

As he later recalled, being in a study class did not necessarily mean Zhang Li did much studying. At the start, he and his twenty "classmates" served as general laborers, moving rubbish and concrete for new buildings around the studio lot. All they seemed to study was how to appear respectful around their superiors. Life had the flavor of boot camp: Zhang Li and the others were only allowed out of the studio grounds on Saturday evenings and Sundays. For the rest of the week they lived together in two big dormitory rooms. Their ages ranged from thirty down to eighteen. At nineteen, Zhang Li, although one of the youngest, was one of several who had spent time in the countryside. The youngest students were fresh from high school. Many of the older members had avoided exile to the countryside through illness, being an only child, or using back-door connections with officials.

When the class got round to studying, they learned the basics of movie making. Zhang Li studied camera lighting for a couple of months and also managed to get some experience in actual filmmaking. In mid-1977 he was selected by cinematographer Teng Xihui as his assistant on a documentary about schistosomiasis, the snail-borne parasitic disease that the Communist regime had made great progress in eliminating from the Chinese countryside.

Peng Xiaolian's life changed in June 1975 when she began her career in the performing arts, not behind a movie camera, but on makeshift stages of small-town halls. Perhaps feeling sorry for Xiaolian, the peasants in Zha Village nominated her for the Jiangxi local opera (*ganju*) class at the art school in Yichun. No one wanted to join the class for local opera, which was considered a backward and dying art, so there was space for the Shanghai girl from the Fengxin hills. She moved to Yichun, a county seat near the western border of Jiangxi, on the railway line that linked Shanghai with Hunan province.

To Xiaolian's immense disappointment, life in the Yichun Art School was in some ways even worse than in Zha Village People's Commune. At least in the countryside she had been free to organize some of her time: the agricultural season had its slack periods, and there had been no supervisors in the fields each day. At the city school, however, her schedule included daily physical training. Xiaolian's legs seemed to hurt more than they had ever done in the fields. There was no spare time except on Sundays: even Saturday afternoons were filled with political study meetings.

Her thirty classmates were all educated youths from Shanghai, other parts of Jiangxi, or Yichun county town itself. In class the students learnt how to perform local opera. Part of the tradition was the "tea-picking" performance (*caicha xi*).[40] As it was 1975, this and other local dramas bore only slight, largely formal resemblance to their originals. Like the flower-drum songs of neighboring Hunan and the clapper songs of the North China plain, they had been reshaped to tell the stories of the "model performances" promulgated from Beijing.

In the spirit of the Party's current emphasis on "open-door schooling" (*kaimen banxue*), Peng Xiaolian and her classmates often travelled in the countryside to perform for villagers grateful for even these performances that at least looked like the traditional dramas. On these expeditions into the countryside, Peng and her classmates would put on stage make-up and parade during the day on the back of a three-wheel tractor, if one could be found, to draw an audience. In remoter locations peasants would walk more than ten kilometers in order, they said, "to see colorful folk" (*kan caise ren*).

The curious mix of public tension and private boredom that

characterized Chinese national life in 1976 gave way to general excitement in October that year with the arrest of the Gang of Four.[41] Superstitious country people with whom Xiaolian spoke were confused: the fall of Jiang Qing, widowed a month earlier on Chairman Mao's death, suggested that the world had been turned on its head. Xiaolian's own celebration of the news she kept to herself, for people at the art academy did not like her, as she read too many books and spent too much time alone.

Things got worse when Peng Xiaolian graduated in the summer of 1977 and was assigned to the Yichun County Drama Troupe. At least at school she had been surrounded by young people. In the drama troupe not only were the people older, but their thinking was also old-fashioned. Young actresses like Xiaolian were expected to pour hot water for the male percussionists to wash their feet before retiring for the night. If an actress did not oblige, come the next performance, the gong player might not manage the right rhythm and ruin an aria. As small-time actresses, the women wore a lot of make-up and gaudy clothes. They felt something was wrong with Xiaolian, with her plain ways and book reading. In exercising at the bar, she would prop up her leg and read a page or two. Changing legs, she would turn a page and keep her nose in the book. Once, in a futile effort to be like the other actresses and to try the newly fashionable novelty, all the rage after the puritanical styles of the Cultural Revolution, she had her hair permed. The results so horrified her that she went to another salon and asked the hairdresser to cut her hair. Even proffering free tickets to the troupe's performance could not persuade them to cut off the permanent waves. Xiaolian rushed back to her room and cut her hair short herself.

Peng Xiaolian did not fraternize much with the rest of the 200-member troupe. Most of her social contact came through the letters she wrote to friends elsewhere. One day she wrote twelve such letters, and on another day, to the puzzlement of her colleagues, received as many letters. She and her distant friends would try to recycle stamps by covering them with an invisible layer of paste. This made it easy to wash off the post office's franking ink. With this treatment one stamp helped carry ten letters, until it eventually dissolved from the wash. As well as letters, Xiaolian also began to write short stories during her time with the Yichun drama troupe.

In such a big troupe, Xiaolian only played minor parts, perhaps appearing in major crowd scenes at the beginning and end of a performance. All the performances were "tea-picking plays" rather than modern, spoken plays, for the Jiangxi townspeople did not like the unfamiliar, foreign style of the latter.[42] In early 1978, about six months after she first joined the troupe, Peng Xiaolian learnt that she was on a list of players who were to be dismissed. A corps of two hundred, even in China's generally overstaffed artistic ranks, seemed too numerous to the leaders of the county's Cultural Bureau. The plan was to send the first group to be dismissed to a department store, where they would work behind the counters. Xiaolian had two months to think about whether she wanted to be a shop assistant.

Meanwhile university entrance examinations were about to restart across the nation for the first time in a dozen years. Peng Xiaolian's mother, who had worked as a humble gate-keeper at the Shanghai Film Studio despite her education, urged her to begin to study for the exams. Xiaolian felt her memory did not suit exam taking, so she did nothing. That May she took time to return to Shanghai to try her luck at exams for the Shanghai Drama Academy. There the teachers told her that at almost twenty-five, she was too old for the acting class and had no hope.

Peng Xiaolian's future directing class colleague Tian Zhuangzhuang had meanwhile returned to life at a film studio, though not the one in which he had grown up. By the mid-1970s a lot of soldiers were being demobilized and assigned to jobs in the civilian sector. Tian Zhuangzhuang had risen to officer rank in Baoding, spending a year as a cadre in the political department at the 38th Army headquarters. But, he later noted, the collectivist life in the military did not appeal, even if he was fascinated by military strategy. He was happy to be demobilized, and not just because it meant he could return to living with his mother in Beijing.

Like Chen Kaige, another son of filmmakers demobilized at about the same time in late 1975, Tian Zhuangzhuang was assigned to a film enterprise. As a demobilized soldier, he had a claim to priority in job assignments. Moreover, he had eighteen months' experience as a photojournalist. The Beijing Film Studio and the adjacent Central Newsreel and Documentary Film Studio did not need more staff, so he was sent to the Agricultural Film Studio, whose main output was educational documentaries for farmers.

Twelve years later Tian recalled an incident early in his time there. Working on a film crew for the first time, Tian was asked by his cinematographer mentor to try taking a couple of shots. They were shooting a film on crop turning as fertilizer in Jingmen county in Hubei province. "I sat behind the camera. The flashing light [in the viewfinder] moved something in me. As I reached up for the lens, the veins in my arm seemed to expand. It was a feeling [of power] like when Sun Wukong [the mischievous 'Monkey King' of traditional Chinese popular culture] changes when the priest, his master, speaks to him. It sounds odd, I know. But it was a really strange feeling. Nobody else I've spoken to seems to have had this feeling."[43] After such an unlikely epiphany, Zhuangzhuang had a sense he would stay in the film business. He was proud of his work as a cinematographer's assistant and was even allowed to direct a ten-minute film in Zhanjiang, a port on the Guangdong provincial coast.

In the early spring of 1978 the studio leadership sent Tian Zhuangzhuang to Dazhai. This village in the Taihang mountains of Shanxi province was trumpeted by the media in the mid-1970s as the nationwide model for revolutionary, "mass line" advances in agriculture. The poor peasants in the production team there had transformed their mountainous territory into highly productive terraced fields. Zhuangzhuang had shot footage at the Daqing oilfield in the northeast, which was the equivalent model for China's industrial sector. He was acquainted with agricultural Dazhai, having travelled there twice before. The first time was on the winter "Long March" he had taken with his brother and friends in 1966–67. They had stopped in Dazhai on their way back to Beijing from Yan'an. As a soldier he had also visited Dazhai with his brigade, for even the military could "learn from Dazhai," as the slogan painted on countless buildings across the Chinese countryside proclaimed. On this third visit cinematographer Tian was assigned to the Dazhai Production Team's "reporters' station" (*jizhe zhan*).

The regimentation of life in the terraced, row housing that had replaced the peasants' previously scattered homes struck Zhuangzhuang as tougher than life in the army. The Dazhai zealots, ever conscious of their model status for the rest of China, allowed no freedom even to visitors. The local people got up before 4:00 a.m. and spent an hour of political study. At 5:00 a.m. the day's work in the fields began. At 10:00 in the evening there was another hour of study before lights-out at 11:00 p.m. The hollowness of this frenzy of political consciousness raising was exposed in 1979, when official reports admitted that the Dazhai miracle had been achieved not through fervent study of Marx and his followers, but through massive disguised state subsidies and record-keeping fraud.[44] Zhuangzhuang was extremely well treated, supplied with his own car and driver to take him anywhere to collect materials and expose the seemingly endless meters of film provided him. He rather enjoyed the attention and might have found an excuse to extend his stay in such relative comfort. But he noticed that a woman seemed to be following him about, which made him rather nervous. She was not attractive, he noted later in telling this story.

Chen Kaige followed this same path from the military into the film industry in the mid-1970s. His father's position at the Beijing Film Studio was looking more secure. In 1974–75 Chen Huaikai was one of three directors of *Haixia*, a story of militia women on the south China coast. Upon its completion in 1975, *Haixia* came under attack from Jiang Qing for its alleged failure to follow Cultural Revolution artistic policy. Mao himself had ordered the film released. In the same year Kaige managed to arrange demobilization and a transfer back to his home town in a move similar to Tian Zhuangzhuang's shift to the Agricultural Film Studio in Beijing. Unlike Tian, Kaige ended up in a laboratory in the Film Processing Factory. At least it was part of the film industry and was just across Beijing's Third Ring Road from the Beijing Film Studio. The continued ill-health of his mother and his father's resumption of work were factors in his being allowed to return home.

Until he took the Beijing Film Academy entrance examinations in the late spring of 1978, Chen Kaige's life was a mix of drudgery at work and some stimulation in his leisure time. Living in his parents' apartment in the film studio compound, he regained something of the relatively privileged conditions of his boyhood. But Kaige, like so many of his generation, had seen a lot of his society and knew he could never, metaphorically speaking, go home. In these years he passed the time in the company of other young people who had been sent to the remoter parts of the country in the late-1960s and had managed to return to Beijing. He renewed his friendship with Zhong Acheng, the son of a Rightist film critic, who had worked in a neighboring team on the state farm in Yunnan. Zhong had begun to write fiction drawing on his life in exile. Chen also met Zhao Zhenkai, who was making a name for himself as an underground poet, writing under the pseudonym Bei Dao. Zhao had worked in a Beijing factory during the Cultural Revolution. The experience they shared shaped their attitude to the changes in the two years between the arrest of the Gang of Four in October 1976 and the advent of the so-called pragmatist leadership of Deng Xiaoping in 1978.

The future Beijing Film Academy classmates had each managed to survive and even excel in the Cultural Revolution. Those from privileged family positions before 1966 by 1978 were mostly back in the cities and bidding time prior to resuming their educations. Some, like Zhang Yimou, did not enjoy special social connections. Their futures would require more struggle.

5. The Film Academy Examinations

When the Beijing Film Academy joined other universities in conducting entrance examinations in the spring of 1978, the academy staff were looking forward to the first degree class since graduation in 1968. After ten years without regular students, the demand for places at the academy would be high and competition to enter fierce.[45] The academy had always attracted interest from prospective students, given the glamor associated with the film industry, in Communist China as much as anywhere else.

Gaining entry into the film academy in 1978 involved participation in several days tests at only three examination centers: Beijing, Shanghai and Xi'an. Those candidates who made it to the test centers had already been adjudged as of sufficient academic aptitude and potential. Even so, at the Shanghai center about four thousand students started the lengthy exam process for all departments: acting, directing, cinematography, sound recording and production design.[46] About thirty candidates travelled from Sichuan province to the Xi'an exam center.[47] For applicants from other cities, the cost of getting to the exam centers was hard to meet. In Xi'an many candidates turned up with as many as 200 eggs to sell to make money. Some stretched limited funds by sleeping in the railroad station waiting-room. Members of the class of '82 later recalled shared feelings of apprehension and determination as they took these steps towards their future careers.

Liu Miaomiao was one of the youngest candidates and, having just turned sixteen by the fall, was the youngest member of the new class. She took her exam in Xi'an, after travelling by bus all the way south from her home in Ningxia. A bra borrowed from the wife of one of her high school teachers was intended to suggest maturity to the examiners. In the classroom at the Shaanxi Art College, she clutched a small hand towel: "When I get nervous, I sweat a lot." The examiners did not look much better: several had only recently been released from detention or returned from farms where they had been sent in the late 1960s. The exams were an opportunity for them too.

Analysis of a piece of fiction or a painting was a major part of the exam. Liu Miaomiao explained the functions of a character in a story by

Lao She, a May Fourth era writer who had committed suicide under Red Guard pressure in 1966 and was now being posthumously rehabilitated. Visual skills in the exam were tested through analysis of a painting. Confronted by the reproduction of a Cultural Revolution oil in grandiloquent style, Liu Miaomiao drew circles with her finger showing how the Cultural Revolution artistic theory of the "three prominences" (*san tuchu*) gave concentric emphasis on the heroic figures in the painting. At the Beijing exam center, Chen Kaige was invited in the preliminary round of the exams, to outline how he would go about filming a simple object, like a hat or a cup on a table.[48]

Writing skills were obviously important for future filmmakers. Liu Miaomiao was given the title "A comb and a button." She took an O. Henry story she could remember and changed the characters to a brother and sister in pre-1949 China. After the exam Situ Jiaodun asked her if she had read any O. Henry. Liu Miaomiao ruefully admitted the plagiarism. Chen Kaige in Beijing was given two hours and up to two thousand characters to write an essay titled "Standing on the Golden River Bridge." As he noted two years later, some of the one hundred or so finalists for the directing department did not realize that the Golden River was the name of the extension of the Forbidden City moat that ran across the northern side of Tian'anmen Square. Chen, like other successful candidates, gave his essay a strong political flavor.

Noting that the entrance requirements for the acting department seemed to emphasize physical attributes (height, length of ears, size of nose), Hu Mei chose directing, despite coming from an army dance troupe. In an exam essay she retold the story of the excitement around a late-night film show in a mining town that her troupe had stayed in. In similar vein Peng Xiaolian in Shanghai chose directing, despite her acting experience. She only learned of the film school exams a day late, having returned to Shanghai to take the Shanghai Drama Academy entrance exam. But she managed to sweet-talk a teacher in the film academy's temporary office in Shanghai to get special permission to make a late application.

Candidates for the cinematography department, in a preliminary test, were required to show their drawing skills. Zhang Li, who had journeyed with two others from Changsha to the Shanghai exam center, could not draw to save his life. In the exam he copied, stroke for stroke, the still-life of an applicant from Anhui province. He managed four out of five points and went on to a week of further tests. Tian Zhuangzhuang was put off applying for the cinematography department, despite his work at the Agricultural Film Studio, because of the technical requirements and the drawing skills expected. He chose directing instead, returning from location at Dazhai to take the exam in Beijing.

Film analysis and writing skills were tested by having candidates watch and write about a feature film. In Xi'an Liu Miaomiao watched the popular 1962 rural comedy *Li Shuangshuang* in an auditorium full of applicants. The film was as old as her. As with most film writing in China at the time, her essay dwelt on the political messages of the film and said little about its style. In Beijing, Chen Kaige and others watched a screening of *Heroic Sons and Daughters*, a 1964 adaptation of the veteran writer Ba Jin's novel set in the Korean War. Chen Kaige had seen the film several times, as it had been re-released in the mid-1970s, even before the end of the Cultural Revolution.

A final step in the exam invited the applicants to perform: telling a story or presenting a short skit. Liu Miaomiao managed to cry effortlessly in memory of the virtually canonized Zhou Enlai in a playlet titled "Where is Premier Zhou?". She later claimed even the schoolboys peering into the auditorium through broken windows had been moved to tears. Chen Kaige in Beijing was given the topic "A Postage Stamp" and half an hour to prepare something. He did not do as well as one candidate, who had the examiners and onlookers laughing at the start and sobbing by the end. At this stage the candidates were asked to explain why they wanted to go to film school. One young woman responded blandly that she wanted to fill the gap caused by a lack of students. She did not go on.

One future filmmaker who almost did not pass was Zhang Yimou. He tried and failed the entrance exams to enter a physical education college (drawing on his basketball skills) and for fine art college.[49] The film academy felt like a poor substitute. He knew little about films, only the film versions of the Cultural Revolution model operas and ballets, and the three "war" (*zhan*) films shown over and over again in those years: *Tunnel Warfare* (*Didao zhan*), *Mine Warfare* (*Dilei zhan*) and *Fighting North and South* (*Nan zheng bei zhan*). But film school would be a way to develop his interest in cameras.

The conditions for entrance to most of the film school departments included an age limit of twenty-two years. Only the directing department made allowance for the ten-year gap in film training, revising the age limit to twenty-five. Zhang Yimou was already twenty-seven years old and wanted to enter cinematography. He tried to register for that department at the Xi'an examination center, bringing a portfolio of his photographs to persuade the teachers. They were impressed by his obvious talent, but he was refused for being over age. Zhang took the train to Beijing, and twice went to the academy to try to register there. But the teachers explained that, while his photographs showed great promise, the age limit was national policy and he could not be registered to take the entrance exams. Feeling sorry for the dejected Zhang, several teachers wrote letters of recommendation to the Xi'an Film Studio for Zhang to be taken on as a still photographer.

Having come this far, Zhang was determined to try anything. Later that summer, in a last-ditch effort, he wrote to Huang Zhen, the Minister of Culture responsible for the film academy. Huang was so impressed by Zhang's photographs and his argument that age should not deny him an education that he sent a note to the film academy ordering it to accept Zhang in the new class. The academy staff were shocked: this smacked of "backdoor-ism," in which the untalented used personal connections to gain special privileges. When they discovered that he had not improperly pulled strings to get ahead but had done it simply on talent and persistence, Zhang Yimou was accepted as a probationary student, on the understanding that, after two years at the school, the faculty would help him get a job. By the time Zhang made his way again to Beijing to enter the film academy, both the Xi'an Film Studio and the China Film Association had heard of this talented photographer and separately asked for him to be assigned to them. It was too late: Zhang Yimou had begun classes in the cinematography department, the oldest among more than thirty classmates.[50]

Young Liu Miaomiao heard the news of her admission to the film academy in August. Early the following month she travelled by bus south to Xi'an again and then took the train to the capital. Arriving at Beijing Railway Station, Miaomiao was overwhelmed by the crowds and confusion. On the broad, rain-puddled concourse in front of the station, she noticed another young woman with a bedroll and enamelled washbasin beside her. With a serious look on her face, she was scribbling in a notebook as she gazed around at the people going in and out of the station, apparently noting what people were wearing and carrying. Liu Miaomiao must have been staring at her for some time, for when it started to rain, the other woman raised a tattered black umbrella and called her over. It was Peng Xiaolian, newly arrived from Shanghai. They made their way north across the city to the film academy together.

Part Two

THE BEIJING FILM ACADEMY

—⁓—

If some members of the class of '82 thought they had at last moved to a big city, they were soon disabused of any romantic notions.[1] The campus of the Beijing Film Academy was surrounded not by the *hutong* and grey roofs of urban Beijing, but by wheat fields, irrigation ditches, and lines of birch trees. Their new school was a 45-minute bus journey out of the city northwest of Desheng Gate. A place of birdsong and the smell of fertilizer, Zhuxinzhuang was not the most obvious place for a film school.

Some of the new degree students were familiar with the location, at least as a bus stop on the way to the Ming Tombs. Half of the twenty-eight new students in the directing department, for example, came from Beijing. Six others were from Shanghai. From the several hundred candidates examined in Xi'an the directing department took only three students and the cinematography department six students. Beijing and Shanghai, the two metropolitan centers of China, dominated the student body. The average age of the class was twenty-five, although ages ranged from sixteen-year-old Liu Miaomiao and seventeen-year-old Zhao Jin (son of the well-known film actor Zhao Dan) to Zhang Yimou, at twenty-eight, the oldest among the twenty-six cinematography department intake. The art department was the largest single group, numbering almost forty. There were more than thirty enrollees in the most technical department, sound recording. The thirty-two new acting students only took some of their classes at Zhuxinzhuang. They spent most of their time in the city at the department premises in Xinjiekou, just outside the northwestern corner of the old city.

Beijing in the fall of 1978 was alive with political rumor and excitement. Deng Xiaoping had returned to power the year before and was intent on vanquishing the conservative Party leaders who were still in power almost two years after the arrest of the Gang of Four. Indirect suggestions had begun to appear in the official media that even Mao Zedong's legacy was open to public criticism. For four winter months, starting in November, a nondescript brick wall beside the Xidan shopping district in downtown Beijing became known throughout China and beyond as "Democracy Wall." Critical thinkers of similar age and backgrounds to the film students out in Zhuxinzhuang put up posters and published mimeographed magazines and books conveying the political and artistic ferment of the times. These months marked the melting of the ice that had constricted Chinese society through most of the 1970s. Despite the subsequent tearing down of the wall, they were also a first indication of the social and artistic experimentation which formed the background to Chinese cinema's New Wave in the mid-1980s.[2]

1. The Academy

The film academy in September 1978, like so many other Chinese institutions, was in the midst of reorganization and reassessment. The academy traced its origins back a quarter-century. In 1951 a film school attached to the old premises of the Beijing Film Studio in Xinjiekou had begun instruction to train a new corps of Chinese filmmakers rather than rely on old hands from the pre-Liberation Shanghai studios.[3] As in other areas of Chinese life, the model for the training of filmmakers came from the Soviet Union. Four Soviet teachers began teaching two-year classes in directing, acting, cinematography and production management in 1955. In June 1956 the Beijing Film Academy officially opened its doors. Short-term courses were also offered, chiefly for staff members sent by studios for special training. About 2,500 had students attended the Beijing film school between 1952 and 1968.[4]

Determined to train a new group of art workers untainted by what they regarded as the bourgeois humanism of the pre-Cultural Revolution generations, Jiang Qing and her allies had established in the late 1960s a May Seventh Art University to take over the functions of existing academies.[5] The new art academy took over most of the campus and buildings of the Agricultural Academy in Zhuxinzhuang. The May Seventh Art University included music, dance, and opera departments to train students in the new-style, contemporary Chinese operas. The art and drama departments found premises closer to the city. A film department joined the music and opera sections at the Zhuxinzhuang campus. Lighting and cinematography were the only specialities offered by this truncated department. The faculty were recruited from among the film academy's staff.[6]

With the arrest of the Gang of Four in October 1976, the shaky edifice of Cultural Revolution cultural efforts collapsed. It took time for the film industry, however, to struggle out of the wreckage. New films, particularly in the highly centralized production system requiring Beijing's approval from the story-idea stage onwards, only slowly emerged. Chinese audiences did not see many new films immediately after 1976. Instead they could watch the re-release of more than two hundred titles made between 1949 and 1966. Most of the few newly made films were released to official and private criticism of their "Gang of Four" qualities: a wooden unrealism promoting repudiation of the "leftist extremism" of the Gang.[7]

The arrival of the new degree class marked the full restoration of the Beijing Film Academy that had been officially announced in early 1978. But eighteen-month and similar specialist courses continued while the degree class was at the academy.

2. The Curriculum

As in the rest of the Chinese university system, teachers were assigned to teach only one group of students through its four years at the academy. In addition to their specialties, the 120 students in Zhuxinzhuang also attended some general classes as a group, joined by the acting department students bused north from in town. The courses for the students of the directing class, the most innovative of the specialities, can illustrate the experience of the whole class.[8]

The future directors began their training with acting classes. The underpinning of the course was the Stanislavsky method. Their teachers had all been trained in the Soviet style (in some cases by Russian experts) in the 1950s. Some students debated with their teachers whether directors should learn acting. Even those, like Chen Kaige, who agreed with the proposition, began to baulk when so much of the first-year class was spent in acting short sketches. Videotaping scenes from such classic May Fourth plays as *Thunderstorm* (*Leiyu*) and a stage adaptation of the novel *Rickshaw Boy* (*Luotuo Xiangzi*) helped relate these exercises to their directing speciality. But by the second year in Zhuxinzhuang most of the directing students firmly believed that too much of their time was spent in acting class.[9]

A good proportion of the students in the department, in contrast, argued that directors should be able to write film scripts, convinced that one major fault in their predecessors' work was the excessive respect paid to scenarios written by others. Some, like Chen Kaige, felt directors might sometimes best write their own scripts. "If the subject or contents of a script don't inspire you, what can you do?"[10] In the first semester the students began with short written exercises on lighting and camera problems set by their teachers.

The directing students in their first two years at the film academy learned to be stage directors. The plays they selected were usually again some of the well-known plays which had introduced spoken drama to China in the 1920s, such as Cao Yu's *Thunderstorm*, a gothic story of incest and suicide. The concentration on plays from a half-century earlier was a reflection also of the condition of official Chinese playwriting in the late 1970s.

In the second year the directing students had already attended many classes in directing, acting, and montage with students from the other specialist departments. Montage had been reified at the center of Soviet film training since the days of Sergei Eisenstein. Indeed, *mengtaiqi* is one of the few foreign words (curiously, two others are "humor" and "logic") directly transliterated into Chinese, rather than translated. The class of '82 started their montage course as a group in their second year. Each student had ten camera shots in which to present a painting. Cameras and film or videotape were not readily available, so they had to write and sketch out on paper a plan of where they would start and of the sequence of shots. Later in the course students used a still camera and told a story in fifteen black-and-white shots.

In these first two years at Zhuxinzhuang, the class of '82 attended several joint courses involving all departments. These combined lessons included Communist Party history, philosophy and political classes, courses on Chinese and foreign art and film history, English classes, and physical education.[11] Party history presented a challenge as the assessment of Mao Zedong's historical legacy and other issues were debated internally.[12]

Peng Xiaolian found herself foiled by the twists and turns in the Party line. As her first-year politics exam approached, she had expected to churn out the familiar, Cultural Revolution rhetoric against former president Liu Shaoqi and former army head Peng Dehuai. Then, inconveniently, the Party rehabilitated Liu and Peng Dehuai. To help her with the new line,

Peng had written some crib notes on the palm of her hand, but her nervous sweating dissolved the notes. She ended up writing about official politics and popular politics, which proved unacceptable to the academy's Party committee. They insisted that she re-sit the exam, suggesting that if she did not, they would have to expel her. Despite the threat, Peng Xiaolian never took the make-up exam. Her academic record included an incomplete for Party history.[13]

The academy's Party history course was discontinued. The teachers explained that the absence of settled interpretations on key aspects of that history made it impossible to teach. A philosophy course served in their second year as a rather unsatisfactory replacement. Soon the diet of dialectical materialism caused student complaints and requests that they be introduced to a range of Western philosophical schools.

In a related effort to reinforce the political correctness of their outlook, the school arranged field trips to expose the students to a range of life experiences. The directing class, for example, spent one month living on a commune in their first year. In the spring of 1979 the same class stayed for a month at a naval training school in Dalian, an industrial port and resort city on the northeast coast. The students had few concrete tasks, and passed their time taking photographs, sketching, and generally having a pleasant time. Chen Kaige buried his head in a notebook. Peng Xiaolian took her oil paints to record the seaside vistas. Such "experiencing life" (*tiyan shenghuo*) had been enshrined in Party policy since the 1940s as a means to expose intellectuals and artists from often urban environments to unfamiliar parts of society. For the students who had experienced a great deal before their arrival at film school, these visits to communes and factories had little point. Soon after the Dalian sojourn Chen Kaige noted that he had gotten drunk for the first time in his life there.[14]

In their first year the whole class also attended a course in foreign (principally Western) art history. A separate class on art theory, with a more Marxist emphasis, was also obligatory. Students of all departments came together in addition in a technical class, introducing the basic principles of filmmaking at a stage in their degree work in which access to cameras was not possible. These introductory courses included an outline of world cinema history.

Even for students entering the production side of the industry, film theory is a central part of film studies in the United States and Europe. It did not feature in the Chinese course. In the late 1970s and early 1980s, few translations were available of writings on film theory since

Eisenstein's time. Besides exposure to the latter's writings in montage class, theory was given short shrift. Only after the fifth-generation filmmakers graduated did more contemporary Western theoretical writings become available.

In their own time, outside their formal classes, the students devoured anything they could find in translation. Freud, Balzac, Kafka, and more recent Western poetry and novels, different from the previous standard Russian classics, found eager readers in the Zhuxinzhuang dormitories.

Some teachers felt that the most effective way to educate new filmmakers was to allow them to see as many films, foreign and domestic, as possible. In the Cultural Revolution virtually the only imported films on China's screens came from North Korea and Albania, hardly major centers of world cinema. The students soon found that the stereotyping and bombast that characterized the few new Chinese films were typical also of the newly re-released pre-Cultural Revolution product. The class developed a reputation for rather direct expression of their criticism, whose bluntness had its roots in their overexposure to such empty propaganda.

Of much more interest to the class were films from abroad. More than earlier or later film-school classes, the students watched foreign films regularly. During their first two years at film school a wide range of films was imported for restricted, "internal" (*neibu*) screenings for film professionals. The relative looseness of Party ideological control in these years made possible importing on an unprecedented scale. Their teacher Xie Fei, himself a fourth-generation director, later recalled the extent of foreign-film viewing, including films none at the academy had seen for thirty years.[15] By the mid-point in his third year at the academy, Jiang Haiyang had not even seen the script of *Kramer versus Kramer* (1976), but he and his classmates had watched works by Fellini, Bergman, Kurosawa Akira, Yamamoto Satsuo, Sergei Gerasimov, Vasili Shukshin, Bertolucci, and Bruce Beresford.[16] Shukshin's *The Red Snowball Bush* (1973) may have had a powerful influence on several of the students. Its story of an ex-convict suggests that the modern city is a source of corruption: only by returning to their pure, rural roots can people find a source of morality to rebuild their society.[17] Here may lie part of the inspiration for the blasted landscapes of fifth-generation cinema.

Hollywood films from the 1930s and 1940s were presented by their teachers as objects for study and mastery. These and many other films were loaned by the China Film Archive, headquartered at Xinjiekou near the acting class.[18] The students voiced complaints against the archive for its notorious reluctance to lend out prints of films.[19]

By their second year at film school, the class of '82 was watching two or three films a week. On their own initiative they organized discussion sessions after the screenings. There the students could voice their assessment of what they had seen, free from any need to acknowledge their teachers' views. A routine was soon established. "When we heard we were to see a film, our first question was 'What year?'."[20] Films from China's pre-1949 film legacy were not readily available from the archive and did not initially have much appeal to the students. They were mostly interested in new films, particularly those made by the talents from the fourth generation, their Beijing Film Academy predecessors twenty years earlier. "We could appreciate them, but we were not satisfied. Watching these films, we formed a determination to exceed the fourth generation."[21]

In their last two years at the academy, greater restrictions were placed on the importing of foreign films, prompted by budget comptrollers rather than censors in the Film Bureau. The students saw a film from abroad perhaps once every two weeks. Sometimes a whole month went by without a foreign movie to view and discuss. By this time the older Chinese filmmakers in the studios had picked up the pace of production and there were more local features to see. The class in these years strengthened its reputation as blunt critics. Several fourth-generation and more senior directors have somewhat mixed recollections of discussion sessions out at Zhuxinzhuang.

The acting department students spent their first two years of academy courses in the city, with bus trips several times a week to the Zhuxinzhuang campus for general course lectures. The directing, cinematography, art, and sound-recording students out at Zhuxinzhuang often found it difficult to think of the acting students as schoolmates. Distance was perhaps the major factor, although the acting students themselves were a rather distinctive group. Whereas only about a quarter of the directing class were the offspring of established film and other artists, about half of the acting class came from such backgrounds. Dormitory living in isolated Zhuxinzhuang in the midst of considerable political change in society created something of hot-house atmosphere. The acting students missed out on this additional experience. Moreover, students from Beijing, who formed a large group among the trainee actors, attended class in Xinjiekou but lived at home.

In some respects the most lively departments for the class of 1978 were the cinematography and art design specialities.[22] Their directing and acting colleagues were being taught in a modified Soviet style not much different from the training which their predecessors had undergone in the 1950s and 1960s. In contrast, the Chinese art and photography world in the four years of their academy training reflected more immediately than other cultural areas the explosion of innovation that occurred after the loosening of many Cultural Revolution strictures. The cinematography and art students spent a lot of time attending the numerous painting, sculpture, photography, and other exhibitions that opened in Beijing during these years. Years later cinematographer Zhang Li mentioned going into the city to see a ground-breaking exhibition of new paintings as a major influence.[23] His classmates and their teachers had much to talk about, including a great deal of newly published theoretical and other writings on Western, non-Western, and Chinese art. Innovation was less obvious in the directing and acting fields, for art exhibitions were easier to mount than innovative dramatic works.

3. Student Films

In their third year at Zhuxinzhuang the students from all five departments came together in making actual films. The cinematography students, for example, finally got their hands on 16 mm cameras at the beginning of their third year of study. In the course of the year the students made each more than forty 15 to 20 second pieces. Each work was roughly equivalent to a single shot in a feature film. They were simply an opportunity to work on focus, exposure, and other basics.[24]

Another way to overcome the shortages at the academy was to send the students to the studios to practice what they had learned. In the fall of 1980 the campus at Zhuxinzhuang was practically deserted, but for the students from the Agricultural Academy.[25] Jiang Haiyang, for example, returned to his native Shanghai to work as an assistant director on *Back Alley* (*Xiaojie*), directed by Yang Yanjin, a then innovative, fourth-generation director. Some other members of Jiang's class dispersed to television studios, in Beijing and other places. At the start of the new decade, television broadcasting in China was on the threshold of a great upsurge in production to match the acceleration in private television set ownership in these years.[26] After their graduation, these young filmmakers would join their older colleagues in confronting the challenge for audience share that television's expansion brought with it. But at the end of 1980 television offered the fifth-generation classmates a chance for two or three months practical experience. For their part, the managers of the television studios welcomed production assistance even from untried students. Tian Zhuangzhuang, for example, pulled some of his illustrious family connections to shoot a TV drama with the eminent actor Jin Shan and his wife, the adopted daughter of the late premier Zhou Enlai.[27]

Earlier, Tian had joined two of his directing classmates and shot a 50-minute video film. Tian Zhuangzhuang, Xie Xiaojing (who also took one of the lead roles), and Cui Xiaoqing directed *Our Corner* (*Women de jiaoluo*) from a script they had adapted from a short story. Tian used his connections with the television station to let him and his classmates make the film.[28] *Our Corner* gave early indication of some central concerns of several fifth-generation works, the relationship between individuals and society and the question of alienation. In the film, three handicapped young men work in a sheltered workshop which offers relief from their lonely existence in a community which is indifferent or even hostile to them. A young woman, Wang Xue, joins them as a helper and impresses them with her warmth and liveliness. Their happiness does not last long, however, for Wang Xue passes her university entrance exams and prepares to leave for college. The naturalism of acting, lighting, and setting also hinted at what was to come.

Earlier, in the summer of 1980, Chen Kaige and Peng Xiaolian went to Fuzhou to shoot a 70-minute drama for Fujian Television. *Goodbye to Yesterday* (*Xiang zuotian gaobie*) told of a young man's life and rehabilitation after being released from jail. Unhappy with the script they were given, Peng and Chen rewrote it extensively. But the experience at the TV station was not a happy one. Peng later noted that afterwards she and Chen never spoke to each other on campus.[29]

Feature film studios, including the People's Liberation Army's August First studio in Beijing, the Pearl River studio in Guangzhou, the Changchun studio in the northeast, and the small and newly reopened Fujian studio in Fuzhou, also accepted some third-year students. The opportunities to make films, however, were greater in video. Chen Kaige headed off for the Hebei television studio in Shijiazhuang in November. Like many of his classmates he had made the connection with the station himself.

Having returned to the Zhuxinzhuang campus, the students in the directing and other departments spent a good deal of the 1981 spring semester making 16 or 35 mm black-and-white short films of about

15 to 20 minutes in length. Because only a few films could be made, the students formed groups of about twenty people from different departments and shared the work. Naturally the students tried to avoid assignment to the parts of a script, for example static conversations, which they felt were least interesting and would provide little opportunity to impress their teachers and fellow students.[30]

In the manner of the video film *Our Corner*, several of these works served as a reflection of their makers' own lives. *Our Fields* (*Women de tianye*) couched the narration in a flashback from the present to the Cultural Revolution years.[31] The very title carried elements of nostalgia, for *Our Fields* was the title of a popular children's song from the 1950s, when, at least in retrospect, socialist idealism knew no bounds. Chen Xi'nan, a college student, feels a disquieting nostalgia for the hard years he spent with a close-knit group of educated youths in an undeveloped wilderness in the northeast. The harrowing deaths of two friends in a fire make the hero's remembrance of these years a mixture of nostalgia and bitterness and a contrast to petty concerns in present-day Beijing.

A third work, *The Courtyard* (*Xiaoyuan*), was directed by Tian Zhuangzhuang, Xie Xiaojing, and Cui Xiaoqing. Zhang Yimou served as one of the cinematographers on *The Courtyard*. The 40-minute, 35 mm black-and-white film was a modest, domestic drama filmed in an actual home near Jishuitan, one of the lakes that stretch northwest from the center of Beijing. A woman narrates the experiences of four young couples who live in a crowded house around a courtyard. Like the students who made *Our Fields*, the makers of *The Courtyard* made a particular effort to avoid the falseness they detested in contemporary Chinese films. A good deal of the story was filmed at night with a minimum of extra lighting. While much of the student acting seems stilted, Zhang Jianya from the directing class drew on his acting experience at the Shanghai Film Studio for a careful performance as a struggling musician living in the courtyard. Its naturalistic atmosphere and concentration on the ordinary, even petty, concerns of a group of neighbors help make *The Courtyard* reminiscent of the best films from the Shanghai studios in the late 1940s.[32]

In their last two years at the Film Academy, the students of the class of '82 also made three 35 mm color films. As production intensified in their final year, these films became the class's graduation projects. Acting students played the four leads in *We Are Still Young* (*Women hai nianqing*): three young male factory workers and the young woman whose arrival at the factory affects the three buddies' friendship. When one of the men hears that the girl has had an affair before, he breaks off their relationship. One of his friends has always loved the girl. A practical joke by his other buddy gives him an opportunity to express his feelings. The film ends a year later with their wedding at which the three young men are brought together again. The four friends realize that they have outgrown old-fashioned thinking and matured from this experience.

Marriage (*Jiehun*) was also considered one of the class graduation films, although the end credits include the names of seven academy teachers, as well as those of three directing and four cinematography students. The 55-minute story of *Marriage* is told in flashback. Apart from its relative novelty in previous Chinese films, the frequent use of flashback at this time may be connected to filmmakers and their audiences' habits of recollecting episodes from their immediate, Cultural Revolution past.[33]

Marriage presents two country brothers, the younger of whom goes to the city in the mid-1970s for higher education. The contrasts between the brothers are drawn in sometimes maudlin fashion. The older brother sets aside his own hopes of finding a wife in order to help his brother make an advantageous marriage into an urban family. Through his wife, the younger brother will be able to change his residence certificate to the much sought after urban category and escape the countryside. The clumsy script gives the younger brother a speech of self-criticism at the wedding reception his older brother has paid for. The flashback ends and we return to a train carriage in the present. The urban, educated brother with his wife and child is on his way back to the village to see his older brother. The script allows *Marriage* to take on something of the rural-urban melodrama typical of "mandarin duck and butterfly" middle-brow fiction popular among urban Chinese readers in the first half of the twentieth century.[34] But innovative dark, natural lighting and other efforts at filmic naturalism are an indication of things to come.

In making their 45-minute graduation film, *The Target* (*Mubiao*, a.k.a. *Benci lieche zhongdian* "This train's last stop") the members of the class of '82 drew upon their Cultural Revolution, educated youth experience. Several of the four directors and five cameramen, for example, had undergone rustication after 1968. The hero of *The Target* is keen to return to Beijing: at the start of the film his voice counts off the thirteen years between 1968 and 1981. As he tells his mother at one point: "This is my last chance." At age eighteen he had been sent to the countryside, then worked in a mining area, and ended up as a teacher among the nomads of the grasslands in the northwest. When he achieves his aim of returning to Beijing, however, his troubles do not end. He starts work in a car factory. Being reunited with his brothers provides no solace: his older brother sneers at his earlier political naivety as an enthusiastic supporter of the Cultural Revolution, while his younger brother is single-mindedly engrossed in study, under pressure to do well in the forthcoming university entrance examinations. Their mother begins to pester the returned brother about marriage, now that he is in his thirties. Her efforts at matchmaking have an additional purpose: with the middle brother married off, living arrangements would be easier at home.

Our hero keeps recalling in flashback a young woman riding a white horse on the grasslands. When he finds her in the city, she is not the stuff of his dreams: she is married with a child. The relatively unencumbered life on horseback on the wide grasslands and the camaraderie of dwelling among the Mongols haunt the memories of several characters. The city cramps physically and emotionally. At the end our hero resolves that he will not go through with a Beijing marriage and transfer permanently to the city. In voice-over he asks himself: "Could this have been my purpose? I should have a higher, more distant aim." The open space of the grasslands will allow this. This final ambivalence toward Cultural Revolution rustication and the suggestion that life today lacks purpose are forerunners of central qualities in future fifth-generation films. The crashing, intrusive music is a less promising harbinger of later trends.[35]

Three longer feature films from 1982 were also considered graduation works. But, as they were made at studios in close collaboration with their academy teachers, the class of '82 regarded them as more mainstream films in which their input was more limited. *Chen Huansheng Goes to Town* (*Chen Huansheng shang cheng*) was a co-production of the small Xiaoxiang studio in Changsha, where the cinematography department's Zhang Li had been working, and the film academy's own Youth Film Studio. The latter was set up in 1979 as an adjunct to the school to earn money and provide faculty and students with filmmaking opportunities. The eponymous hero of *Chen Huansheng Goes to Town* is a middle-aged peasant who is sent by the country factory owned by his commune to the city to serve as a purchasing agent. The contrast between Chen's earthy honesty and the craftiness of the town factory staff is the focus of the film. As one of their cinematography professors noted years later, much of the film was the work of their teachers.[36] This and its studio origins help account for the somewhat clichéd qualities of the film.

The same is true of *Probationary Lawyer* (*Jianxi lüshi*), made at the

Youth Film Studio. A law student goes on an internship in a small town and serves as defence attorney for a criminal. The young lawyer soon realizes that society is as much to blame as the young man for his crime. Peng Xiaolian worked on this project as her graduation effort, serving as an assistant director (although she later noted she was little more than a log keeper, noting details of each shot as it was filmed). Her classmate Jiang Haiyang was more successful in asserting himself as an assistant director on the project. Acting department students played the young adults in the film. They all travelled to Hangzhou and Suzhou, two tourist locations, during the filming, and also lived for a time in the law students' dormitory at Peking University. Although directed by an older director, Han Xiaolei, *Probationary Lawyer* shows the influence of the class of '82. The film was an exercise in the use of long takes: the 90 minutes is made up of little more than 300 shots, much fewer than most features.[37]

Tian Zhuangzhuang again used his connections to set up the other graduation film made at an outside studio, *The Red Elephant* (*Hong xiang*). His mother, the actress Yu Lan, was by now a senior executive at the newly established Children's Film Studio in Beijing. Tian, the art directing student He Qun, Zhang Yimou with four others from cinematography, the directing department's Zhang Jianya, and several classmates went to Xishuangbanna in Yunnan province in the far southwest. Like much of the southwest, Yunnan was peopled by several ethnic minorities. *The Red Elephant* tells how a group of Dai minority children find an unusual elephant and make friends with it by saving its tiny offspring.

The Red Elephant differs from most Chinese films made for children in its deft touch. The Dai children and adults are played by Dai, rather than Han Chinese impersonating them. The usual talking down to youthful audiences is not strong in this work. Zhang Jianya recalled later, however, that the teachers had obliged the students to include a sequence of the adults looking for the child heroes, to show young audiences how much adults were concerned about them.[38] The art and photography skills of He Qun and Zhang Yimou anticipate their collaboration on *One and Eight* and *The Yellow Earth* two years later. The minority setting also turned out to be a dry run for Tian Zhuangzhuang's first films after graduation.

Compared to American and other Western film students, the members of the class of '82 had less direct practice in filmmaking in their four years at the Beijing Film Academy. Equipment limitations obliged the students to work in groups. But the Chinese film students benefited from working in 35 mm, something less common in Western film schools. The Chinese students also gained direct experience of production conditions and working in studio systems. The students in the acting department began early appearing in regular films and television dramas. Zhang Fengyi, a student from Guangzhou, for example, shot to instant fame by playing the lead role in the Beijing Film Studio's *Rickshaw Boy*, released in August 1982 just two weeks after his graduation.[39]

Even if much of their training was practically oriented, each student had to write a graduation thesis and undergo final examinations. Jiang Haiyang, for example, wrote on the relationships between plot and mood, drawing on his experience during his third year on the set of *Back Alley*. Liang Ming from the cinematography department produced an essay on color and tone in film art. Zhang Fengyi used his *Rickshaw Boy* performance for a thesis on the actor's self and the characters he or she plays.[40] In mid-June 1982, each department held oral examinations on the theses. Faculty, students, and film people from outside the school attended these ritualistic gatherings. But sometimes the exchanges could be lively. A report in the following year's *Film Yearbook* speaks pointedly about the independence and novelty of many of the students' views.[41] The accompanying lengthy extracts from seven theses is prefaced by an editor's note that the views expressed are not fully matured and their analyses should not be treated as necessarily correct.[42] Liu Miaomiao, at nineteen the youngest graduate, managed to produce one of only five theses in the entire class to receive the full five marks available.[43] On 19 July 1982 one hundred fifty-three students of the class of 1982 graduated.[44] They were the first graduates of the Beijing Film Academy since its opening in 1956 to be granted bachelor's degrees.

4. Classmates

It would be misleading to present a picture of a tight-knit cohort of young filmmakers moving smoothly through their four-year degree training at the Beijing Film Academy. As the first degree group in ten years, in an era of considerable political and social change, the class of '82 and their teachers had to spend time establishing what their education should embrace. The 153 students were not a particularly united group. Artists, even those in training, often have well-developed egos. The class of '82 earned a reputation for questioning and impatience that extended beyond the Zhuxinzhuang campus and the Xinjiekou acting department headquarters.[45]

One of the two major groups into which the classmates spontaneously divided themselves had been largely educated before arriving at Zhuxinzhuang. The label "social youths" (*shehui qingnian*), which identified this group, did not mean that the older students showed good manners and were adept at the social niceties. If anything, the reverse was true. "Social youths" referred to the shared experience of forced exposure to society during the Cultural Revolution. This "social experience" affected the older students in the class of '82 in several ways. Jiang Haiyang recalled later that they had a greater sense of responsibility and a maturity that their younger classmates lacked. The older students knew how hard it had been for them to get to the campus at Zhuxinzhuang. Many felt it was their last chance to make good.[46] This greater social experience could sometimes lead to frustration with the discipline of the classroom. Wu Ziniu later claimed that in 1979 he seriously thought about giving up his studies and going to live in some natural landscape somewhere.[47]

On the other hand, the older students may not have been as swift as the high schoolers in grasping new ideas and fashions of thought. Chen Kaige, Tian Zhuangzhuang, and even Zhang Jianya were embarrassed at not knowing how to dance socially, at a time when ballroom and disco dancing became the rage for young Beijing. But the older students could draw on years of experience to produce perhaps more thoughtful, deeper analyses of academic and social questions. Indeed, the younger students would occasionally seek out a "social youth" to talk over a personal problem.[48] The cinematography and sound-recording departments included a higher proportion of the younger students: the sound department had made knowledge of physics an entrance requirement, which worked against educated youths. Two-thirds of the directing students were "social youths," as was half the acting class and about a third of the art and cinematography departments' students.[49]

Cutting across this difference in maturity and experience were a number of other divisions in the class of '82. Four years after graduation, Wu Ziniu recalled social distinctions among his classmates. Some were the sons and daughters of high officials, or from families active and well-known in the art and performing worlds. Ordinary folk, among whom he included himself as his father was a college teacher, were a minority.[50] Few, at least of the more mature students, from among the relatively privileged groups dwelt on their family backgrounds.[51] Most wanted to make their own way on their own merits. Upon graduation, however, a high proportion of those students assigned to studios and television stations in Beijing enjoyed good family connections. Others, like Zhang Yimou, of less illustrious parentage found themselves assigned to more distant studios.

Communist Party membership was another potential distinguishing factor among the students, although it seems to have mattered little during the four years at the academy. Years in the army was a standard route in the mid-1970s into Party ranks. Chen Kaige, Tian Zhuang-zhuang, Zhang Junzhao, and Hu Mei in the directing department had all served in the People's Liberation Army and carried Party cards. But this distinction did not necessarily unite: several of their classmates noted later that Tian and Chen's mutual distaste for each other was evident in these years.

On a scholarship of twenty-two *yuan* a month (less than US$10) with fourteen *yuan* of that spent on the monthly meal plan in the cafeteria, Peng Xiaolian and many of her classmates needed to stretch their resources as far as their ingenuity would allow. Once during a power blackout, Peng Xiaolian and friends made a dash for the pile of cabbages stored for the winter beside the dining room and made off with armloads. A rickety old sewing machine did sterling service in making genuine looking perforations in the counterfeit movie tickets some students made to get into special screenings.[52]

Distance limited the students' participation in the poster writing and publishing activities associated with the Democracy Wall in the winter of 1978–79. The film academy was even further out of the city than Peking University and the other schools in the northwestern suburbs. But some film students did manage to take part. The unofficial magazine *Today* (*Jintian*), for example, published poems by class members. Liu Miaomiao, Zhang Li and others visited the wall, combining their political curiosity with an urge to check out the nearby Xidan shops. Zhang Li ten years later recalled the students' excitement at the Democracy Wall activities of self-taught, former sent-down youths, although he pointedly noted that the students felt "those people were very brave."[53]

The openness which the Wall symbolized extended to all areas of intellectual and artistic endeavor. The newly established Academy of Social Sciences joined the effort at introducing a range of writings on new aesthetic theories.[54] This was a welcome change from the stale, Stalinist and pre-Stalinist theory which had been the usual fare since 1949. After three decades of tightly circumscribed political limits and constantly repeated orthodoxy, these months seemed extraordinarily open and unusually directionless. Even after Deng Xiaoping suppressed the Democracy Wall movement, ordering the arrest of its leaders such as Wei Jingsheng in the spring of 1979, the possibilities it had opened up could not be forgotten.

The combination of this novel atmosphere and the ambition on the part of the students at the Beijing Film Academy to make a break in Chinese cinema proved powerful. The students were a lively group, and earned a reputation among intellectual Beijingers for not tolerating nonsense. "We liked to argue," noted Wu Ziniu several years later, "we were a stubborn lot. We didn't even believe in table manners."[55] Not surprisingly, outsiders sometimes perceived them as an arrogant group, with whom cooperation was difficult.[56]

On occasion the students came into conflict with cautious leaders. One of the youngest members of the directing class was Zhao Jin. His father, the actor Zhao Dan, died in October 1980 shortly after his outspoken artistic will had been published in *People's Daily* under the heading "Rigid control ruins art and literature."[57] Zhao Jin had a reputation for wildness and had a far greater enthusiasm for dance parties than his fellow students. He also tended to lead the others against Party caution, inspired perhaps by his father's dying example. In 1982 his graduate thesis in the directing department argued that truth had no objective criterion. Deng Xiaoping himself had made much of the slogan "Seek truth from facts" in his efforts against Party conservatives standing in the way of economic reform. But Party orthodoxy, at a time when Deng's dabbling in support for the Democracy Wall was long gone, emphasized the class and material bases for truth. The academy's Party Committee almost refused Zhao Jin permission to graduate.[58]

Their teachers had less influence on the formation of this fifth-generation cohort than the academy perhaps would have liked. In discussing the class of '82 four years after their graduation, Ni Zhen, one of their most respected professors, confessed that their teaching had had little to do with the way the class turned out. His former students agreed. Wu Ziniu and Zhang Yimou, among others, echoed Jiang Haiyang's view: "They didn't have much to teach. In a sense teachers and students were all learning in those years."[59] Jiang felt that the class learned most simply from seeing as many films as they could. When the teachers lectured about the films, they dwelt on the story and contents of the works, spending little time on assessing the films as films. In this the faculty lectures resembled almost all critical writing on Chinese cinema since 1949.

As Zhang Yimou observed of their foreign film viewing: "The teachers hadn't seen these films either. They were seeing them for the first time too."[60] Tian Zhuangzhuang concurred: "We learnt by watching films," then added with a measure of typical flippancy, "The teachers had nothing to teach."[61] Certain faculty members encouraged the free discussion that followed film screenings. Ni Zhen later remarked, perhaps a little ruefully, that it was a deliberate strategy to help destroy the vestigial influence of the narrowness of the Gang of Four years.[62] After ten years of disruption, many faculty had trouble presenting a systematic education to their students. Before 1966, Soviet-style film education had been standard. At the time of Dengist reform, the Soviet model was no longer accepted, but the new system was not clear.[63] Zheng Guo'en, professor of cinematography who had taught at the film academy since 1956, chose what he described as a Buddhist expression to characterize the role of teachers like himself with the class of '82: "The master takes the student to the door, but the student must go through it himself."[64] Again the distance between the Zhuxinzhuang campus and the city played a part. The teachers only took the staff bus out to school on the days on which they had classes to teach. Otherwise the class of '82 was left alone. As Zhang Yimou later remarked: "You might say we trained ourselves."[65] Despite the divisions in the group, several classmates later recalled how much they had learnt from each other in these years.[66]

5. Graduation

As graduation approached in July 1982 the students learned to which studio or television station they would be assigned after leaving the academy. In a system of work assignment and limited interchange between work units, the announcement of assignments was greeted with some dread. The Pearl River Film Studio in Guangzhou had not asked for anyone from the class of '82, and so got no-one. Initially the Shanghai Film Studio had not asked for any assignees, although the leaders there later changed their mind and took several of their former employees, including Zhang Jianya and Jiang Haiyang. Jiang soon married the daughter of Chen Zhigu, one of the heads of the Shanghai studio. Connections like this naturally figured in assignment decisions.

Some students found that their new work units were small,

undeveloped studios in distant provinces. Zhang Yimou was assigned to one such studio, the Guangxi Film Studio in Nanning. This news added to his confusion, for, he later claimed, he had seriously thought around graduation time about giving up films all together and returning to his first love, still photography. On learning of the Nanning assignment, he felt it was too far away. Zhang thought to contact the editors of *Shaanxi Pictorial* (*Shaanxi huabao*) magazine to get a job as a photographer.[67] Other graduates remained in Beijing, at the feature film and documentary studios, and in television. This was true for the film blue-bloods in the class, Chen Kaige and Tian Zhuangzhuang, who had grown up in the grounds of the studio. The Changchun Film Studio, in the northeast, was something of a booby prize. The studio was notorious for producing films of the most egregious, modified Stalinist style. As if to mollify feelings of disappointment, cinematography professor Zheng Guo'en told the students that earlier graduates had waited an average of seven years before being able to work independently. His advice was for the graduates to put their heads down: "Work hard and keep quiet" (*duo zuo shao shuo*).[68]

In retrospect, the graduation of the class of '82 was filled with promise, although their real grasp of film had to wait until after they had produced their first films in the studios. Of course not all of the 153 graduates who left Zhuxinzhuang in July 1982 were going to be great talents. But, as one of the most successful graduates observed four years later, the academy teachers could feel satisfied if about a quarter of the 28 directing department graduates turned out to be accomplished directors.[69]

The importance or otherwise of the Beijing Film Academy in this achievement is difficult to assess. The four years spent at Zhuxinzhuang were not inconsequential. Their teacher Ni Zhen emphasized how 1978–82 saw considerable political and intellectual change and innovation, albeit sometimes temporary.[70] The academy classrooms provided some practice in filmmaking techniques. But the most important learning for the class of '82 came from outside any classroom. Most of the future achievers in the group came from among the "social youths" who had learned a great deal from their experiences during the Cultural Revolution. The combination of the discussion of these issues at film school with the earlier experience of society lies at the core of any explanation of the fifth-generation achievement.

Part Three

THE FILMS OF THE FIFTH GENERATION

—ᴍ—

The class of '82, proceeding to their work assignments in film studios and some television stations, faced uncertain careers. Film industry leaders were starting to notice the impact of rising television ownership on box-office income. If the experience of previous new arrivals at the studios was any guide, the new graduates could expect to spend years in minor positions on crews before being allowed to take full responsibility themselves. But, at several studios on the margins of the film enterprise, opportunity came earlier than expected. The forcefulness and determination that these graduates had shown in getting to the film academy and in their years at Zhuxinzhuang also helped force change.

The following discussion of the films of the fifth-generation filmmakers is organized around the individual careers of nine members of the class of '82. An auteurist approach to film history has obvious limitations in any country: this study makes no special claims to its validity. The focus on directors recognizes the reality of how films got made in China, for all of these films required special determination by their directors in a social and political environment where personal relationships had considerable importance. This approach allows us to trace the shared trajectory of the careers of this age cohort. The experiences of individual artists in different studio contexts make clear the broad history of Chinese filmmaking in the 1980s and 1990s. It also shows the interplay between individual experience and wider political and social developments that shaped Chinese film history in these years.

For most of these filmmakers the account ends in the late 1980s, when it can be argued that the fifth generation as a coherent force for artistic change had faded. Some of these directors' careers are traced through the

1990s: most discussions end in the late 1980s. The Beijing massacre on 4 June 1989 signalled the end of the cultural liberalization in which the fifth-generation filmmakers emerged. The aftermath of June 4th added further political cautions to the financial problems hitting the film studios that had become obvious over two years earlier. By the 1990s changing circumstances in Chinese life, entertainment choices and increasing commercial pressures were beginning to make much of film's New Wave seem an anachronism. With a few notable exceptions, the explorations of the national crisis that had propelled the rise of the fifth generation had begun to seem like a throwback to the aftermath of the Cultural Revolution. New opportunities in seaboard and urban China, coupled ironically with a response to the June 4th Tian'anmen events, drew public attention elsewhere.

By the 1990s most of the directors discussed here no longer enjoyed the scope to produce "exploratory" (*tansuo*) films like their first works and went on to make more commercial films and television dramas. Several directors, including Chen Kaige and Zhang Yimou, continued in more exploratory vein in the 1990s, with help from international investors, perpetuating the fifth-generation legacy. Two films that served to announce the arrival of the fifth generation merit special attention. We start with them.

1. First Films: *One and Eight* and *The Yellow Earth*

Strictly speaking, the first fifth-generation film was Wu Ziniu's *The Candidate* (*Houbu duiyuan*, Xiaoxiang studio), a children's film which was formally certified for distribution on 15 December 1983. Tian Zhuangzhuang's *September* (*Jiuyue*, Kunming studio) received Film Bureau certification in May 1984.[1] But two other films, certified in October and December 1984, announced the arrival of the fifth generation on China's screens. The breakthrough came not from the big, established studios in Shanghai, Beijing, or Changchun. *One and Eight* (*Yige he bage*) and *The Yellow Earth* (*Huang tudi*) were both made at the Guangxi Film Studio in Nanning, the capital of the Guangxi Zhuang Autonomous Region which borders Vietnam.

Throughout China's history, innovation and vigor have arisen from the outer limits of the Chinese pale. New dynasties, for example, generally arose in borderlands before conquering the Chinese heartland and claiming imperial power. The Guangxi studio was one of the newest studios. A producer of newsreels since its inauguration in 1958 through the 1970s, the Guangxi studio had also a strong sideline in dubbing Mandarin Chinese films into Zhuang and other languages of the province. It remained a small studio: the employees at Guangxi numbered 303. On a per capita basis, they were somewhat more productive than their Beijing colleagues, each year producing four or five features. In contrast, the three thousand or so artists, technicians and workers employed at the Beijing Film Studio in 1984 made seventeen feature films (up from eleven the previous year).[2]

The smallness and newness of the studio in Nanning were crucial factors in the fifth-generation breakthrough from Guangxi. The established studios in Beijing, Shanghai, and elsewhere were overstaffed. Low levels of annual production meant that some directors spent a decade or more without making a film. New graduates of the directing department could look forward to several years working on continuity or as a director's assistant before being able to serve even as an assistant director at one of the big studios. In contrast, Guangxi had far fewer directors, established or otherwise, competing for the opportunity to practice their craft. Moreover, the directors who were there by definition were less established, with less clout in demanding the opportunity to make films.

Although the Guangxi studio leadership initially asked for twelve

1982 graduates from the film academy, the classmates baulked at the prospect of such a remote place, aware that work assignments in China were difficult to alter. Eventually Nanning got four rather reluctant assignees: Zhang Junzhao from the directing department, Zhang Yimou and Xiao Feng from cinematography, and the art designer He Qun. Having grown up in remote Xinjiang in the far northwest, work assignment to the far southwest was not totally disagreeable for Zhang Junzhao. Wei Zheng, the head of the film academy's cinematography department and himself a member of the Zhuang minority, had some influence on Zhang Yimou's assigned workplace. Recognizing Zhang's potential, Wei was keen to secure him for the Zhuang autonomous region.[3] Wei Bida, the head of the studio, was determined to give his new, young colleagues an opportunity to make a good start. Also an ethnic Zhuang, Wei had been studio head for only a short time and was nearing retirement. He readily acknowledged that he knew little about films.

Six months after their arrival in Nanning the four graduates had found a script for their first effort together. It was based on a long poem, "One and Eight," written before the Cultural Revolution by the innovative writer, Guo Xiaochuan. On 1 April 1983 Wei Bida called a general meeting of the studio staff to formally announce the formation of the Guangxi Film Studio Youth Filming Group (*qingnian shezhizu*). Wei asked the studio personnel to give the young people every encouragement and co-operation. Such exhortations were necessary, for immediately after the meeting some older staff members began to complain that they had had to wait three to five, even ten, years after graduation to start their first independent production at Guangxi or prior to moving there. Leaving behind these disgruntled colleagues, the Youth Filming Group set off for Ningxia province in the northwest. As a sign of their resolution to succeed, the all-male group shaved their heads.[4]

Like many of the typical fifth-generation films that followed it, *One and Eight* was set during the War of Resistance to Japan. Nine prisoners are being held by a group of Communist Eighth Route Army soldiers. One of these captives, Wang Jin, is himself an Eighth Route Army man, a former political instructor falsely accused of treason. The other prisoners are three bandits, three army deserters, a young traitor, and a convicted well-poisoner. In the course of attempting to make their way with their army captors to safer territory, the prisoners begin to show a grudging respect for Wang Jin. Also impressed are the army section chief, who leads the band of soldiers and prisoners, and a young woman who serves as medical officer. The Japanese savagery in a ruined village hastens the change of heart of all but the well-poisoner and young traitor: Wang Jin's example has begun to encourage a sense of patriotism among the eight. When the group is completely surrounded by the Japanese, Xu Zhi, the section chief, grants the prisoners' request to be armed alongside the Eighth Route Army soldiers. A prisoner even carries the wounded section leader Xu on his back as they attempt to break through the surrounding enemy. Eventually Wang Jin, now carrying Xu, and one of the prisoners make their way to safety. Several of the others are not so fortunate. One of the young deserters, an old bandit, and the army medic encounter a band of Japanese soldiers. The young man is shot and the woman is about to be raped when the old bandit, unseen by the Japanese, saves her from violation by shooting her. Apart from Wang Jin, only one of the original prisoners survive at the rather bleak ending. On a treeless plain he hands his rifle back to Wang Jin and pledges never again to regard the Communist Party and Eighth Route Army as his enemy. Supporting section leader Xu, Wang Jin watches as the reformed bandit makes his way into the distance.

One and Eight prefigured many other fifth-generation films not simply in artistic terms, but in encountering problems with the censors. All Chinese films needed certification by the central Film Bureau before they could be released. The Film Bureau insisted that the encounter between the woman medic and the Japanese soldiers be remade. In the new version the old man, instead of shooting Yang Qin'er to save her from rape, is shown shooting at the Japanese, implying that Yang Qin'er and the others escape to catch up with Wang Jin and Xu Zhi.[5] The censors in the Film Bureau (then under the Ministry of Culture), approved the re-edited One and Eight reportedly because, at one level, the film shows how a Communist Party member helps reform the eight other prisoners, even if Wang Jin is himself a prisoner.

Because of these delays, One and Eight was not released, like most other 1983 films, early in the new year, although it was completed in November 1983. At this time a campaign against "spiritual pollution" appeared in the official media.[6] Advocated by diehard conservatives in the top Party leadership, the campaign was directed at new, mostly foreign, influences in economics, society and popular culture that were emerging from Deng Xiaoping's economic reforms. High among its targets were women's make-up, bell-bottomed trousers and rock music. By mid-1984, the campaign had fizzled out, but by then it was perhaps too close to the thirty-fifth anniversary celebrations of the founding of the People's Republic on 1 October to allow a controversial film like *One and Eight* to be released. The Film Bureau may have feared the film's artistic innovation would overshadow the feature films and documentaries produced to commemorate the anniversary. The film was finally given limited public release on 8 October 1984.

One and Eight was like no other war film made in China since 1949. The war film has a long pedigree in modern Chinese cinema, reaching its apogee in the early 1970s, when the Red Army heroes were even more brave, perfect, immaculately dressed, and caring for the masses than ever. This story was different: the young Guangxi filmmakers were attracted to the subject precisely because it used a wartime setting to deal with larger issues and with protagonists who were apparently less than heroes. The initial presentation of Wang Jin among the eight other prisoners does little to help the audience differentiate him from the others. All nine men are considered traitors, not worthy of respect. Through Wang Jin's forceful example, the eight real criminals turn good. The nine men all share a common humanity and capacity for goodness, which on occasion must also involve cruelty, as when the old bandit feels he must shoot the young medic to save her from rape. Zheng Dongtian, their directing department teacher at the Beijing Film Academy, had advised Zhang Yimou and Xiao Feng against choosing that story for their first film, for it would be hard to satisfy typical studio heads with such subject matter. He ruefully acknowledged his error in an interview fifteen years later: "Who would have thought they would come up with a film like that?"[7]

The screen images in *One and Eight* reinforce its message. Cinematographers Zhang Yimou and Xiao Feng seem to have drawn upon the style of super-realist (or photo-realist) paintings. These enjoyed a brief vogue in the early 1980s in China while they were at the film academy and were typified by Luo Zhongli's monumental *Father*. Close framing, sharp focus, and natural lighting enhance the "realism" of the film. The film starts with the prisoners in a makeshift underground prison. Monumental bare torsos and heads fill the frame, as the viewer tries to sort out who is the Communist Party member and who are the rest. Later, as the band of soldiers and prisoners makes their way through a deserted landscape devoid of trees or much human habitation, the telephoto shooting anticipates some of the style of *The Yellow Earth*. Most of the frame is filled with sky, leaving a narrow strip of earth at the base of the frame along which the characters trudge. At other times, the desert fills much of the screen, leaving only a narrow strip of sky. In an explanation of their plans prepared before they left Nanning to start shooting, Zhang Yimou and Xiao Feng constantly used words like "an aesthetics of strength," "bold," "strong," and "terse." Color, for example, would be reduced as much as possible to contrasts between black and white. They confronted the universal aesthetic concern for beauty (*mei*), which in much of Chinese film history had been an excuse for contrived unnaturalness: "If we can, in that battle in such a harsh environment, make every character stick in the audience's mind, then we feel: 'We've expressed beauty.'"[8] Art designer He Qun, his film academy classmate, recalled fifteen years later that the watchword for the look of the film was "terseness" (*jianlian*).[9] Nothing so visually striking had been seen in Chinese cinema since at least 1949.

There are resonances of Soviet cinema in parts of *One and Eight*. According to director Zhang Junzhao, the crew read Soviet war literature as they developed the script for the film.[10] The physicality and monumentality of the human beings reinforce this sense. When the band of prisoners, armed with knives and makeshift weapons, rush out of a ruined temple in slow motion, Soviet film images again come to mind, as does Kurosawa Akira's *Seven Samurai*. The class of '82 had seen some Soviet war films at Zhuxinzhuang. The filmmakers' relative restraint with music—a few seconds of massed, angelic chorus to back the slow motion rush at the enemy, and on a few other occasions—enhance the deliberate naturalism of the film.

Because this is the first major fifth-generation film, viewers of *One and Eight* feel an urge to relate the theme and impact of the film to the background of its makers. The theme that labels of criminality or honor matter less than a shared humanity has considerable post-Cultural Revolution relevance. Long before 1966, for example, Zhang Yimou's father had been labelled as an "historical counter-revolutionary." Other film academy classmates had parents who were accused by Red Guards eager to follow the very first sentence in Mao Zedong's 1,400-page selected works: "Who are our enemies?"

But even without direct reference to the histories of the filmmakers, *One and Eight* was clearly a film of its time, boldly reflecting on screen for the first time the new irrelevance of the Communist Party. For young people in particular, the Cultural Revolution's denial of a human nature that transcended class differences was nonsense. Wang Jin and his eight companions prove they have as much right to join society as their captors.

They are all trapped in a war and on an earth that show no mercy: to fuss over political legitimacy is to render yourself powerless to act. Chinese filmmakers both before and after 1949 have found it easier to address issues of contemporary relevance through stories set in the past. *One and Eight* was distinctly a film for the 1980s.

One and Eight, however, was not the international break-through film for the fifth-generation filmmakers. Because of the Beijing authorities' caution about the novelty and ambiguity of *One and Eight*, the class of '82 was introduced to Chinese and foreign audiences through another Guangxi studio film. *The Yellow Earth* was unlike any Chinese film these audiences had seen. In its consummate integration of theme and form *The Yellow Earth* is a superb reflection of the innovation of this generation.

Chen Kaige had been assigned to the Beijing Film Studio (where he had grown up) upon his graduation from the film academy in mid-1982. He assisted fourth-generation director Huang Jianzhong on two films, *The Fragile Skiff* (*Yiye xiaozhou*, 1982) and *Twenty-six Girls* (*Ershiliuge guniang*, 1983). Discouraged by the lack of independent directing opportunities, Chen leapt at the invitation to direct his first film at Nanning. Zhang Yimou had proposed the idea to the studio leadership in September 1983, as the Youth Filming Group was completing post-production on *One and Eight*. Chen journeyed down to Guangxi in November and began to look for a script or film idea. Zhang Yimou had a script from the Xi'an writer Zhang Ziliang which the Xi'an Film Studio had already turned down. Zhang, Chen, and the others felt it had potential. With the preliminary approval of Wei Bida and the Guangxi studio leadership, a small group of five (Chen, Zhang Yimou, Zhang Ziliang, the art designer He Qun and the composer Zhao Jiping) travelled to northern Shaanxi province in January 1984 to find a suitable location.[11] They used the wartime Party headquarters town of Yan'an as their base for more than two months' exploratory work on a film which would deconstruct the Party's cinema.

The urge to innovate shines through in the statements that Chen, Zhang Yimou, and He Qun prepared in Nanning in late March, prior to returning to Shaanxi for shooting.[12] Unusually for a Chinese film, little happens in the script that Chen Kaige worked up. Dialogue is at a minimum, in contrast to the usual reliance on the spoken word. The close link between modern spoken drama and film in the pre-1949 film industry was compounded after 1949 by the careful attention of censors to film scripts. The censors subscribed to the notion that dialogue, even in excess, could carry clearer messages to mass audiences than mere images.

As they had resolved in making *One and Eight*, simplicity and solidity would be watchwords for *The Yellow Earth*. But, Zhang Yimou pointed out, where *One and Eight* had emphasized active force (*li*), the new film would have a quiet, still strength. Chen and Zhang were both struck by the apparent stillness of the Yellow River, which defined the eastern border of much of Shaanxi province. The river seemed to embody an enormous and unstoppable strength. The significance for the filmmakers of the setting in the heartland of Chinese civilization is made clear. The yellow earth beside the Yellow River gave birth to the yellow race. But the old-style filmic bombast this might lend itself to was not for these artists. As Chen noted, the style of the film could be encapsulated in one word: "concealed" (*cang*), a word also associated with things stored up. *The Yellow Earth* would have the quiet power and subtlety of the river.[13]

The film's setting is northern Shaanxi, several hundred kilometers from Yan'an, in 1939, in the midst of the War of Resistance to Japan, although war seems far away. Gu Qing, an Eighth Route soldier from Yan'an, comes to a poor village near the Yellow River. His assignment is to collect local folksongs to be reworked into songs to promote the Communist cause. Gu Qing is billeted in the man-made cave house of a poor peasant whose family includes a thirteen-year-old girl, Cuiqiao, and her ten-year-old brother, Hanhan.

The outsider from Yan'an does not stay long, but has an unsettling effect on the closed world of this peasant family. Cuiqiao learns about the Communist Party's policy of treating women as equals. Like her older sister before her, Cuiqiao is faced with marriage to a much older man. Her father is saddened to see his daughter leave, but the marriage was arranged long ago: Cuiqiao will eat better in her new home, and her bride-price will provide the funds for her brother's eventual marriage. The son's marriage is the more important, as he will continue the family line. Presently Hanhan's family is so poor that no parent would allow their daughter to marry into it. In the second wedding sequence of the film, Cuiqiao moves to her new husband's home. Meanwhile Gu Qing has returned to Yan'an, where he watches a vigorous men's waist-drum dance to farewell new army recruits.

The Yan'an that Gu Qing had described to Cuiqiao offers the girl a way out of her marriage entrapment. She says goodbye to her brother in a long sequence beside the Yellow River where Hanhan now draws the water she used to carry to their cave house. Having handed her brother her cut-off braid, symbol of her newly married status, Cuiqiao rows out into the waters. As in earlier sequences when she drew river water, her song about her miserable life as a woman fills the soundtrack. This time there are additional lyrics about the promise of the Communist Party policies. The song is suddenly cut off in mid-lyric and images of the silent yet powerful currents are replaced by a beached boat-shaped rock or log on a sandbank. The final sequence in *The Yellow Earth* shows the village men at a massed prayer for rain. Hanhan is among them. He seems to see Gu Qing appear over the horizon and tries to run towards him. The film ends before we can confirm Gu Qing is really there and whether Hanhan reaches him.

From the first shots, *The Yellow Earth* is different from any Chinese film made before it. Here is a film using the full power of the medium, not a respectful adaptation of a short story or play. The audience is taken into a village wedding in the barren north Shaanxi hills. The bright reds of the wedding party, and of the jacket of the girl Cuiqiao who watches the ceremony, are in contrast to the blues, blacks, and greys of the other villagers' clothes, and the yellow loess earth of the hills. Tight framing, on the red wedding sedan and the faces of some of the villagers, reinforces the reality of the people's actions and the artifice of the filmmakers' presentation.

To an extent not seen before in Chinese cinema, image and theme are powerfully integrated. Telephoto shooting makes the characters appear to emerge out of and merge into the yellow landscape. People rarely step into the frame. In these landscape shots, they often climb out from behind a dip in a hill in the middle of the screen. These villagers are part of the landscape, trapped in a place made poor by the refusal of the land to yield more. The framing of the shots is one of the most distinctive features of *The Yellow Earth*. They are strongly reminiscent of traditional Chinese landscape painting, with its relative freedom from the strict reproduction of reality evident in Western painting since the Renaissance and reinforced by the invention of the camera. Ni Zhen has noted this debt to the "flattening of space and its boundless extension" of classical Chinese painting.[14] This appropriation of the creative methodology of Chinese artists is further elaborated by Chris Berry and Mary Farquhar, who suggest that this use of traditional aesthetic codes provides the means for a powerful rejection of socialist realism.[15]

In landscape shots typically four-fifths of the frame is taken up by the yellow ground. The top fifth is left for the sky. Human figures sometimes walk along the line between earth and sky, overwhelmed in nature. As shot follows shot, some viewers are reminded of turning the pages of a Chinese picture book or comic story. The intention was to emphasize the heaviness of the earth.[16] The people of this place are in effect weighed-down and trapped by the land. The emptiness of the landscapes is in fact a burden, rather than a suggestion of scope for the imagination, as in traditional Chinese painting. This use of tradition is the major emphasis in the superb discussion of the film by Jerome Silbergeld, who warns that all readings can be over-readings of this pioneering film.[17]

In an industry that was starting to struggle to compete with fast-paced action films and television programs from abroad, Chen Kaige and his colleagues chose a deliberately slow pace and a carefully worked simplicity. The story itself is far from complex. Its telling captures well the unchanging nature of its subjects' lives. Here at last in a Chinese film are real peasants, not the garrulous persons of Cultural Revolution films, instantly mobilized to revolution. Cuiqiao's father allows Gu Qing to stay but utters few words of welcome on the soldier's first night in the cave house. The cave is lit by little more that an oil lamp and the fire from the stove, adding to the authenticity of the scene. Cuiqiao takes a long time to overcome her reserve. Gu Qing makes a bad impression on her by accepting her father's invitation to wash his feet in water she has just carried two kilometers from the river. Her brother says nothing at all until the following day when he belts out a crazy song about bed-wetting.

The Yellow Earth hints where its predecessors declaimed. At the opening wedding the newly arrived Gu Qing is invited to join the feast. The "fish" in the main course are crudely fashioned from planks of wood, and covered with a cooking sauce. The village head offhandedly remarks that fish are hard to come by in such a poor place, and it's the thought that counts. At Cuiqiao's own wedding, her husband is not seen: the grizzled hand which reaches into the frame to remove her wedding veil is indication enough of her predicament.[18] Yan'an, the cradle of revolution, is presented in an almost dream-like sequence of massed, waist-drum dancers. Zhang Yimou's camera moves for almost the first (and one of the few) time in the film, in some shots hand-held among the ranks of dancers, the vigor of the camera movements matching that of the drummers. It is as if Yan'an, and all that it implies in terms of heroism and sacrifice, is a dream not just for Cuiqiao but also for the fifth-generation makers of the film, born after the victory of the revolution in 1949. Cuiqiao's drowning, on her way to the Yan'an of her imagination, is only implied. The ambiguity of her interrupted song, "The only thing that will save me is the Commun ...," is startling. Followed by the massed rain prayer, the ambiguity in the presentation of the ability of the Communist Party to save these people is quietly made.

The presentation of Gu Qing is quite novel for Chinese cinema. He is a solitary Communist. Even in the brief sequence that seems to place him in Yan'an, he is barely seen with any comrades. In more usual films such figures arrive in villages in teams to arouse the locals to revolution or resistance. Gu Qing, in contrast, seems passive, aware that he has prompted expectations in Cuiqiao's mind that he cannot fulfil. He even makes himself squirm with his weak promise to return later for the young woman. Lu Xun, twentieth-century China's greatest writer, is famous for his creation of inadequate male figures, often as narrators of his stories. *The Yellow Earth*, of equivalent importance in Chinese film history, presents a similarly confused and decentered, male central character. Gu Qing's return to the village, too late to help Cuiqiao as he had promised, is unresolved. His figure appears on the horizon, disappears, then emerges again. Gu Qing may have come back from Yan'an or he may just be a figment of Hanhan's desperate imagination.

In responding to the novelty of the film imaginary some Western scholars have attempted to mine Chinese historical aesthetic and philosophical concepts to describe its meanings. In an early study, Esther Yau turns to Daoist notions of great formlessness and silence by way of explanation. Yau argues that Western analyses, with their concentration on narrative, are inadequate when confronted by *The Yellow Earth*'s images.[19] Mary Farquhar goes further, applying the *yin/yang* (female/male) dichotomy to the film.[20] Rey Chow usefully cautions against a what we might call such nativist reading of the film's aesthetics and "in terms of the politics of identity formation." Instead she offers the view that the music, namely Cuiqiao's songs, are a key to the film's rupture of revolutionary expectations.[21]

In China upon the film's completion the discussions of *The Yellow Earth* by critics, filmmakers, and cultural bureaucrats in China avoided reference to these careful political ambivalences and aesthetic roots. Conservatives did not wish to give the politics legitimacy by acknowledging their existence. Supporters of the film could not draw attention to them for fear of getting the filmmakers into trouble. Instead, in ritual statements that as usual concentrated more on the film's content than on its style, the opponents of the film complained that they were most upset by the film's impression of backwardness and poverty without suggesting ways for amelioration.[22] For many Chinese audiences, even young viewers, this lack of concern for "beauty" that the film shared with *One and Eight* made *The Yellow Earth* an unsatisfactory and unsettling experience. Certainly Chen, Zhang, and their team set out to create, as some of them had already done in *One and Eight*, a harsh, muscular beauty. In Chinese aesthetics this is called "hard beauty." The "soft" beauty of watery, verdant landscapes was more typical of Chinese cinema.[23] For foreign audiences, the Chinese critics argued, the poverty in the film would give the wrong impression about China and the role of the Communist Party in its development. The rain dance sequence was the last straw for the critics. Since 1949 official writers on film naively imagined that to present something on screen without clear signals of disapproval (villains with ugly, off-color faces and the like) was to endorse it. These critics rejected the real meaning of the sequence as a final, most effective expression of the need for change through revolution.

There are problems with the film, to be sure, but they are not political. The use of a full Western string orchestra at certain emotional points in the story grates, at least with Western audiences. The power of local song and other music elsewhere in the film serves to emphasize the clumsiness of the lush chords. Indeed, Zhao Jiping's reworking of local folksongs, particularly those sung by Cuiqiao, lends the film a special appeal. The

Shooting *The Yellow Earth*

girl's song lyrics, largely the work of Chen Kaige himself, are rich with small images of domestic farm life, filled with the birds and plants absent from the film's images. The songs balance the somewhat distancing quality of the carefully contrived images.

Aware of the film's difference and novelty, the China Film Corporation gave the film only limited release. Few provincial and regional film distribution companies cared to spend money to buy copies for distribution in their territories. The Chinese distribution system was not geared for "art house" films that might find less than a mass audience. By the time *The Yellow Earth* and *One and Eight* appeared, film distributors were deeply troubled by the slump in audience numbers as private television ownership surged.[24] Only after *The Yellow Earth* had created a sensation among audiences at the 1985 Hong Kong International Film Festival in April, four months after its formal domestic release, was the film taken more seriously in China. Several awards at film festivals in Locarno, London, Honolulu, and Nantes later in 1985 added to the renewed attention within China. Eventually thirty copies were printed for limited re-release.[25] As elsewhere, a new audience had to be cultivated to appreciate this new kind of film.

It is tempting to invest *The Yellow Earth* with greater significance for the fifth-generation filmmakers than it perhaps can really bear, simply because the film was the first public success from the Beijing Film Academy class of '82. Shortly after finishing the film, Chen Kaige spoke of the crew's ambitions when they started work on *The Yellow Earth*. Much of the writing and films of the years since 1976 had centered on individual suffering during the Cultural Revolution. These works were labelled "wound literature" (*shanghen wenxue*). This literary emphasis was fully in line with the political repudiation of the Gang of Four and the concomitant reassessment of the historical role of Mao Zedong. Chen and his classmates, who had gone through similar experiences, felt this literature rather superficial. He hoped in his film to go beyond the limitations of this often maudlin dwelling on suffering. The art of *The Yellow Earth* would express how his generation had matured in the upheavals of the 1960s and 1970s. The film would take a wider view than current fiction to express his generation's capacity for joy and sorrow, their perspective on history, and their sense of identity.[26]

Such a story, set beside the Yellow River in the place where Chinese civilization was thought to have first emerged, was also a striking contribution to the emerging discussion in the 1980s among Chinese intellectuals of the roots of Chinese civilization. This discourse, called "the search for roots" (*xungen*), was led by older members of the Cultural Revolution sent-down youths. In literature Han Shaogong, a writer of short stories, published a seminal article, "The Roots of Literature" (*Wenxue zhi gen*) in 1984. In it he suggested that writers and others look at the marginal, ancient cultures of China's south and east (Han himself was from the south-central province of Hunan), which were conquered by the centralizing Chinese state based in the north. This fascination with cultural origins that might be free of Confucian and other orthodoxies was, of course, in part an indirect way of questioning the contemporary orthodoxy of Marxism-Leninism. *The Yellow Earth* was a pioneer in the film exploration of these "roots." Tian Zhuangzhuang's minorities films, Chen Kaige's *King of the Children* and even Zhang Yimou's directing debut would continue the search.

The filmmakers convey their search for identity through the striking, still images of *The Yellow Earth* and through the metaphor this art elaborates. There is a deliberate timelessness about the film, despite the identification with 1939 in the initial title sequence. The original title of the film, "Silence on the Ancient Plain" (*Guyuan wu sheng*) reflected this quality. The setting in the core of Chinese civilization beside the Yellow River adds to the metaphorical effect. As the art director He Qun noted fifteen years later, the crew wanted to achieve an epic quality in their film, in contrast to the gentle, cultivated, rather smaller-scale feel of many fourth-generation films.[27] In an unconscious way the filmmakers could be said to have absorbed the inflated rhetoric of Cultural Revolution "model performances," seen in Peking opera and films of the early 1970s. While their attitudes and themes were different, the ambition could be described as equally large-scale and universal.

The Yellow Earth is a story of the impact of new ideas from outside upon a closed, static community. It is a metaphor for China, including the filmmakers' generation, in the 1980s. The process of making the film itself reflected this notion. Chen Kaige, Zhang Yimou, and their colleagues had themselves been exposed to a great deal of international cinema while students at the Beijing Film Academy. They had also seen more of society than most previous filmmakers. Their film used this exposure to outside artistic ideas to distinctly local effect, expressing their conviction of the need for social transformation. *The Yellow Earth* richly deserved the attention it brought to this new generation of filmmakers. It was the finest film made in China for at least thirty-five years.

2. The Spirit of the Times: Wu Ziniu's Films

Wu Ziniu was the first of the class of '82 to direct a feature film and the first to win an award for doing so. Starting in 1983 with a children's film, *The Candidate*, followed by a war drama, *Secret Decree*, Wu made *Dove Tree* about the Sino-Vietnamese border conflict in 1985. This film had the distinction of being the first work of the fifth-generation to be banned outright by the Beijing censors. Wu the next year completed *The Last Day of Winter*, set in the prison camps of Gansu in the far west, "China's Gulag." *Evening Bell*, a pacifist and nationalist essay, also set in the harsh landscape of the northwest, followed in 1988. Wu Ziniu in the 1980s seemed perhaps the least ready to compromise of the class of '82. But by the 1990s he had been obliged to work in a more commercial vein. Eventually he directed films on the Nanjing massacre and the Communist revolution that earned the approval of the authorities he had been so inclined to provoke a decade earlier.

Lacking the social clout that allowed Chen Kaige and Tian Zhuangzhuang to remain in Beijing upon graduation, Wu Ziniu wanted to join Zhang Yimou in Guangxi, but was assigned to Changsha, capital of Hunan province in south-central China. The Xiaoxiang Film Studio in Changsha had a shorter history than the studio in Nanning, but feature film production at Xiaoxiang was on a stronger footing. Founded in 1971, and beginning news documentary production in 1972, the Xiaoxiang studio produced its first feature film in 1980.[28]

Eleven graduates, including Zhang Li, who served as cinematographer on Wu Ziniu's first two films, went down to Xiaoxiang in September 1982. Several had worked at the studio earlier in the year on *Chen Huansheng Goes to Town*, one of their graduation films. Like the studio in Nanning, Xiaoxiang's small size and newness enabled the newcomers from the Beijing Film Academy to begin work on their first film relatively soon. The newcomers' performance on the earlier project encouraged the studio leadership to move swiftly to set up a Youth Filming Group at Xiaoxiang, the equivalent of the group at Guangxi responsible for *One and Eight* and *The Yellow Earth*. The group in Changsha was in fact established a month earlier than that in Nanning. With an average age of only twenty-three, this was the youngest film crew in Chinese cinema, at least since the 1930s in Shanghai.

The crew first made a 55-minute film for the Hunan television station. *Four Apprentices* (*Sige xuetugong*), a story of two young men and two young women, was reminiscent of the student films *Our Corner* and *We Are Still Young*. Zhang Li, who had worked at the Xiaoxiang studio before going to film school, served as cinematographer, while Wu Ziniu was director. Pleased with the result, the studio leadership gave a script for a children's film to the Youth Filming Group. After three requests, Wu Ziniu reluctantly agreed to take up the project as director, but changed the script, abandoning the original story of children who use martial arts to thwart spies.[29]

The Candidate (*Houbu duiyuan*), like most Chinese children's films, is a morality play, in this case about a schoolboy who learns to balance his love of Chinese martial arts (*gongfu*) with his need to do well in class. Ten-year-old Liu Kezi is in the fourth grade, and not doing well. When his grades improve through hard work, his teacher Song Ping, his classmates, and his mother all agree that Kezi may join the *gongfu* club, but only as a "candidate" member. When school ends for the summer holidays, Liu Kezi takes home a report card with straight A's. At home his mother, an ordinary worker, is too busy trying to find a job for her husband, who presently lives and works in Beijing, to give Kezi enough attention. After a bitter argument about *gongfu*, Kezi runs away from home. The educative effects of the twenty-four hour search by teacher, coach, and classmates are sufficient to restore harmony to Liu Kezi's home. All ends well.

Wu Ziniu and his youthful crew avoided the usual pitfalls in this rather hackneyed material. Most Chinese children's films (and indeed children's literature) talk down to their young audiences. This was true, of course, of many adult films before the emergence of the fifth generation. *The Candidate* treats the story on the level of the child hero: even the camera is more at the child's level than usual in Chinese children's films. Images convey information without excessive dialogue. Zhang Li's decentered camera, often in tight framing, suggests the problem of family separation with shots of people reading homemade notices pasted to lamp-posts seeking to swap homes. Images of lonely, withdrawn children, often framed by doors or windows, indicate a new reliance on the visual in Chinese cinema. The naturalism of the lighting and art direction is in sharp contrast to the glossy, utterly false settings and feel of most of *The Candidate*'s predecessors. These novel qualities earned Wu Ziniu's film a Special Prize in the 1984 Golden Rooster Awards, China's newly instated major film awards.[30]

Wu Ziniu's next project was going to be *Red Shores* (*Hong'an*), a story set on an urban waterfront, when he was assigned a new, rather indifferent script. *Secret Decree* (*Diexue heigu*, literally "Bloodshed in Black Gorge") is a war story set in 1939. A tale of betrayal and bravery, *Secret Decree* is complicated, sometimes confusing, and loaded with meetings, static confrontations, and the dialogue that goes with these. It was not promising material. Commander Wang Chaozong in central China is surrounded by the Japanese and calls on President Chiang Kai-shek to send reinforcements. He receives instead a secret decree calling for "strategic surrender." Wang starts negotiations with the Japanese commander but soon breaks them off, refusing to surrender. The tension increases as Chiang sends a commander from the Guomindang right-wing C.C. clique to get hold of the secret orders. He reaches Wang's Eighty-Fourth Corps and is assassinated. Complications increase as one set of secret orders proves to be a forgery. Wang Chaozong eventually realizes that one of his deputies is a Communist. The film ends with Wang securing the real orders and handing them to his patriotic deputy, who will expose the Guomindang traitors.

What Wu Ziniu did with *Secret Decree* was to turn "revolutionary history" into a thriller. The story proceeds at a fast pace, with the major characters identified on first appearance by on-screen titles. Such fifth-generation devices as tight or unexpected framing and naturalistic lighting add to the effect. Even the musical score is unexpected: rather abstract, uneasy orchestrations replace the usual Romantic and bland grandness of most modern historical film scores. The composer Tan Dun, a contemporary of Wu Ziniu and the fifth generation, contributed to a number of the new-style films in the mid-1980s and later won an American Academy Award for his work on the score of Ang Lee's *Crouching Tiger, Hidden Dragon*. As in the case of *The Candidate*, the studio leadership teamed Wu with an older co-director. Li Jingmin was twelve years Wu's senior but had never directed a film. He had apparently ingratiated himself with the head of the Xiaoxiang studio by presenting him with a refrigerator, which was becoming a popular urban household luxury item at the time.[31]

Secret Decree proved a popular success after its release in early 1985. A fascination with the Nationalist camp during the War of Resistance to Japan seems common to Chinese of any age in China, Taiwan, and Hong Kong. The relative novelty of a film in which some of the Nationalist officers are presented sympathetically and capable of changing Chinese sides should not be discounted. The skill with which Wu and his crew turn a confusing story into an action-filled, often violent, thriller was perhaps the main attraction. *One and Eight* and *The Yellow Earth*, released at about the same time, did not come close to the box-office success of Wu's film. Two hundred seventy-eight copies of *Secret Decree* were distributed, almost ten times the number of copies of *The Yellow Earth*. The film made an unprecedented 1.8 million *yuan* (over US$400,000) profit for the Xiaoxiang studio.[32]

Along with the awards won by *The Candidate*, the popularity of *Secret Decree* gave Wu Ziniu enough personal capital to be able to make a film more to his own taste. There was even further talk of arranging membership of the Communist Party, a considerable honor. The next film, however, had the distinction of being the first fifth-generation film to be banned. After several screenings to film industry personnel in Beijing and elsewhere, the film was locked in a vault in Changsha, by order of the Hunan Propaganda Department of the Chinese Communist Party.[33]

Dove Tree (*Gezi shu*) is set on the Sino-Vietnam border. The 1979 Chinese invasion across the Vietnam border (or "punishment," as Beijing preferred to call it) was a profoundly unpopular event among ordinary Chinese citizens. Soldiers were reportedly sent into battle by officers using maps little changed from the Qing dynasty (1644–1911). Timed to assist the Khmer Rouge-led Cambodian resistance to Vietnamese invasion, the Chinese action was also seen by Beijing as a patriotic diversion from "Democracy Wall" dissent. The short story on which Wu Ziniu's film was based had caused no official alarm when it was published in the January 1985 issue of the major literary magazine *October* (*Shiyue*). Ye Nan, the middle-aged author, is the twin brother of Bai Hua, whose script for the film *Unrequited Love* (*Kulian*) had been officially criticized in the spring of 1981. This criticism, which lasted for six months, was the first official campaign against a writer or artist since the Cultural Revolution. Ye Nan, a more subtle writer than his twin, had written several film scripts since the early 1960s.[34]

Some of Ye Nan's friends wondered whether the original story, titled "The Distant Cry of the Magnificent Bird" (*Huameiniao de wanli jiaosheng*) might cause him trouble. However, encouraged by the relatively relaxed cultural climate after the recently convened Fifth National Congress of Writers and Artists in early 1985, Ye Nan took four days to turn his story into a film script.[35] The Xiaoxiang studio leadership approved the script in two days. They were impressed by the project's combination of a respected writer, a successful director, and a setting with its inherently patriotic quality. The money for the film was available, for one-sixth of the studio profit from *Secret Decree* had been set aside for Wu Ziniu's next project. Upon hearing word of the project, the Film Bureau in Beijing expressed qualms about the film, but by then Wu had already started location shooting.[36]

Dove Tree presents the experiences of a squad of a dozen young Chinese border guards who have been cut off from their main unit, in the course of a single day, from sunrise to sunset. Four of the soldiers encounter a Vietnamese nurse. Surrounded by a thick fog and the forest, the five from the two countries find a common humanity. The nurse attends to the wounds of the soldiers and they talk of their pasts, youthful hopes, and fears.

With a crew of about two dozen, Wu Ziniu's filming entirely on location in border country went smoothly. The crew spent time before shooting interviewing Chinese veterans of the Vietnam border conflict and also met with some Vietnamese prisoners of war. The shooting was completed in thirty-five days, seven of which were used transporting equipment to and from the remote location. Six of the actors who played ordinary platoon members had actually fought on the Guangxi front during the 1979 Sino-Vietnamese border conflict.

One innovation to lend the film authenticity was the use of synchronized sound recording for the entire project. Synchronized recording had not been used to this extent in any Chinese film. Even films shot entirely on a studio sound stage had hardly ever included directly recorded sequences. Such recording is not easy: the *Dove Tree* crew had to fire rifles at the start of shooting to scare the forest birds into silence or flight. In the midst of filming, a certificate arrived from Changsha for the director, recording the studio's selection of Wu as a "model worker."

When interviewed jointly a year later, Wu Ziniu and his scenarist Ye Nan expressed their surprise at the reception the Hunan cultural authorities gave *Dove Tree* upon its completion. The crew had concentrated on their art, and Wu was unprepared for the objections: "We were making a film about people and war. We gave no thought to war or pacifism." But political sensitivity is a necessity for Chinese artists: despite these expressions of innocence, they may have had some inkling of what was coming. Wu reported how his cinematographer Zhang Li, on seeing the completed work, joked how he had never realized the film was so "reactionary." His Party critics, Wu felt, took an opposite tack, looking at the film exclusively from the point of view of national interest. The critics argued that *Dove Tree* was a vehicle to express supra-class feeling and the notion that war is hell. Also objectionable was the excessively sympathetic portrayal of the Vietnamese. As Zhang Li remarked in an interview a year later, if the film had been made in another country or had been set in the War of Resistance to Japan, it might not have run into trouble.[37] Its artistic distinction also drew attention to the film.

Although the audience at one studio screening, Wu reported, sat in stunned appreciation at the end, the Hunan Province Party Committee secretary was among the film's chief critics. The young filmmakers and critics who saw it in Beijing when it was shown to participants in the 1986 annual national conference on feature film creation also thought highly of *Dove Tree*. But Party critics had more power. Fu Zidi, the studio head, a poet who had spent twenty years labelled a Rightist, was fearful of the political consequences for Xiaoxiang. The film was not even forwarded to the Film Bureau in Beijing for final approval. Four representatives of the Film Bureau journeyed to the Xiaoxiang studio and watched the film there. Earlier, in January 1986, a long letter from the Xiaoxiang leaders to the Hunan Province Party Committee acknowledged their errors in the production of the film. The leaders of the People's Liberation Army's August First Film Studio also sent a long, critical letter to Beijing at this time. Word of *Dove Tree*, moreover, reached the highest levels. Deng Xiaoping reportedly remarked that the filmmakers should have gone to Hanoi to make the film.[38] The film was locked away. It will probably be many years before *Dove Tree* can be seen on China's screens.

In February 1986 Wu Ziniu made his ritual "self-criticism," acknowledging that he had not paid enough attention to the political aspects of the film, in front of an audience of 200 studio employees.[39] For their part, the studio heads worried that they could not afford to have even one of the five or six films produced annually banned outright, thereby providing no box-office revenues. They felt some alarm at the setting in a labor camp in the northwest of Wu Ziniu's next film. But the critical and popular successes of *The Candidate* and *Secret Decree* apparently outweighed the unpleasantness over *Dove Tree*.

The Last Day of Winter (*Zuihou yige dongri*) was adapted by Qiao Xuezhu from her own novel, *Oh, Younger Brother, Younger Sister, Older Brother* (*Didi meimei gege, a*). The film relates the visit of three people to their relatives, who are prisoners in a labor reform camp in the far northwest. Each is confronted by the painful recollection of where their sibling went wrong, and the reasons for their criminal lapses. After leaving the prison camp, the threesome meet up again and spend the night at a desert inn. Come morning, they set out back east on the last day of winter. A burst of spring thunder echoes across the empty hills and sky.

Wu Ziniu took a script with moralistic elements—particularly in the flashbacks to when the young people went wrong—and turned it into a powerful contemplation of social morality. Nearing the prison farm, the visiting threesome hitch a ride on an ox cart, which, like all modes of transport in the film, seems to emerge from out of the ground. The old carter tells them: "Don't look at the numbers on their uniforms. Consider the man inside the clothes. . . . I work like them. For me it's work, for them it's reform." Contributing to the symbolic associations Wu works into the story, the landscape is dotted with the eroded ruins of earthen walls of towns abandoned long ago. Suddenly the travellers come upon a huge hole in the ground. In it are a mass of dark-uniformed, shaven-headed prisoners, digging. Almost like dumb animals, they look up as each of the visitors make their precarious way along a board that bridges the hole. When the woman crosses, the sexual tension from the prisoners is clear. The prisoners march at double time across the bleak landscape, a cluster of black ants moving like robots. Reaching the gates of the prison, they roar out their platoon numbers, like machines, to the guards. The latter wear goggles against the wind and cold, reinforcing the impression of a dehumanized society in another world. The prison camp itself seems surrounded by the ruined walls of an earlier age.

Despite having come so far, the visitors are allowed only thirty minutes with their brother or sister. Rather than rely on straight-forward flashbacks for each of these encounters, Wu Ziniu tells the stories of the three families in a relatively complex structure of recollection, including in conversation between the three visitors. The emphasis is on the helplessness of the young offenders and the ways their families, neighbors, and society did little to help prevent them straying from the straight and narrow. These encounters are punctuated with other episodes. The chief guard recalls how he came to the prison at age seventeen, and laments to the visiting woman how he gave up his youth for the sake of the prisoners. In this remote land, he has become something of a prisoner himself.

The travelling threesome is gloomy and ill at ease when they gather at the inn after their visit to the prison camp. Yuanyuan, the young girl, in particular cannot sleep. Suddenly gunshots sound out in the night. Whistles join the shots, as a huge band of flaming torches moves across the dark desert. The visitors' immediate thought is that someone has escaped. They recall the old carter's jocular remark that they shoot those escapees whom they cannot catch. But the innkeeper assures the three visitors that the gunshots accompany the issuing of orders at the camp. No-one has escaped: their siblings are safe. The innkeeper voices an epilogue: "There isn't just one person who has offended. How many people have committed crimes?" This indictment of society in general remains with the travellers until the spring thunder the next morning suggests a new beginning.

Wu Ziniu's *The Last Day of Winter*, like *One and Eight* and *The Yellow Earth*, relies for its impact on a harsh, untamed beauty. Wu and his young cinematographer, Yang Wei, emphasize the inhospitable qualities of the landscape and the ways it dwarfs the human beings trying to survive in it. The power of this film derives from the novelty of seeing on the screen images of a part of Chinese society rarely accessible to Chinese, let alone foreigners. Nowhere does the film label these people "political prisoners." But any audience recalls that Gansu and Qinghai provinces are the places to which were sent protesters of the Democracy Wall movement, such as Wei Jingsheng, sentenced in a Beijing court to fifteen years jail for passing on to Western journalists "secret" casualty figures from the Sino-Vietnam border war of early 1979. Presenting one guard as a friendly individual in *The Last Day of Winter* does not outweigh the extraordinary images of a dehumanized mass of prisoners and their keepers.

The somewhat conventional explanations for the prisoners' past failings—broken marriages and uncaring parents—do not obliterate the startling views of China's Gulag. To the relief of the studio bosses, *The Last Day of Winter* was released in mid-1986 without a murmur. Political conservatives, in China always more concerned with the written text of a film than with the images on the screen, found the moralism of the criminals' stories a suitable lesson for China's film-goers. The film went on to participate in numerous international film festivals, where the images were perhaps better understood.

Wu Ziniu's next project took him to the PLA's August First Film Studio in Beijing. One of the August First deputy studio heads, also in charge of the script department there, encouraged Wu to come to Beijing.[40] This was a chance to live in the capital after three years in Changsha. The Xiaoxiang studio gave him permission to transfer temporarily to the army unit. After all, he had completed three well-received films in Changsha. But the army studio was not an easy place to make a film, as Hu Mei, Wu's directing department classmate, had already discovered. To the usual hierarchy of a studio leadership was added the authority of the PLA General Political Department's cultural apparatus. The August First studio had been established in the mid-1950s primarily to produce films for China's armed forces, including educational and other documentaries.

Wu Ziniu's August First project was titled *Evening Bell* (*Wanzhong*). Wu co-wrote the script with Wang Yifei, a writer in the script department of the Xiaoxiang studio. Its setting is a dry northern Chinese landscape in the fall of 1945, after the Japanese surrender. A five-man team from the Eighth Route Army is going through the gruesome task of collecting and burying corpses when, near a ruined Buddhist temple, they come across a cave where thirty-four Japanese comrades are holed up in an ammunition store. The starving Japanese eat the meagre rations that the Chinese soldiers provide but refuse to surrender. If they are going to die, they want to blow up the ammunition, taking the besieging Chinese soldiers with them. The patience of the Chinese soldiers eventually pays off and the Japanese officer's plan to blow everyone up is thwarted. In the end the Japanese become prisoners of the Eighth Route Army.

Filmed in 1986 by Hou Yong, a film academy classmate who was cinematographer on Tian Zhuangzhuang's first three films after graduation, *Evening Bell* is in some ways a reworking of the themes of the banned *Dove Tree*.[41] A first cut was screened to an audience of August First studio employees in late March 1987. At the end of the film, as the Chinese squad leader emerges over a hill from the exploded cave, carrying a Japanese soldier and grinning broadly, the audience applauded vigorously, an unusual occurrence in a Chinese theatre. Some of the studio leaders present were alarmed at this enthusiasm. Aware as much as anyone of growing cynicism in the spring of 1987 after a winter of abortive student demonstrations in major cities and demands from Party central to root out "bourgeois liberalization" (*zichan jieji ziyouhua*), some studio leaders were convinced that there was something inflammatory about *Evening Bell*.[42]

Wu and his crew were obliged to re-shoot certain scenes. One sequence, for example, in which the cannibalized bodies of several Chinese women are carried out from the cave, was filmed again using male bodies. Studio caution meant that *Evening Bell* was only released in the autumn of 1988, more than two years after shooting had begun. In February 1989 Wu Ziniu received a Silver Bear award at the Berlin International Film Festival for the film.

Evening Bell

Humanity in times of war is the focus in *Evening Bell*, as it had been in *Dove Tree*. But whereas *Dove Tree* was set in the green, misty hills of China's southwestern border, *Evening Bell* shares its landscape with *The Last Day of Winter*. This fascination with the untamed and unwelcoming settings of the northwest emerged in several fifth-generation films. *One and Eight*, *The Yellow Earth*, and *Red Sorghum* all draw upon the otherness of their settings to suggest an absence in Chinese culture. This point is clear when these landscapes are contrasted with the usual representation of Chinese settings as well-watered, inhabited, and often cultivated. This is the landscape of eastern China, especially Jiangnan, the region south of the eastern Yangzi River. Previous generations of Chinese filmmakers had treated this landscape as a typical Chinese setting, as had writers and painters for centuries. These watery settings seldom appear in the fifth-generation films. Instead, the dry, lonely and wild landscapes of the northwest demand a toughness and instinct for survival. In *Evening Bell* the five Chinese soldiers seem to thrive in this unfriendly place. The Japanese, in contrast, cannot tough it out.

The filmmakers imply that toughness is what Chinese civilization now needs to survive in an unfriendly world. For several members of the class of '82 Cultural Revolution rustication was often spent in inhospitable areas where nature was not the soft, verdant Chinese landscape of clichés. But there is more to the otherness of these film settings. These films suggest that the world is hostile and China's place in it far from secure. Like the gentle southern landscapes, the effeteness and softness of Chinese intellectuals, educated in a civilian Confucian tradition, are rejected.

The nation, and indeed the world, also needs to acknowledge its common humanity, *Evening Bell* suggests. Foreign viewers remarked on the film's resemblances to *Harp of Burma* (*Biruma no tategoto*), Ichikawa Kon's 1956 story of a Japanese soldier who chooses to remain in Burma at the end of the war to help bury the dead. Asked shortly before *Evening Bell*'s Chinese release, Wu said he had heard of Ichikawa's film but had not seen it.[43] But in apparent contradiction to this suggestion of the need for a basic humanity is a dialectic between the representation of the Chinese and Japanese in the film. At the start of the narrative, ranks of Japanese soldiers are seen preparing to commit suicide. They give their names and place of origin, not infrequently Hiroshima and Nagasaki, as flames fill the screen. The Japanese officer in the cave and his deputy are presented as nationalist fanatics. Their attitudes undermine the emphasis on humanity of the opening scene by implying that the mass suicide is further evidence of fanaticism.

On the other hand, the five Chinese soldiers have every reason to seek vengeance against the defeated enemy. A series of rapid flashbacks show how each has lost loved ones to Japanese brutality. *Evening Bell*'s plea for more humanity is thus tempered with nationalism. Wu's choice of Tao Zeru to play the leader of the Chinese squad underlines this. After roles in *One and Eight* and *The Last Day of Winter*, Tao brings with him to the screen qualities of a distinct and proud identity. A tough Chinese like him can stand upright in this unfriendly but powerful land. His grin to his companions and to camera at the end of *Evening Bell*, that appealed to the studio audience, plays on this persona.[44]

With his wife working in Beijing, continued secondment to the PLA studio allowed Wu Ziniu to remain in the city. He began planning a film about Chinese nuclear bomb testing, involving a young person lost in the desert near a test site. When the studio leadership objected that there was "too much humanist morality" in his revised script, he dropped the project and began to think of trying a potentially less demanding project.[45]

For his next project Wu Ziniu had only to look at home, where he found a complete change of pace and one that reflected the more commercial demands being made on the Chinese film industry by the late 1980s. His wife Sima Xiaojia, a harpist in the Central Philharmonic Orchestra, had adapted for the screen a lengthy novel written by her father. Sima Wensen had written his novel *Storm on the Tong River* (*Fengyu Tongjiang*) during the eight years after 1955 in which he served as cultural attaché at the Chinese embassy in Jakarta.[46]

Sima Xiaojia's script tried to preserve the episodic, picaresque qualities of the novel's tale of clan feuds, bandits, and Communists in lawless Fujian in the 1930s. The film would be in two parts, *The Joyous Heroes* (*Huanle yingxiong*) and *The Realm Between the Living and the Dead* (*Yinyang jie*). Even with such apparently commercial material Wu Ziniu's core interests come strongly through the film. Here again is a concern for a common humanity that overrides the question of factional or political loyalty. On the eve of leaving Fuzhou to start location shooting, Wu predicted a potential problem arising from his refusal to make unremittingly clear the goodness of the heroes and the evil of the villains. Traditional feuding in the southeastern provinces had made such distinctions mostly academic anyway. Adding an underground Communist to this mix was one of the charges that had been brought against Sima Wensen in the Cultural Revolution. The summer of 1988 was a more liberal time, but Wu Ziniu still half expected trouble.[47]

The two parts were finished in late 1988, passed censorship without major revision, and went on to relative box-office and critical success. In a director's statement after completion, Wu pinpointed his aim in the films: "At the end, apart from the usual 'how the Chinese have suffered,' I hope you can be encouraged to some deeper reflection. If you portray a person as a Communist, that glorious personage is all too familiar (I could cite almost half a century of literary works as proof). On the other hand, presenting a Communist above all as a human being, will certainly create a new impression."[48] Wu Ziniu continued in this vein in his next film, made in the months immediately following the June 4th incident in Beijing.

The Mill (*Da mofang*) was a co-production between the Hong Kong leftist film company Sil-Metropole and Wu's official work unit, the Xiaoxiang studio. As several of his film academy classmates had also discovered, co-production provided some assurance that the completed film would find an audience, at least outside China. Zhang Yimou's *Judou*, made at about the same time as *The Mill,* was a Sino-Japanese co-production. This enabled audiences worldwide to see *Judou,* which was not released in China until three years later.

Wu Ziniu in *The Mill* returned to some of the directness and anger of his films set in the northeast. His new film, however, was set in the hill country of south-central China. A clever interplay between the present and the past points up the contemporary relevance of the narrative. Qingguo, the protagonist, first appears as an old man in his seventies. He is troubled by vivid recollections of episodes in his youth. One day he comes upon a funeral procession for a woman whom he had loved passionately fifty years earlier. His memories come flooding back. These memories become vivid when the older Qingguo encounters his younger self on a misty mountain path. Wu Ziniu uses this device at the beginning and end of the film, framing the core narrative. But the old man also appears several times throughout the film, observing his young self lying drunk in a gutter or taking his revenge.

Back in the 1930s Qingguo fell in love with Jiucui, a young peasant woman. When thugs in the employ of the village head identify Qingguo as a member of a "Red gang," he flees the village, abandoning the water-powered stone mill he used to make paper, and spends a year in the mountains as part of a guerrilla band associated with the Communist Red Army. When he returns, a toughened fighter, he learns that Jiucui has been forced to become a concubine of the village head. Tao Zeru's headman is a paraplegic and opium addict who sadistically abuses Jiucui. Qingguo determines to take a terrible revenge. Over several moonless nights he carefully paints his body and face pitch black, observed at one point by his seventy-three-year-old self. One by one he knocks out the headman's guards and assistants and carries them over his shoulder back to his paper mill. The village is in an uproar over the killer spirit who has stolen away with eleven men. Finally he steals into the bedroom of the headman himself, whose helpless squawks for mercy are soon silenced with a swift blow, and a new body joins the others placed around the mill stone. Then in a moment of operatic vengeance, Qingguo releases the water gate and sets the huge mill stone turning. It literally makes mincemeat of Qingguo's enemies who are either dead or barely conscious before the great stone rolls. Later, to the terrified Jiucui he insists: "They had to die, they had to die," but the young woman flees in horror. The film returns to the present, as the nails are banged into Jiucui's coffin. In a final encounter, Qingguo at seventy-three comes upon himself at twenty-three at the mill itself. They are both in rain capes made of grain stalks. The old man staggers off into the mist.

A turning mill stone made red with human flesh as discordant music roars is a powerful image from any culture. It was too much for the Chinese authorities. The Hunan Province Party Committee, the same body that had taken such an interest in Wu Ziniu's *Dove Tree*, objected to the film, as did the censors in the Film Bureau (since 1986 part of the Ministry of Radio, Film and Television) in Beijing. Completion just six months after the June 4th incident was not the best timing for such a violent story. Reportedly He Jingzhi, the Minister of Culture, heard that the film was controversial and encouraged Li Ruihuan, member of the Politburo in charge of ideological matters, to view the work. Causing specific complaint was the portrayal of young Qingguo. Although the film does not directly identify the young man as a Communist, even its suggestion that Qingguo was a leftist guerrilla drew protest from the censors, who claimed that Communists would not act in such gruesome ways and largely for personal vengeance. *The Mill* was not approved for domestic release. Deferring to contractual obligations and to its pro-mainland political alignment, Sil-Metropole delayed release of it internationally.[49]

In his relatively prolific filmmaking career since film school, Wu Ziniu showed a remarkable persistence and ability to capture the changing spirit of his times. *The Candidate*, although made for children, reflected the optimism of the early 1980s, as economic reform promised an improvement in standards of living for urban dwellers as well as farmers. *Secret Decree*, the two-part *Storm on the Tong River* adaptation, and *The Mill* in their different ways took up the question of the differences between Communists and their enemies at a time when communism was becoming increasingly irrelevant in rapidly modernizing China.

An associated conviction that all people, whatever their nationality or political labels, shared a common humanity informed *Dove Tree*, *The Last Day of Winter*, and *Evening Bell*. This notion was contrary to the Communist Party's usual doctrine that humanism was a "bourgeois" concept that denied the importance of class. *Dove Tree* was banned, but it and the other films spoke for their age, as Party doctrine became the domain of aged politicians and ideologues. On the night of 3–4 June 1989, the latter exacted a terrible revenge on the streets of Beijing and other cities in China. Wu Ziniu filmed *The Mill* in July and August of that year. In a statement after the filming, Wu remarked: "Domestic animals just live for themselves, so they can be sacrificed. There's nothing strange in this. Human beings are born to want to enjoy a happy life. For this reason I have picked out a story from the past, and made a film like this."[50] Like Zhang Yimou's *Judou*, Wu's film reflected a distinctly post-June 4th mentality.

Even for Wu Ziniu, June 4th became a more distant memory as economic growth and the demands of the marketplace increased in the 1990s. In 1991 Wu filmed another script written by his wife. *Mountains of the Sun* (*Taiyang shan*) suggested how much the new decade made some of the fifth generation's concerns seem old-fashioned and how the times encouraged compromise.

In 1955 in Fujian Ah Ning, a schoolteacher, adopts an abandoned baby boy who is unable to speak. She too had been abandoned, by her husband now in Taiwan. The villagers expect Ah Ning to marry Ah Xiang. When he goes missing in the mountains while gathering medicinal herbs for Ah Ning and the boy, the villagers search high and low for Ah Xiang. He is discovered injured but alive, an event that causes the boy to gain the power of speech. Thirty years later the family's peace is shattered by the unexpected arrival from Taiwan of Li Daxi, Ah Ning's former husband. Li realizes he should not stay and quietly leaves. His heart, however, belongs on the mainland. On the eve of the Spring Festival, the four come together as a family. As fireworks burst in the sky, Ah Ning dies, a smile on her face.

The melodrama and sentiment evident from this plot summary are presented with visual effects—gloomy, naturalistic lighting and an emphasis on the landscape—typical of Wu's earlier work. Tao Zeru, who had first appeared in *One and Eight* and had played against type as the evil village head in *The Mill*, plays Ah Xiang. The result is a pastiche apparently designed to serve the Party's policy on relations between the mainland and Taiwan, as Wu Ziniu continued to respond to the broader social and political context.

Wu Ziniu's most commercially successful film from the 1990s, *The Nanjing Massacre* (*Nanjing da tusha*, 1997) managed to serve government needs and reflect the humanism at the heart of his typically fifth-generation style films. The film was made to commemorate the sixtieth anniversary of the Japanese army's atrocities in the former Nationalist capital. The massacre is a continuing source of dispute between Japan and China, with Japanese right-wing politicians denying the extent of the slaughter claimed by the Chinese side. Wu Ziniu produced a film that underscored the horror of events, thus serving Beijing's propaganda requirements. But with an international cast and a sub-plot of desperate diplomacy, the familiar, somewhat ill-defined humanity of Wu's 1980s works finds an echo on the bloody streets of Nanjing. The commercial and political demands of the film, however, outweigh this element. *The Nanjing Massacre* confirmed that the fifth generation's impetus to innovate and challenge had faded in the face of commercial and social reality. In 1999 Wu made *The National Anthem* (*Guo ge*), a bio-pic on the 1931 creation of the song that became Communist China's anthem.[51] This film and Wu's *The Hero Zheng Chenggong* (*Yingxiong Zheng Chenggong*, 2000), an historical epic about the seventeenth-century defender of Taiwan against the Dutch, seemed to seal the incorporation of this director into the political and commercial mainstream.[52] The angry young man of *Dove Tree* had become the establishment director, though a humanist streak remained intact.

3. From the Margins: Tian Zhuangzhuang's Films

With their sparse dialogue and reliance on images, two of Tian Zhuangzhuang's early films typified the revolution in Chinese cinema made by his generation. *On the Hunting Ground* (*Liechang zhasa*, 1984) and *Horse Thief* (*Daoma zei*, 1986) took the ethnic minorities genre in Chinese film in new, unexpected directions. Tian used these settings on the periphery of Chinese civilization to contemplate relationships between individuals and society which concerned many intellectuals of his generation. Tian's films from this period can be described as a cinema of absence or a cinema of distance. Settings on the Mongolian steppe and on the Tibetan plateau are at great physical and metaphorical distance from his audiences and emphasize an absence of the familiar. But even Tian's other films, with contemporary or historical settings in the Chinese heartland, suggest absence and distance. With these concerns, Tian very much spoke for his generation.

While still at film school, in 1982 Tian co-directed *Red Elephant*, a children's film with a minorities setting. Before returning to the minorities genre, Tian directed another film featuring children. Faced, like Chen Kaige, with a long wait for an independent directing opportunity at the overstaffed Beijing Film Studio, Tian Zhuangzhuang took up an invitation in 1983 to make a film at the Kunming Film Studio. In the capital of Yunnan province, where he had shot *Red Elephant* a year and a half earlier, the Kunming studio was small, new, and eager to make a mark with its first films.

Tian's Kunming film, *September* (*Jiuyue*) to a degree was preparation for his later concentration on the relations between individuals and society. The protagonist is Yuan Xiaoyu, a middle-aged music teacher, who has spent a lifetime of service at a children's Cultural Palace. Children's choirs from all over the city are preparing a concert to mark her retirement in September, although the preparations are not going smoothly. One day teacher Yuan receives a letter from a prisoner named Zheng Qitian, who claims to be her former student and asks to meet her when he is released from prison. The teacher cannot recall who Zheng is and fails to recognize the young man when he comes out of the prison gates. Finally the day of the September concert arrives. When Zheng Qitian comes to bid his teacher farewell, Yuan Xiaoyu now recognizes her former pupil. He had been constantly humiliated as a child because of his politically suspect family. Yuan had encouraged him to become an accomplished singer. At the concert Yuan introduces the ex-convict on-stage and persuades him to sing for the children.

Framing his images in ways that set *September* apart from ordinary Chinese films, Tian makes the most of this story. Both the teacher and her former student share a sense of frustration at the lack of interest on the part of parents and students. A career of teaching children to sing revolutionary songs ends with a concert to which few people want to contribute. Zheng Qitian, who has cherished in jail the memory of his kind teacher, finds she has forgotten him. But the political ambiguities inherent in this material are ultimately softened in the ending chorus in which unity prevails.[53]

Tian made his next film, *On the Hunting Ground* for the Inner Mongolia Film Studio, in Huhehot in the Inner Mongolian Autonomous Region. Tian took with him from the Beijing studio his cinematography department classmate Hou Yong, who had shot *September* for him. Tian also invited Lü Yue, another cinematographer from the class of '82, who had been assigned to the Emei Film Studio in Sichuan province.

The film's Chinese title, literally "*Zhasa* of the Hunting Ground," is meaningless to anyone other than a Mongolian speaker or a student of Mongol history, and accordingly an indication of the distancing strategy of the film. *Zhasa* is the Chinese transliteration of a Mongolian word for rules of the hunt attributed to Genghis Khan, Mongol conqueror of China and most of central Asia in the early thirteenth century. The film has the distinction of having only one copy ordered for domestic distribution: a second copy was made by the China Film Corporation for export use. *The Yellow Earth* at least had twenty-something copies made.

What the regional and provincial film distribution companies saw when they previewed the work was indeed unexpected. Watching *On the Hunting Ground* is not an easy experience for any audience. The usual minority film in China featured a lot of singing and dancing, the implication being that non-Han people were "just like us" (the Han, ethnic Chinese majority) although perhaps more prone to burst into song.[54] The people in *On the Hunting Ground* are most definitely not like "us." In an interview in 1988, Tian claimed in his typical, studied cavalier fashion that he gave no thought for his future audience in making the film. His main concern was to convey his personal fascination with Mongol life and the feel of the steppes.[55]

Unlike many minorities films in which a Han Chinese character serves as mediator between the unfamiliar peoples on the screen and audiences, *On the Hunting Ground* is peopled entirely by Mongols, speaking

Mongolian. An off-screen voice in Mandarin Chinese provides limited narration, in place of dubbed dialogue. The intrusion of this non-native voice in fact seems to further distance the people on the screen. We follow the social ostracism of a Mongol hunter after he breaks the steppe hunting rules. The shots and *mise en scène* seem random, as when a lengthy series of slow motion and telephoto shots of steppe animals falling under hunters' bullets are followed by a hunting dog howling and the arrival of the hunters at an encampment. The narrative takes time to become clearer: at first the story seems to be about the return of a cow to the local cooperative. Later the focus on a hunter breaking the rules grows stronger. The violence of the hunt is contrasted with the calm of the encampments and the quiet solemnity of religious rites.

Several years after completing the film, Tian suggested that the rules of the hunt in the film had allegorical meaning: their function was similar to that of Mao Zedong Thought in the Cultural Revolution. As for the Mongols in the film, so for Chinese in the 1960s, the rules had extraordinary transformative powers, commanding a remarkable degree of social conformity. Whoever transgressed the rules was ostracized, be they Mongols on the steppes or Chinese intellectuals exiled for displeasing Mao's disciples. Transgression could be corrected by confession and forgiveness. These themes and the religiosity behind them were to emerge again in Tian's next film. In an earlier interview with a reporter from the mass circulation *Popular Cinema*, Tian emphasized the relevance of the film for modern China, contrasting the rules by which hunters and nomads treat the animals in the film with the lawlessness and betrayal characteristic of relations between humans.[56]

The camera in *On the Hunting Ground* serves to reinforce the audience's sense of alienation and confusion. It moves rarely, tracking the animals being shot, and is still in the often dark scenes at encampments. Frequently when it pans, for example at the religious ceremony at the end of the film, the camera motion has no connection with movement in the frame. Tian Zhuangzhuang seems to be sharing through his camera movements the disorientation and need to explore that he felt when he was sent down to the eastern edge of the steppe in Jilin province in the late 1960s. The film's distancing and mystery remain to one of the last shots in the film, a full-circle tracking around a deer head on a pole: a massed, Western-style choir is heard as four hunters stand with bowed heads at the pole. As if to lend a timelessness and remoteness to the film, a title at the end quotes Genghis Khan's rules of the hunt.

On the Hunting Ground was so unusual that Chinese critics and filmmakers were at somewhat of a loss in responding to the film on its completion in early 1985. Many seized upon its documentary qualities: sheep are shorn, yurts are erected and adjusted in rain, a market day is held. With only one copy made for domestic exhibition, few Chinese viewers, even in Inner Mongolia, managed to see the film. Conservative critics and others seized on this as further evidence of the fifth generation's failure to find an audience. At a national meeting in early 1986 to summarize feature film production in the previous year, Ding Qiao, a senior leader in Party cultural activities with a special interest in cinema, singled out several fifth-generation films and artists for comment. He characterized *On the Hunting Ground* as deliberately making the theme, characters, and story boring (*danhua*, literally desalinated). He quoted Tian Zhuangzhuang's earlier response: "Comrade Ding Qiao, don't worry. We young comrades are concerned about the question of audiences."[57] Despite these official grumblings, a small group of critics and commentators defended the film for its experimental subtlety and power.

Before he started work on *On the Hunting Ground*, Tian Zhuang-zhuang had seen the script of *Horse Thief* at the Beijing Film Studio, based on a short story set on the Tibetan plateau about a father and son who were both thieves. Prior to going off to Inner Mongolia, Tian and the script writer Zhang Rui worked together on revising the scenario, based on Zhang's novel. Zhang Rui had lived a number of years in Qinghai province, north of Tibet and inhabited by a great many Tibetans. But the Beijing studio leadership wanted a prettified and commercial presentation of the story, and showed no interest in Tian and Zhang's revised version. Zhang Rui had also sent his original script to the Xi'an Film Studio, where it attracted the interest of Wu Tianming, a fourth-generation film director who was to play a vital role in nurturing the fifth-generation "New Wave." Wu, the newly installed head of the Xi'an studio, with a unique mandate to effect the reformist "director responsibility" management system in the studio, was in a position to act on his interest. Unlike the heads of the other film studios, Wu had considerable power to decide what got filmed and who would film it. Tian Zhuangzhuang began filming in Qinghai and Tibet in the spring of 1985 for the Xi'an Film Studio. Hou Yong and cinematographer Zhao Fei, another class of '82 graduate, joined Tian on the project.[58]

Horse Thief is a more accessible film than *On the Hunting Ground*:

Tian described the latter as objective and the Tibetan feature as subjective. In *Horse Thief* the mystery of a non-Han culture still dominates the film, but the audience is invited to feel sympathy for the hero. The film follows the story of Norbu, a serf who has been expelled from his clan for stealing an official's temple gifts. When Norbu's young son, Tashi, dies from sickness, Norbu makes penance for the death and his stealing. A second son is born, but he too is lost, as Norbu seems to leave society.

More important than the rudimentary story are the stunning images created by Tian, Hou and Zhao. The surreal representation of Tibetan customs—the scattering of paper across the land (paralleled later by snow drifting across the plains), the prayer banners and other structures in a mostly empty landscape, the burying alive of sheep—is different from the expected exoticism of the older minorities genre. Here, things are neither explained nor relegated to the safeness of colorful, ethnic customs. In sharing his confrontation with this difference, Tian Zhuangzhuang shows an honesty usually absent from the genre but typical of the early fifth-generation films.

Confronted with the bizarre images of Tian's film, many critics and fellow filmmakers were confused. Since the film did not fit into the minorities genre, reviewers tried to relegate it, like its predecessor, to the category of documentary. Many of the images were indeed filmed as documentary footage, and shortly after completing the film Tian spoke of his frustration at not being able to direct his subjects. In Tibet he was obliged to film as best he could at religious ceremonies and in holy places. While he left the film with a deliberate timelessness, the Beijing film authorities insisted that a title at the beginning situate the film in the pre-1949 era. The primitiveness that Tian so obviously relished should not be ascribed, the censors deemed, to Tibet since its "liberation" by the People's Liberation Army in 1950. Tian selected the date 1923 at random, choosing two years after the founding of the Chinese Communist Party, and filled the screen with it in unnecessarily huge numbers. A lengthy sequence of a sky burial, showing vividly the cutting up of a human cadaver and vultures feeding on it, was severely shortened at the censors' insistence. Distribution organs ordered only about a dozen copies of *Horse Thief*, which prevented the film from finding much of an audience. These copies were all dubbed into Mandarin Chinese in an effort to increase the film's accessibility. Chinese audiences do not read subtitles: all foreign films are dubbed. Tian's film, however, was made with an all Tibetan cast, speaking their native tongue.

When asked what attracted him to minority peoples, Tian Zhuangzhuang cited several reasons. Difference is expected in the minorities genre: "If I did these things in a Han Chinese setting, people would get suspicious and ask, 'What are you up to? What are you trying to say?'"[59] This reasoning positioned Tian firmly with his Chinese filmmaking predecessors, despite the innovation of his visuals and narrative. After 1949, minority settings allowed artists to address themes, like love stories, which were rare in mainstream, non-musical feature films. Tian was also attracted to non-Han subjects because he felt they were "strong" (*qianglie*). This adjective, which also conveys intensity and violence, was a favorite of many of his film academy classmates. It referred to the powerful images and harsh beauty seen in films like *One and Eight* and *The Yellow Earth*, as well as the films of Wu Ziniu and Tian Zhuangzhuang. Tian's preference, which he again shared with the others, to rely on images rather than dialogue is natural in settings where the characters lead relatively simple lives and speak a foreign language.

Horse Thief

The images of *Horse Thief*, confusing as they may be, direct us to consider themes beyond the immediate purview of ethnic minorities. Three relationships seem central to both the Tibetan and Mongolian films: humans and nature, humans and the gods, and, perhaps most important, humans and society. Those fifth-generation filmmakers, like Tian, who had been expelled from their urban homes in the Cultural Revolution, perhaps took a special interest in this third relationship. The deliberate distancing in these films and their effort to frustrate much emotional identification are designed to force audiences to think about what they are seeing. Tian Zhuangzhuang, in this respect, might be called a Brechtian filmmaker. This approach is apparent from the very first shots of *Horse Thief*, in which a row of monks ring bells and rock hand drums. The sound viewers hear has no obvious synchronization with the images, inviting us to contemplate from a distance. A decade and a half later Tian Zhuangzhuang wrote of the challenge of trying to present the relationships between human beings and religion. He chose to use a device of piling up or repetition (*diehua*), simply adding images one after the other to produce an accretion of puzzlement.[60] Tian in fact regarded the Tibetan setting in some respects as incidental, speaking of the film as a portrait of the nation's (*minzu*, literally the race or people) backwardness, hardships, dignity, and aspirations.[61]

The fascination with the primitive in Tian's two minorities films reflected a wider movement in artistic circles in China in the 1980s. Several deliberately primitivist films appeared in mid-decade, set in the Xia and Shang dynasties in the first two millenia before the Christian era. In painting, the turn to pre-literate folk motifs was another indication of this trend, as were the number of short stories set in pre-historic or pre-literate societies. In effect this artistic movement was an effort to understand humans, as it were, "before the fall." Some writers produced speculative pieces which questioned even the cultural bases of Chinese life. The alienation of those Cultural Revolution years, and the official denial of a supra-class human nature, encouraged some Chinese to wonder what mankind was like before literacy, education, Confucianism, feudalism, Marxism, and Leninism, as it were, messed things up. Life and society before or at least somewhat beyond these distortions of civilization are central concerns of these two films by Tian Zhuangzhuang.[62]

Just as *Horse Thief* was proving its lack of appeal to audiences,[63] a reporter interviewed Tian about his films for the September 1986 issue of the mass circulation monthly, *Popular Cinema*. The interview was published under the heading "A director who is trying to change audiences."[64] Through it Tian Zhuangzhuang immediately became the best known of the fifth-generation filmmakers throughout China. The journalist, Yang Ping, indirectly accused Tian of failing to connect with audiences and suggested that most people found *Horse Thief* utterly incomprehensible. Determined to respond with equal bluntness, Tian provided readers of the magazine with a memorable remark: he made *Horse Thief*, he suggested, "for audiences of the next century to watch." Tian's typical and somewhat facetious retort became a lightning rod for a whole range of critics, from professional commentators to magazine readers confused by the new cinema after *The Yellow Earth*. Deng Xiaoping, top leader of the Chinese Communist Party, was credited with the retort that if Tian was going to make films for twenty-first century audiences, he might care to wait until then to collect his wages.[65]

Tian Zhuangzhuang was tough enough to survive this controversy, but realized that it would be politic to choose his next project carefully. Having made two art films set in minority areas, Tian chose not to essay a purely commercial work, which might to his critics have seemed the opposite extreme. He selected instead a literary adaptation. In so doing, Tian returned to the Beijing Film Studio and the Chinese mainstream, completing *The Drum-singers* (*Gushu yiren*) in 1987. In the back of his mind was a wish to prove he could make an orthodox literary adaptation, a major genre for earlier filmmakers, including his parents. The film was based on a novel by Lao She, a writer known for his depictions of Beijing life, who committed suicide in the summer of 1966, after Red Guard attacks on his politics. Lao She's *The Drum-singers* is about a family that practices the north China art of drum song, but the story is set in the Nationalist wartime capital of Chongqing. The novel was first published in English translation in New York in 1952, but the original Chinese manuscript was lost. The book was only published in China in 1980 in a re-translation into Chinese.

The film in some way resembles those of Tian Zhuangzhuang's minorities films, for its central figure is marginal and is also forced to flee from settled society. The hero, a middle-aged tea-house performer, is uprooted from his home in the north, flees with his family from the Japanese invasion in 1937, and ends up running a teashop in Chongqing. There he struggles to keep the family together as Japanese bombs, gangsters, and worries over his daughters' virtue make his life miserable. The film begins with the family arriving by boat in misty Chongqing. It ends after the Japanese surrender with what is left of the family leaving the city by boat on the first stage of returning to their Beijing home.

With *The Drum-singers*, Tian Zhuangzhuang self-consciously tried to suggest to skeptics that he could be a director of intelligence and restraint. While the story was distant from his own generation's experience, the setting was not as exotic and hence distracting as those of his minorities films. Tian excels even in this more orthodox mode and with subject matter of much less personal interest to him. The economy of the film is striking: every shot counts, with a constant focus on the hero, Fang Yuqing, at the core of every development. For a film about artists, there is surprisingly little art on display. On the rare occasions when one of the drum-singers sings on screen, Tian's camera tends to concentrate on the artist's face. His interest lies in exploring the inner lives of artists rather than their social function and connections with audiences. Other directors might fill the film with highlighted performances to a crowded teahouse. Only after over 100 minutes, and just 5 minutes from the end of the film, do we finally see and hear a drum song performed in front of an audience. Fang's younger daughter, who is living with a gangster and has just borne his child, sings a song at the insistence of her abusive husband. But Tian's most effective performance scene comes earlier and is to an audience of one, when Fang sings a sad song alone at the grave of his brother, killed in a Japanese air raid. Even with relatively orthodox material, Tian found ways to take a decentring approach, almost excluding songs from a film about singers.[66]

Having suggested his versatility, Tian could not resist goading his critics further. In the summer of 1988 his *Rock 'n' Roll Kids* (*Yaogun qingnian*, literally "hip-swinging youths") explored one of China's newest minority cultures: unlike the officially enumerated fifty-five ethnic minorities, this was one not recognized by the authorities.

Youth subcultures had always existed in socialist China, but low spending power and an underdeveloped consumer sector tended to limit youthful expressions of identity and communal attachment. With economic reforms after 1978 providing spending power and the goods to feed it, Chinese consumers took to the market with vigor. Choice of consumer goods expanded rapidly, as did choices in entertainment, recreation, fashion and life-style. By the late 1980s, urban young people adopted the musical tastes and styles of dress and manner that they understood to be the mode in Hong Kong, Taiwan, and further afield. Twenty years earlier, their counterparts generally accepted a diet of heroic stories of youthful martyrs to the Party's cause, such as the selfless soldier Lei Feng, famous for mending the socks of his comrades. By the mid-1980s Michael Jackson and Madonna had millions more devotees than Lei Feng and his kind. The subculture had developed to such an extent that there were even conscious efforts to sinicize it. The *Red Sorghum* phenomenon, discussed later in connection with Zhang Yimou's film, helped shape in 1988 a youthful popular culture with Chinese characteristics.

Into these cultural developments Tian Zhuangzhuang inserted *Rock 'n' Roll Kids*, which he made at the film academy's Youth Film Studio. Having been accused of ignoring his audiences, Tian showed ill-concealed glee in setting out to cater to youthful tastes. Break-dancing, a form of street aerobics that enjoyed a brief vogue in the United States in the early and mid-1980s, was the vehicle for Tian's exploration of youthful alienation in contemporary Beijing. Long Xiang, the protagonist, lives in a world of motor bikes, fashion modelling and dancing. Feeling confined by the old dances he has to perform in his state-run dance troupe, he quits his work unit. Long (a surname meaning "dragon") becomes an individual entrepreneur (*geti hu*), seeking work in the fashion industry by pushing his idea of combining dancing with runway modelling. He also has problems with his love life. Yuanyuan, his girlfriend, walks out on him, accusing him of selfish devotion to dancing. When he discovers that Yuanyuan has married, Long reaches a low point. Another young woman, a painter of revolutionary-style wall posters who becomes a nude model instead of going to university, assures Long Xiang: "It's not what you do, it's what you think of yourself." Long goes on to triumph at a big dance performance. The story ends with the suggestion that the painter and Long have a future together.

Into this world of fast motor bikes and faster dancing, Tian injects some elements that reflect both the times and some typical fifth-generation concerns. Films need not be set in the barren northwest or on the banks of the Yellow River to be able to address questions of Chinese patriotism. In the final big sequence, Long Xiang and the other performers sing proudly, in the rock style of northern Shaanxi folk songs popular in the summer of 1988, about themselves and their audience being of "the yellow-skinned race." Periodically the band of bikers and dancers meet and dance in front of the Meridian Gate (Wumen) which marks the southern entrance of the Forbidden City in the heart of Beijing, suggesting both the newness of their subculture and their pride in China's historical heritage. In a statement on the release of the film, Tian contrasted his own youth with that of present-day young people. He hoped that youth would not feel under the pressure (he expressed it as tiredness, *lei*) that his generation had felt. In a comparison that revealed the attitude of a lot of his contemporaries, Tian saw parallels between the former emphasis on "worshipping a god" (*bai shen*, meaning Mao) and the 1980s "worship of money" (*bai jin*). He made *Rock 'n' Roll Kids*, he said, to encourage young people to "lighten up" (*qingsong dianr . . . kaixin dianr*).[67]

Visited on the set of one of the major dance sequences, on a sound stage in the August First Film Studio, Tian Zhuangzhuang was highly conscious of critics' skepticism about the project. When asked why he was filming this, he responded with typical facetiousness, "Why shouldn't I?" He went on to explain that the mixture (*shijin*) of elements appealed to him. He also acknowledged that after three films exceptionally unsuccessful at the box office, he had to show he could make a commercial movie.[68] Upon its release, the film certainly did better than *On the Hunting Ground*, *Horse Thief* and *The Drum-singers*.[69]

Tian returned to a script that he had been working on since completing *Horse Thief*. *The Great Waters* (*Dashui*) was a contemporary story set beside the Yellow River. The script was by Mo Yan, the original writer and adaptor of *Red Sorghum*, and Liu Yiran, who had written *Rock 'n' Roll Kids*. Tian had not been keen on the original script which the Beijing studio had given him in 1986, but in the intervening years he had made considerable revisions. When he had time to start production in earnest, however, there was no money for the project and it was abandoned.[70]

Events in the spring and early summer of 1989 intervened. When the People's Liberation Army seized Tian'anmen Square on the night of 3–4 June 1989, ending the student protests of that spring, Tian Zhuangzhuang was in Europe. Unlike many of his generation, and to the alarm of many of his friends abroad, Tian returned to Beijing within weeks. In late 1989 he completed a television drama, *Illegal Lives* (*Feifa shengming*, a.k.a. *Tebie shoushushi*, literally "Special Operating Room").[71] By this time he had begun work on his next feature film. Jiang Wen, star of *Red Sorghum*, and Liu Xiaoqing, one of China's leading actresses whose career had begun during the Cultural Revolution, asked Tian to direct them together in a film.

In post-June 4th China, writers and artists needed to exercise great caution. Tighter political restrictions coincided with increased financial difficulties for most of the state-owned feature film studios. Tian's new project addressed these two questions: it was a co-production between the Beijing Film Studio and a Hong Kong company and it was safely set in the past.[72] *Li Lianying, the Imperial Eunuch* (*Dataijian Li Lianying*) is in a sense a prologue to Bertolucci's *The Last Emperor* (1987). It tells the story of the relationship between Cixi, the Empress Dowager (who dies at the start of Bertolucci's epic), and the powerful eunuch Li Lianying, chiefly during the Guangxu emperor's reign, 1875–1908. The empress dowager, a hated figure in modern Chinese history, served as regent to the infant emperor at the start of his reign and wielded great power over him. Towards the end of his rule, she had him virtually imprisoned in the palace, and his death within days of Cixi's is thought to have been from unnatural causes. In all these intrigues, Li Lianying had to balance loyalty to the emperor and service to the empress dowager. The film covers the Hundred Days of Reform in 1898, when the emperor tried to introduce systemic changes inspired by the Westernizing ideas of Kang Youwei (1858–1927) and Liang Qichao (1873–1929). The empress dowager ruthlessly put an end to the reforms, executing many of the reformers. In 1900 the court fled Beijing as the Eight Nation Army of the Western powers and Japan besieged the city in response to the anti-foreign Yihetuan (Boxer) rebellion.

Tian Zhuangzhuang (left) shooting *Li Lianying, the Imperial Eunuch*

These were spectacular events, but Tian's focus is rather different from Bertolucci's. Whereas the latter gave great play to spectacle by filming in the grand spaces of the Forbidden City, Tian concentrates on the more domestic settings of the palace: in its backrooms and private chambers, Li Lianying plots and flatters his way into the affections of the Empress Dowager. Jiang Wen plays Li as both a repulsive and sympathetic person who is neither man nor woman, capturing the mostly closeted pretensions of an imperial servant who daydreams of himself as emperor. Liu Xiaoqing, Jiang's real-life partner, gives one of the best performances of her career as she ages through her imperial role. The narrative frequently flashes forward, to the aged Li Lianying sometime after the fall of the Qing dynasty in 1911, living with a small boy in a house at the Qing imperial tombs in Dingling. At the end of the film, disturbed by his memories and the lives he had to snuff out on imperial orders, he takes down the basket that contained his boyish genitals, cut off at the age of nine, stuffs the dried object into his mouth, and staggers out towards the tombs. He collapses on the marble steps under a ceremonial archway.

Allegory has long been a device for Chinese artists to comment on politics. The Cultural Revolution can be said to have begun in 1965 over the allegorical commentary in a play set in the fifteenth century, *Hai Rui Dismissed from Office* (*Hai Rui ba guan*), which was a thinly-disguised criticism of Mao Zedong. In 1991, sensitive viewers could interpret *Li Lianying, the Imperial Eunuch* as a devastating commentary on post-June 4th politics. Imperial intrigues and vicious rivalries, often divorced from the world beyond the palace walls, was one way of looking at the central Party and state leadership in the 1990s. Like the Qing dynasty at the turn of the century, this was a system riddled with corruption and ambition, apparently unwilling and unable to reform itself.

Given the political climate after the June 4th incident, the filmmakers could not acknowledge an allegorical reading of *Li Lianying*. But Tian had earlier, in less restricted times, made claims for a broad reading of *On the Hunting Ground* and *Horse Thief.* "A lot of people take these films to be stories set among Mongolians and Tibetans. In fact, I made these stories about human beings. Every Chinese—every Chinese who has been through the Cultural Revolution—can find themselves in *On the Hunting Ground* and *Horse Thief.* To make a wild statement, these films can be described as autobiographies of today's Chinese."[73] Tian made *Li Lianying* to some extent as a personal favor to his friends Jiang Wen and Liu Xiaoqing,[74] but a remarkable consistency pervades Tian Zhuangzhuang's films. In his two minorities films he went to the margins to comment upon Chinese society; in Li Lianying, a man-woman on the margins of the ceremonial space of the imperial palace, Tian found another means to add to a continuing discourse on Chinese culture and society.

In 1992 Tian filmed *The Blue Kite* (*Lan fengzheng*), the story of a Beijing family during a tumultuous era. In defiance of the domestic banning of the film, it was shown at the Cannes Film Festival in May 1993 to critical acclaim. This proved to be one of the most accomplished film accounts of the Cultural Revolution experience made by any Chinese filmmaker, and, unexpectedly one of only three such essays in Cultural Revolution history by fifth-generation directors.[75]

The Blue Kite recounts the family history of a boy, Tietou (literally "steel head"), from 1953 (and the death of Stalin, which delayed a marriage) through the Anti-Rightist Campaign in 1957 to the mid-1960s, when Red Guards beat the boy into unconsciousness in the closing scene. Tietou's mother lives successively with three men. The first, the boy's father, is sent away as a Rightist. One of his work companions, distraught at the casual way in which her husband was so labelled, supports the mother and son for the next few years. Tietou calls him Uncle. He dies of liver disease. Then, on the eve of the Cultural Revolution, Tietou gains a stepfather when his mother marries a high Party cadre. This move makes the family vulnerable to Red Guard attack.

What characterized Tian's film is a remarkable tact in dealing with momentous and, indeed, horrendous events. Like his contemporaries in Taiwan, the directors Hou Hsiao-hsien and Edward Yang (Yang Dechang), Tian presents history from a personal viewpoint. With this focus on a family, major events occur off-screen. Lesser directors might present the ghastliness of starvation and accidental death in climactic scenes. Tian Zhuangzhuang instead has a character read an official letter describing the death of the alleged Rightist in a forestry accident, while the screen is full of calm shots of tree-covered mountains. This low-key approach adds enormous power to the account. A second device reinforces the impact of the film. It is narrated by the voice of a young boy, presumably twelve-year-old Tietou after he has fallen to the ground on being beaten by the Red Guards.[76] Simple, infrequent music based on children's songs enhance the effect. The last shot is of a paper kite caught in the branches of a tree against a leaden sky. Essentially the way in which the film presents its subject matter amounts to a distancing effect, not inconsistent with Tian Zhuangzhuang's earlier films.

The Blue Kite's boldness in presenting the impact of the Cultural Revolution and its preliminary political skirmishes on the lives of real people infuriated conservatives in Beijing. Tian was accused of conspiring with foreign residents in smuggling the shot film out of China to complete post-production in Japan. The acclaim at Cannes compounded the problem. As a result the Film Bureau of the Ministry of Radio, Film and Television issued a decree in the spring of 1993 that Tian (along with several other film directors, including the sixth-generation Zhang Yuan) should not be allowed to make any more films. Nor was he to be allowed any access to filmmaking equipment and premises. It was a remarkable reaction, though Tian affected nonchalance. Two years later his production office in the Beijing Film Studio was decorated with a framed copy of the official statement revoking the earlier ban, now that Tian (and the others banned) had shown necessary contrition. Tian's response to being asked about contrition is unprintable.[77]

By the mid-1990s Tian Zhuangzhuang had stopped directing and become a producer, encouraging the work of several younger filmmakers who were identified, somewhat against their will, as members of the sixth generation. This new, so-called generation lacked the shared experiences growing up that helped define the earlier group. But they were labelled sixth-generation to acknowledge the emergence of a new cohort in Chinese film. They were also determined to make as striking a mark on Chinese cinema as their predecessors. Many of their works tended to be small-scale, urban portraits of intimate relations, unlike the blasted landscapes and large themes of early fifth-generation productions.[78]

For Tian Zhuangzhuang producing was not an easy task. Lu Xuechang's *How Steel is Made* (*Gangtie shi zheyang lianchengde*), a story of a young man growing up to become a petty gangster, took more than three years and several re-editings to pass censorship. Ironically titled after a popular Soviet novel, the film follows its hero from late Cultural Revolution enthusiasm to cynical despair. Tian Zhuangzhuang himself appeared as a wise old train driver who tries to guide the boy. Likewise, *So Close to Paradise* (*Biandan guniang*, literally "Shoulder-pole Girl," a.k.a. *Yuenan guniang*, "Girl from Vietnam"), directed by the sixth generation's Wang Xiaoshuai, took four years to reach its audiences in 1998.[79] Like its stable-mate, the film explores the underbelly of society undergoing economic transformation. Wang's film is striking for the naturalism of its acting and directing, a worthy successor to the contemporary feel of the domestic scenes in his mentor's *Rock 'n' Roll Kids*.

These were frustrating times for Tian, especially as the ending of *The Blue Kite* suggests a sequel would follow. In the spring and summer of 2000 he shot a documentary among the minority peoples of Yunnan province in southwest China. *Delamu*, a superbly constructed account of people on the ancient tea and horse trading route between Yunnan and Tibet, seemed like a return to the margins of his work from the 1980s. Its release in 2004 was a typically roundabout way to show his critics, both artistic and political, that he still meant business.

True to earlier form, Tian marked his return to feature-film making in an unexpected way in 2001. He remade one of the classics of Chinese cinema, the 1948 *Spring in a Small Town*, directed by Fei Mu (1906–51). The earlier film had been in effect banned in China for more than four decades, because Fei Mu was categorized as right-wing on three counts: his remaining in Shanghai during the Japanese occupation, his directing during that time of a biography of Confucius, and his move in 1948 to Hong Kong.[80] The 1948 film presented a post-war love triangle, told in part with voice-over from the woman caught between her sickly husband and a former lover, who comes visiting after many years. The emotional tension that Fei created through simple but stylish *mise en scène* lent the film the hallmarks of a masterpiece. Tian Zhuangzhuang's version is in color, does not make use of the world-weary voice-over, and seems somewhat tedious in comparison with the original.

Critics responded to the new work by wondering why Tian bothered to remake what many regarded as close to perfection. His response was to talk of homage to a great Chinese film and filmmaker.[81] On one level, the modern version is indeed an exercise in using color, a more mobile camera and other novel devices in telling an older story. But at heart Tian's version of *Spring in a Small Town* was a commentary on his own predicament at the turn of the twenty-first century. As a remake, the film draws attention to the richness of the Chinese film heritage, significantly that from before 1949. It also underscored how difficult it was, in contemporary political and commercial climes, for modern-day Fei Mus to make films from the heart that would stand the test of time. Once again, Tian Zhuangzhuang used the margins or distance in the past to make a subtle but powerful point about the present.

4. A Women's Cinema?: The Films of Hu Mei, Peng Xiaolian and Liu Miaomiao

Dai Jinhua, cultural critic and something of a public intellectual in China, was convinced in the 1990s that there was no such thing as a Chinese feminist cinema. She argued that

> in the last fifty years … the true "women's film" (*nüxing dianying*) is rare, if not completely absent. In the majority of female-directed films, the female gender not only rarely manifests itself as a narrative position or a visual vantage point, but it also seldom emerges as a distinct feature characterizing the film's material structure, plot development, characteriza- tion, narrative style, and cinematic language. In contrast to the literary works of contemporary women writers, most women directors have not turned their gender position into the motivating force for their creative work.[82]

Three women directors of the class of '82 created works with a focus on personal psychologies and relationships that encouraged their identification by Dai's fellow critics as part of a "women's cinema" (*nüxing dianying*) trend in the 1980s.[83] Hu Mei, Peng Xiaolian and Liu Miaomiao spoke of a degree of frustration in making their films that seemed less obvious for their male classmates.

Hu Mei returned to army life on being assigned to the August First studio in Beijing.[84] After working as a log keeper and assistant director, Hu Mei co-directed her first film, *Army Nurse* (*Nüer lou*, literally "The Women's Quarters") in 1984. This immediately established her as a maker of psychological dramas with a distinct feminist tone. Hu Mei's films examined the inner worlds of her, often female, characters.

Hu Mei later reported that the studio leaders seemed to regard her as "a slip of a girl," and therefore unlikely to cause trouble.[85] This made it easier for her to gain approval for the script of *Army Nurse*. Based on a short story by Ding Xiaoqi, a woman friend of Hu Mei, *Army Nurse* told the story of nurse Qiao Xiaoyu in terms of a choice between love and revolution.[86] The head of the August First script department recommended the script to the top leadership. Hu Mei and Li Xiaojun, a male fifth-generation classmate, were ordered to co-direct the film.[87] Not to be outdone by the Guangxi and Xiaoxiang studios, August First also formed a "Youth Filming Group" to make *Army Nurse*.

The result is a highly subjective film. As a rather weary female voice begins an off-screen narration, a bright and energetic Qiao Xiaoyu joins the army as a nurse in an isolated rural hospital. The tone of the narrator's voice suggests that a more complex character will emerge. After several years working at the hospital, Qiao falls in love with a handsome young patient, Ding Zhu. She finds it difficult, however, to express her true feelings to the soldier. In a moment of great anguish and emotion, she lets her head fall onto the soldier's shoulder as she is bandaging his naked torso. Her emotions are never fulfilled, however, for such an affair would be against army regulations and Qiao Xiaoyu is too much of a good soldier to allow her emotions to take charge. Friends try to arrange a match with another soldier, but Qiao by now has lost the courage to pursue happiness, fearful of the responsibility of having her own family, with no leaders above her or women friends constantly around to give her guidance. She decides to return to the small hospital, where there is no need for her to show individual will.

Hu Mei likened Qiao Xiaoyu's life to that of a nun. The pressure on nurse Qiao is initially from outside, but like a nun, Qiao Xiaoyu internalizes others' expectations and leaves the greater society behind. She digs a hole for herself, and buries her love in it.[88] Interestingly, as she discussed the film six months after its completion, Hu Mei slipped frequently back and forth between talking about Qiao Xiaoyu and about herself. Hu Mei shared with her fifth-generation classmates a concern for the relationship between individuals and society, but unlike those who chose to examine this relationship in historical or unusual settings, Hu Mei set her films firmly in the present.

After Hu Mei and Li Xiaojun completed filming *Army Nurse*, working with two cinematographers also from the Beijing Film Academy class of '82, they still had to ensure studio and higher level approval. Army officials emphasized that the film should present a pleasant (*mei*), rather than a grey (*hui*), impression of army women. They wanted the "contradiction" between love and career to be made more emphatic, "for the education of the troops."[89] Small points caused large concern. The absence of any clear motivation for Qiao's liking for Ding Zhu was one such point, as if sexual attraction to the handsome soldier was an unacceptable reason. A new scene was added in which Ding gives blood for a transfusion for an old patient, a former proletarian revolutionary. The old man was originally in the script simply to serve as go-between between Qiao Xiaoyu and the shy young soldier. In the revised version, Qiao is impressed by Ding Zhu's sense of service.

Hu Mei found her intention thwarted in other ways. To Hu Mei, the small boy to whom Qiao gives a soda and food seemed an unnecessary addition to show that the heroine had natural, maternal instincts. Less emphasis was put than Hu Mei had planned on the highly charged episode in which Qiao rests her head on Ding Zhu's bare shoulder. Apparently one (male) studio leader felt that the male should make the first move in such an encounter.[90] Nonetheless this episode is still striking, as Jerome Silbergeld makes clear in a masterful analysis of the sequence with the handsome Ding:

> Their physical encounter is brief and so chaste as to scarcely qualify as a sexual encounter in America; but initiated by a girl, narrated by a woman, and representing a whole culture so starved for personal affection after ten paranoid years of destroying all internal enemies, the brief ten seconds when army nurse touches military patient became one of the most emotionally charged moments in modern Chinese cinema.[91]

For Hu Mei, a key element in the film's intimate psychological portrait was the narration. The idea of using a weary voice was hers. She also hoped that as much as possible the picture on the screen would have little relation with what was said in the off-screen narration by Qiao Xiaoyu's voice, to set up a dynamic dialectic between image and sound. Her initial idea was for the film to proceed according to Qiao Xiaoyu's feelings, rather than tell a story. The narration, she hoped, would consist of thoughts aroused by people and memories of events. Women, Hu noted in an interview, like to remember the past.[92]

Hu wanted in her directing debut to establish in Chinese film an emphasis on feelings which she saw as characteristic of Western cinema. Most Chinese films concentrated on social relations. This focus on women in society situated *Army Nurse* in the broader development in Chinese cinema in the mid-1980s of what was called "women's cinema".[93] *Army Nurse* shared the highly subjective element of a voice-over narration with, for example, *Sacrificed Youth* (*Qingchun ji*), also a 1985 film, directed by Zhang Nuanxin, one of the fifth-generation's film academy teachers.[94]

The personal meaning for Hu Mei of both *Army Nurse* and her next feature is clear. In recalling her life before film school, Hu described her sense of having a public and private personality. To her schoolmates, high-school teachers, and army dance-troupe officers, Hu Mei was a vivacious young woman, enthusiastic in her participation in political movements and performances. But privately Hu could not ignore the trouble her family encountered in the Cultural Revolution. She also could not overlook the chauvinism of some of her superiors.[95] Qiao Xiaoyu is not Hu Mei, but the autobiographical significance of the subjective approach in *Army Nurse* deserves acknowledgment.

Far from War (*Yuanli zhanzheng de niandai*), also made at the August First studio, is an intimate examination of an army family of four in Beijing: an instructor at an army staff college, his wife, a singer of Western opera, their young son and the officer's elderly father, himself a war veteran. The old man suddenly leaves home, returning to the northern village of his youth to present the local school with his life's savings. He is deeply troubled by an episode in the War of Resistance to Japan. In a recurring flashback the old soldier recalls his relationship, as peasant soldier, with a brave young peasant woman. Having saved her from being raped by a Japanese soldier, he fell and rolled down a long grassy bank with the girl. The young man finds himself physically aroused and has sex with

Far from War

her. The old man has a gnawing sense of guilt about this episode, and the generous gift to the school is an effort to salve his conscience. He gives the money in memory of the young woman, whose recent death he has read about in a magazine. Meanwhile his son and daughter-in-law are searching for him, realizing the loneliness which is the lot of many older people. Eventually there is an emotional reunion, as the family resolves to allow each other more room for their lives as individuals as well as to live more harmoniously together. The redecoration of their apartment which had started the film is completed.

Far from War is a more consistent work than *Army Nurse*, but as with her first feature, Hu Mei had to live with studio concerns. One was the implication that society was not properly looking after senior citizens. The scene in which the peasant guerilla and the young woman roll down the bank confused some of the older officers of the studio. One asked, upon seeing an early cut of the film, why the two young people were wrestling after escaping from the Japanese. When the other studio inspectors realized that the young man in effect rapes the young woman, Hu Mei was obliged to reshoot and recut the scene to make the episode less obvious.[96]

To a greater extent than in *Army Nurse*, images are a major part of the film's impact. The cinematography was by her classmate Zhang Li, who had shot Wu Ziniu's *Dove Tree*. Art design by Su Zhou, another classmate from the art department and Hu Mei's husband at the time, helped the integrated look of *Far from War*.[97] Veteran actor Huang Zongluo gives a highly restrained reading of the old man's character, avoiding a temptation to milk the part for maudlin sympathy. His scenes with Wang Xueqin, who plays his army instructor son (and had played Gu Qing in *The Yellow Earth*), have a subtlety that is a credit to the actors and their director.

Like *Army Nurse*, *Far from War* is about belonging. The family members each have individual doubts about whether they should be where they are. The grandfather feels discarded by society and a nuisance to his son and daughter-in-law. His recurring memory of events over forty years ago typifies his sense of isolation. His son wonders if he deserves to be teaching at the officers' academy when he has had no experience of real war. His daughter-in-law is troubled that her family does not give her the security of belonging that she thinks it should. She is rehearsing the part of Cio-Cio-san in Puccini's "Madama Butterfly," the story of a woman abandoned. Hu Mei was unusual among her classmates in presenting these sorts of quotidian unease in contemporary society. Her direct presentation of the characters' complexity was also not typical. Hu Mei's contribution to China's "women's cinema" in the 1980s owed less to the rhetoric of human liberation coined by Mao Zedong and his propagandists and more to an awareness of the gap between rhetoric and reality.

After completing *Far from War* in 1987, Hu Mei was unable to continue in this vein. Much of her energy was spent in trying to leave the August First studio and army ranks. Finally, in the spring of 1989 she was able to leave the army studio, after making another film, *The Marksman* (*Wuqiang qiangshou*), which she described as simply churned out for the studio to make some money.[98] Now calling herself China's only self-employed (*geti hu*) film director, Hu Mei spent much of her time on television dramas and serials. An independent director could find work more easily there than at the overstaffed, near bankrupt film studios. By 2000 she had established a Shanghai branch of her own film production company, to match the headquarters in Beijing. Funds came from the commercial success of a historical drama series for television set in the early Qing dynasty (1644–1911).[99] Meanwhile, upon her divorce from Su Zhou, she had become the partner of an ambitious writer and art collector of about her own age called He Xin. He Xin is best described as a "court philosopher," much used by Premier Li Peng and the more conservative members of the top Party leadership.[100] He served to present their orthodox vision of a modernizing China, in a world which made the fifth-generation views of the mid-1980s seem distinctly out-of-date.

While Hu Mei's first films combined psychological complexity with social naturalism, at the Shanghai Film Studio Peng Xiaolian found it difficult to avoid a Shanghai gloss in her work. In Shanghai-made films since the 1930s and even after 1949, apartments seemed larger and brighter, people healthier, and lives faster paced. Her directing debut was a mature working of the Shanghai style in a contemporary, teenage story. For her second film Peng removed the story and setting from Shanghai and tried to present a specifically female point of view. But her Shanghai roots were difficult for her to ignore.

Having worked as log keeper on one film and frustrated at the lack of prospects in Shanghai, Peng took paid leave for more than a year while she edited her father's writings in Beijing, under the auspices of the Chinese Writers Association. While in Beijing she married an aerospace engineering student. Soon afterwards her husband went to the United States for further study, and the marriage came to an end after two years. Back in Shanghai in 1985, Peng Xiaolian worked as one of two assistant directors of a remake of a notable Shanghai film from the 1930s. *The Song at Midnight* (*Yeban gesheng*) had been first filmed in 1937 by a team of left-wing artists under the direction of Maxu Weibang and had become a cult film, a cherished memory for older generations of Shanghai film-goers. A Chinese version of *The Phantom of the Opera*, the 1937 *The Song at Midnight* combined the story of a ghost haunting a theatre with a patriotic call for social and national unity against an unnamed Japan.[101] Quite why China in the 1980s needed a remake was not clear. Peng Xiaolian found working with director Yang Yanjin eminently resistible. Her particular task was supervising the dance sequences in the film, including overseeing rehearsals and other preparations for the scenes in which thinly clad young women cavorted for Yang's camera.[102]

Her first opportunity to direct came in late 1985. Despite its Shanghai setting, *Me and My Classmates* (*Wo he wode tongxuemen*) has little connection with the reality of life in the city. In some respects the film looks like a Chinese version of a contemporary Japanese teenage film. The young actors in their unstructured jackets or spotless sportswear look as if they were found in Shibuya or Harajuku. Bu Lan, in the first grade of senior high school, is nominated as a joke to be class sports monitor and unexpectedly wins election. At first reluctant to serve, she is encouraged by her mother and by one of the boys in her class. Bu Lan's enthusiasm inspires the boys to win the basketball league championship.

Although the story was not new, some of the social implications of *Me and My Classmates* were an interesting reflection on developments in China in the 1980s. Much of Bu Lan's initial immaturity is ascribed to the absence of her father. This absent parent motif, usually involving the father being sent overseas on a modernization mission, appeared as an explanatory device for youthful transgression in a number of Chinese films from the 1980s.[103] One of Bu Lan's classmates is from a private entrepreneur household. His family works long hours at its retail business, but can afford a private telephone and prominently displayed English books.[104] Compounding the modernism, Bu Lan's mother teaches modern dance.

To complete the Shanghai or fantasy dimension of the film, the high school, housed in a pre-1949 building, is magnificently equipped. At a time when few urban schools had even a single computer, there are classrooms full of them in Bu Lan's school. Even the original title of the film, abandoned at initial script-approval stage, *The Disco Queen and Her Classmates*, is reminiscent of the combination of fantasy and fascination with the modern of many progressive films of 1930s Shanghai. As Peng noted about her film: "It deliberately avoids the sharp contradictions of reality to present an idealized, lyrical picture of the life of high school students today."[105] Such fantasy had its appeal, at least for officials and some critics who gave it several awards.[106]

Peng Xiaolian's second feature, made in 1987, was set far from Shanghai, and addresses the "sharp contradictions of reality" with considerable directness. *Three Women* (*Nüren de gushi*) is based on a script largely the work of Peng herself, rewritten from another writer's scenario. Peng had started work on the script in 1984, completing it in 1985. Only having done the teenager film was Peng entrusted with her original script.[107]

In *Three Women* Peng drew upon her years in the countryside as a sent-down youth and leader of a women's team on a commune. The film presents the story of three women from north China who journey first to Beijing and then to Chongqing, selling in free markets the synthetic knitting yarn produced at a factory near their home. The youngest woman is avoiding marriage to an idiot forced on her in order for her brother to marry the idiot's sister. The oldest woman is a country bumpkin who acts as mother to the group. For the third woman, the journey offers a chance to help her orphaned family of four sisters. After several months in Chongqing, they return with a lot of money and a great deal more self-confidence to the village.

More than the highly sanitized version of reality in *Me and My Classmates*, *Three Women* is of considerable interest, particularly on the question of the position of women. Even in the 1980s the system of arranged marriages had not been eliminated from north China villages. During the train journey to the southwest they meet a woman in her second pregnancy (against family planning regulations) determined to bear a son. When the three women return to their village, they pass near the ancient, now ruined arch erected to commemorate a chaste widow whose name was forgotten long ago. The arch was prominent in the earlier village scenes. At the end of the story, the idiot brother-in-law and another young tough walk threateningly towards the three women. In the last shot of the film the camera pans skyward, upwards to the Great Wall and on to the blank sky. The proximity of the women and the wall reminds Chinese audiences of the ancient legend of Meng Jiangnü, whose grief for her husband who had been killed constructing the wall is said to have caused part of the Great Wall to collapse. Its appearance in Peng Xiaolian's film serves as a final, ironic comment on the way women are still treated.

The general directorial restraint positions this fifth-generation director in a classical mode of filmmaking exemplified by some older Shanghai directors like Bai Chen. Peng's direction of the scenes of the free market on the Chongqing waterfront brought a lot of admiration from her Shanghai colleagues. Xie Jin, the pre-eminent third-generation director, told Peng he found it hard to believe these scenes with large numbers of extras were actually staged.[108] But, despite some deft touches and Peng's own experience with country women, *Three Women* is not a fully convincing film. The ups and downs of the narrative have an artifice that

Three Women

many of the film's other elements seem to belie. The forced marriage, the swindling of the older woman by a Beijing trickster, the encounter with the pregnant woman desperate for a son, and the episodes with the construction workers in Chongqing are presented with acting, editing, and music that makes them seem false. Ultimately, *Three Women* cannot leave behind its origins in the Shanghai film world. Like her male classmates Zhang Jianya and Jiang Haiyang, Peng Xiaolian was trapped in a Shanghai mode.

For her next project, Peng Xiaolian planned to make a film about the Cultural Revolution experiences of the writer Ba Jin (1904–), one of the most popular May Fourth writers and a friend of her late father. The central narrative would be about a film director making a film about Ba Jin's experiences, incorporating documentary footage from the time. But the Shanghai studio leadership were unenthusiastic about the subject matter, fearing it might be too controversial. No feature film had documented the Cultural Revolution experiences of a well-known artist. Meanwhile, Peng Xiaolian made a two-month visit to the United States in late 1988. A few months after the June 4th incident in Beijing, she returned to the States to enrol in a master's program in film at New York University. In late 1991, under the auspices of Japanese documentarist Ogawa Shinsuke (1935– 92), she began pre-production for a documentary on Chinese students living in Japan. Ogawa's death put the project on hold.

Having secured American permanent residency, Peng Xiaolian returned to Shanghai in 1996 to work as a director. Among completed films, chiefly for television, were the detective story *A Dog to Kill* (*Quan sha*) and *Once Upon a Time in Shanghai* (*Shanghai jishi*). She also continued her fiction writing, publishing several collections. A source of particular pride was her commissioning, by the late director's commune, to make a biographical film about Ogawa Shinsuke. *Manzan Benigaki* (2001) was a combination of Ogawa footage shot over sixteen years and interviews, shot by Peng, of his filmmaking commune members. The mix of devotion and frustration among Ogawa's followers made some viewers think of another charismatic leftist leader in a different field: Mao Zedong. Less a source of pride was her work, in the summer of 2000, on a children's feature film starring an animated kite, inserted through computer manipulation into live action. But *The Magic Umbrella* (*Keke de mosan*, co-directed with Hu Yijiang) served to confirm that Peng Xiaolian's days as a distinctive fifth-generation director, like those of her classmates, were long gone.[109]

Being the youngest student in the class of '82 was an indication of the kind of determination Liu Miaomiao took to her new workplace on graduation. In her almost three years at the Xiaoxiang studio in Changsha before making her first feature, Liu Miaomiao was only able to direct a single television play. For the rest of the time she worked as a log keeper and assistant to directors. One such director was Chen Lu, Wu Ziniu's nominal co-director on *The Candidate*, when he co-directed *Behind the Movie Screen* (*Zai yinmu houmian*) in 1984.[110] As their graduation exercise, a group of film students is preparing to shoot a film about the efforts of a textile mill's Party secretary on behalf of troubled young people. Sent to live at a textile mill, the cynical film students learn to respect the young factory workers they befriend. Their graduation film takes on new significance as a tribute to the young workers. Liu Miaomiao was not alone in seeing the film as a veiled criticism of her film-school classmates, whose rebelliousness had been notorious during their time at Zhuxinzhuang.

Liu Miaomiao made her first feature in 1985 at the Fujian Film Studio in Fuzhou. It was China's newest feature film studio, having begun production only a year earlier. None of her crew, apart from the actors, had worked on a feature film before. *A Merchant Shipping Tale* (*Yuanyang yishi*) had started out as a script about shipboard safety, funded by a shipping company. When offered the chance to direct, Liu reckoned she was in no position to decline. "If I did, who would ask me to make any other film?," she commented in an interview after completing the work.[111] Inexperienced cinematographers, art directors and other crew had made the shooting a nightmare. The completed work did not satisfy Liu Miaomiao. In talking about it several months later, she insisted, between cigarettes, that the responsibility rested squarely on her own young shoulders. She should have been more circumspect about accepting the project in the first place. Having taken it on, her lack of experience in organizing a shoot and in finding artistic solutions to script problems meant that *A Merchant Shipping Tale* could not succeed.

Liu Miaomiao's youthful efforts at a directorial style are ill-served by the weak script. There is somewhat forced homage to Antonioni here. The three different, surreal color schemes in the flashbacks involving the apartment of the central protagonist, a ship's captain, are an interesting fifth-generation denial of the "realist" tradition in Chinese cinema. The frequently confrontational camera similarly serves the innovation Liu cherished.

Liu Miaomiao's next project confronted the attitude that she was just "a slip of a girl" head-on. *The Sound of Hoofbeats* (*Mati sheng sui*) could be described as a female reworking of *One and Eight*, the breakthrough fifth-generation film. The rugged masculinity of *One and Eight* became in Liu Miaomiao's hands a paean to female toughness. The film's title came from a line in Mao Zedong's poem, "The Long March." In 1934–35, escaping the Nationalist blockade, the Red Army made its way on a 12,000 kilometer journey from the southeast through some of the most inhospitable territory on the borderlands between Sichuan province and the Tibetan plateau and then north to Shaanxi and eventually Yan'an. Party history emphasizes the heroic accomplishment of the Long March as the trial in which the Communist Party was reborn under Mao's leadership. Liu Miaomiao's film representation of the experiences of a band of female soldiers on the journey salutes simply the heroism of survival.

Of the 20,000 soldiers who reached northern Shaanxi only a handful were women. Many more had started the journey or joined later. Most of these women were abandoned because of injury or weakness, married off to local farmers, or presented as slaves to some of the minority chieftains in western Sichuan. Liu Miaomiao learned almost accidentally of these women soldiers, for they do not figure in the official history books. She was intrigued by their stories, and angry that they had not been recognized beyond, in some cases, a miserable twenty *yuan* (about US$5) monthly pension.[112] In her director's statement, written before starting shooting, Liu stressed her interest in presenting the ordinary soldiers' view of the Long March in contrast to the usual concentration on Party leaders.[113] As in *One and Eight*, much of the film is shot with a close, decentered camera. Zhang Li, Liu Miaomiao's classmate and now former husband, was one of the cinematographers on the project, made for their Xiaoxiang studio.

The result was a typical 1980s fifth-generation film, except that the sweaty, ragged heroes are mostly women. When the eight women first appear on screen, staggering across the harsh landscape, it is difficult to tell that they are female. Of the male soldiers, only the commander seems willing to help the women on the journey. But when he hands over his spare pair of straw sandals to the leader of the women, several other men do the same. The women had been cut off from the main body of their army and have joined up with a small squadron of men. The sheer instinct for survival drives the soldiers on. At one point the senior officer, whose leg has been amputated, commits suicide lest he slow down the group. The soldiers watch in horror as captured Han Chinese settlers are sold into slavery to the local Tibetans. A similar helplessness prevents the women from doing anything as local armed men rape other women soldiers. Two women are lost trying to drag a dead horse across a swollen river to feed their comrades. The soldiers are so hungry that they even consider eating an old goatskin coat. The leader attempts to urge them on: "We'll keep going. Is there anything else we can do? Is there anywhere else to go?"

All this is a far cry from the orthodox screen representation of the Long March, which praised popular, multi-ethnic support for the Red Army marchers. The women soldiers in *The Sound of Hoofbeats* cower from the terrain, the weather, other soldiers, and the local inhabitants. Their heroism consists in simply surviving. This is a distinctly post-Cultural Revolution view of Party history. Liu Miaomiao's 1987 film had difficulty surviving the censors. The novel by Jiang Qitao, on which it was based, had been published without problem. But the cultural authorities continued in the 1980s to ascribe to film a power over audiences unmatched by books. The film passed censorship inspection in November 1987 but had only limited release: provincial distribution managers decided audiences did not want to see such a gloomy, uncommercial film. Only seven copies were ordered.[114]

The distributors' assessment seemed accurate, at least when Liu Miaomiao proudly showed her film at the China Film Archive in the summer of 1988 to three young boxers being cast for her next project. The young men seemed unimpressed. Boxing had been banned in China in 1958, allegedly after premier Zhou Enlai declared it too brutal. The beginning of the 1980s saw a revival of boxing, part of the flourishing of youth subcultures that also featured male and female body building. *The Boxers* (*Quanji shou*) told the story of two generations of boxers, one of whom seeks to redeem himself for accidentally killing his friend in the ring in the 1950s by coaching the dead man's son in the 1980s.

Liu Miaomiao planned a commercial success, commissioning five popular songs for the film,[115] but *The Boxers* did only modest business. The youth audience she sought seems to have been turned off by the 1950s beginning and the older characters in the film. Like Wu Ziniu's Fujian films from 1988, *The Boxers* was evidence of a fifth-generation response to the demands of the marketplace. It also showed how difficult responding could be in a film enterprise in financial crisis, even for a director of Liu Miaomiao's youthful determination.

In 1992 Liu Miaomiao wrote and directed *Innocent Babbler (Za zuizi)* at the Youth Film Studio. A country tale, its look and feel was reminiscent of the ruggedness and directness of *The Sound of Hoofbeats*. The central protagonist is a young boy with a hare-lip who manages to overcome adversity. For the authentic atmosphere in the film, shot in Ningxia, Liu drew upon her own experience as a child visiting cousins in the countryside.[116] The film turned out to be one of Liu Miaomiao's successes, winning an award at the Venice film festival.[117] It was followed in 1993 by another modest critical success, *Family Scandal (Jia chou)*, a joint production of the Beijing Film Academy's Youth Film Studio and the Ningxia Film Studio, where Liu Miaomiao transferred in the mid-1990s to serve, at one point, as studio head.[118] All three films lacked major male characters, an indirect assertion, perhaps, of Liu's feminism.[119]

Two other women from the directing department class of '82 also made their mark. Li Shaobai, who had been an army medic during the last years of the Cultural Revolution, followed a path similar to that of Hu Mei and Liu Miaomiao. Her *A Man at Forty (Sishi bu huo)* had the psychological interest and complexity of *Army Nurse* and *Far from War*. Li's *Blush (Hongfen)*, with a script by Ni Zhen, won a Silver Bear at the 1995 Berlin film festival. It explored women's position in an historical setting similar to that of Zhang Yimou's *Raise the Red Lantern*. Earlier, Li had filmed *Bloody Morning (Xuese qingchen)*. Set in a remote northern village, the film follows a police investigator as he reconstructs the brutal killing of a young man. It was a Chinese reworking of Gabriel García Márquez's "Chronicle of a Death Foretold." Its look and feel reminded viewers of the primitivism of *One and Eight* or Liu's *The Sound of Hoofbeats*. Hu Ying suggests that the film demonstrated that

> one powerful way of inserting the "Real" into the film's texture while inscribing a gendered perspective is to depict women's marginalization forcefully, at the same time providing the means of filmic identification with that marginalized position for both the other characters and the audience.[120]

In contrast, Ning Ying focused on intimate portrayals of contemporary urban dwellers: elderly opera fans in *For Fun (Zhao le)* and overworked policemen in *On the Beat (Minjing gushi)*. Ning's seven years studying in Italy immediately after graduation from the Beijing Film Academy seem to have encouraged a reworking of a tradition of neo-realism that owed a debt also to progressive Shanghai cinema of the 1930s.

Dai Jinhua may be right in asserting that a truly feminist cinema has not yet emerged in China, though her question might be equally applied to other national cinemas. She insists that "women's success rested on their ability to master those subjects and materials that characterized the work of male directors."[121] But the pioneering efforts of third and fourth-generation women directors since the 1950s found worthy successors in the class of '82. In an industry not exactly welcoming of female talent or innovation, these new filmmakers did not have in effect to become men to succeed. Hu Mei and her female classmates were able to extend the subject matter and approaches of their films in new directions that were of particular interest to both women and men.

5. The Rise of the Entertainment Film: Zhang Jianya and Jiang Haiyang

Two classmates returned to Shanghai to embark on careers that were directly in response to the growing commercial pressures on the film studios in the 1980s and 1990s. Faced with a massive rise in television ownership, increased consumer choice in entertainment and leisure, and declining cinema audiences, the Shanghai Film Studio felt well equipped to respond to audience tastes. Shanghai has always been a pioneer in Chinese cinema.

Despite the number of studio employees, Zhang Jianya rose rapidly, being appointed in less than three years as head of one of three creative groups to which all the studio's artistic personnel belonged. He had first served as log keeper for older directors on two typical Shanghai films. *Under the Bridge* (*Daqiao xiamian*, 1983) was directed by Bai Chen, a sixty-two-year-old director who has been called the Billy Wilder of Chinese cinema. It tells the story of an unmarried mother who returns to Shanghai after spending the Cultural Revolution years as an educated youth in the countryside. In Shanghai she meets a young man who is self-employed as a bicycle repairman. Their growing affection survives the woman's eventual disclosure of an illegitimate child. With its concentration on the urban lives and country misfortunes of middle-class citizens, *Under the Bridge* has elements of the "mandarin ducks and butterfly" middle-brow fiction popular among urban Chinese readers in the first half of the twentieth century. The Shanghai film industry had grown in the 1930s appealing to this kind of audience.[122]

The second production on which Zhang worked as log keeper was the improbably titled *Romance in Philately* (*You yuan*), by the veteran director Sang Hu. Sang, almost seventy, first entered the Shanghai film world in the 1940s, when he made a name for himself in comedy. Despite his association with the pre-1949 Shanghai film world and his prominence in the 1950s, in 1972 he was chosen to direct the film version of Jiang Qing's "model ballet" *The White-Haired Girl* (*Baimao nü*).

In March 1985 Wu Yigong, as president of the Shanghai Film Corporation, appointed Zhang Jianya to head the newly established Third Creative Group (*chuangzuo zu*) at the studio. Each of the three groups was responsible for the total film production process, from script preparation and studio approval to finished film. Zhang Jianya's elevation to head one of the three new groups was a gesture by Wu towards breathing new life into Shanghai's creative ranks. Zhang's group included Sang Hu, Bai Chen and Xie Jin, perhaps the most widely known Chinese film director before the rise of Zhang Yimou. Zhang discovered that these older directors had a confidence lacking in fourth-generation directors. The latter had had little chance to practice their craft in the turmoil of the 1960s and 1970s. The annual meeting of film studio heads and the Film Bureau in Beijing had set nineteen films as Shanghai's production quota for 1986: eleven of these were in the hands of Zhang's group.

That year Zhang completed his debut directing effort, *Ice River* (*Binghe shengsixian*, literally "The Line of Life and Death on a Frozen River"). *Ice River* seems untypical of the usual Shanghai film and has some of the "hard beauty" characteristic of other fifth-generation directors. One reason for this impression is the setting, on a frozen stretch of the Yellow River between Shanxi and Shaanxi provinces in northwest China, close to the setting of *The Yellow Earth*. The script of *Ice River* had lain around the Shanghai studio for two years: Zhang took it on with cinematography classmate Shen Xinghao. The film presents an assortment of passengers and crew on a cross-river ferry trapped in an ice floe. While they wait for rescue or an icy death, each of the trapped individuals learns something about themselves. The mix of local country folk with educated passengers serves as a microcosm of Chinese society.

Although director Zhang presents the passengers and their stories with considerable skill, the film tends to lose its sureness of touch when it moves to the river bank. The rescue mission, under the leadership of the county Party secretary, stresses the risks taken by army helicopter pilots. When the local farmers, including relatives of the trapped passengers, appear en masse to wring their hands in front of the Party secretary, many viewers are reminded of similar scenes in earlier Chinese films. The Party secretary's headquarters tent includes tables covered with white table-cloths and complete with porcelain tea mugs and high-quality cigarettes. These touches may seem improbable, but do make a sly point about some local Party secretaries being small-time, local emperors (*tu huangdi*).

This mixture of visual motifs from the fifth-generation palette with an obviousness more typical of older films marked Zhang Jianya as a transitional figure. As he himself noted in an interview as he completed the film, it was difficult being a fifth-generation filmmaker at the Shanghai studio; at the smaller, newer studios, innovation was probably easier.[123] Tian Zhuanzhuang told Zhang that *Ice River* marked the first time that a director of their generation had managed to present a range of characters

Ice River

interacting as a convincing group, without a single dominant character.[124] On the evidence of *Ice River*, Zhang might be called a member of the fourth and a half generation of Chinese filmmakers.[125]

Zhang Jianya's next project was a harbinger for a change of direction in his directing career. Under the general supervision of Wu Yigong himself, he directed a comedy, *The Tribulations of a Chinese Gentleman* (*Shaoye de monan*), based on a novel by Jules Verne. Jin Fu, the profligate young master, finds himself bankrupt soon after inheriting his father's wealth in Shanghai in 1915. He takes out a huge insurance policy and tries to die in order to repay his lovely fiancée, Lianhua. Two Western insurance agents are equally determined to prevent Jin Fu's death, and after several mishaps, Jin Fu realizes that money does not mean happiness.

The Tribulations of a Chinese Gentleman was an effort by the Shanghai studio leaders, ever conscious of their city's cosmopolitan tradition, to reach a popular international audience. Lianhua is played by a Chinese-American actress. As the two insurance salesmen, two West German comics bring old-fashioned, music-hall styles to the film. The young master is played by Chen Peisi, the son of Chen Qiang, a notable specialist in villainous and comic roles in Chinese cinema since the 1950s. The

Germans chase Jin Fu across China, stopping briefly at such tourist attractions as a Taoist temple in Nanjing, a treasure-filled imperial tomb in Henan, and the Great Wall. The most appealing element in the film is one for which Zhang Jianya took special responsibility: the music is a crazy blending of Beethoven and music-hall goofiness.

Wu Yigong had another motive in this co-production with a West German producer. As head of the Shanghai film studio, he felt a need to foster an alternative cinema to the efforts of Wu Tianming at Xi'an. Wu Tianming was encouraging filmmakers like Tian Zhuangzhuang and Chen Kaige to explore new paths for Chinese cinema. He was also pushing the idea of the "Chinese Western," films set in the untamed, dry northwest around and beyond Xi'an. Wu Tianming had also made an impact as an outspoken critic of cultural conservatism and political restriction. In Shanghai, Wu Yigong saw himself as defender of cinematic traditions that his studio had played such a large part in creating. His outspoken criticism was directed particularly at the more exploratory works, which he charged with elitism and intellectualism.[126] He proudly contrasted the number of copies struck of Shanghai-made titles with the minimal distribution numbers for films like *The Yellow Earth* and *Horse Thief*. Wu Yigong's statements suggest jealousy of the fifth-generation's rapid critical success: he himself had had to wait twenty years after graduation to direct his first film. He made *Tribulations of a Chinese Gentleman* "to prove by making a comedy film that box office value and the pursuit of entertainment do not have to be seen as 'vulgar' and 'low'."[127]

Wu Yigong's alternative view coincided nicely with the Party's criticism of "bourgeois liberalization" in the spring of 1987. The Party organized this campaign after student protests in favor of educational and political reform in several major cities in the winter of 1986–87. The demonstrations suggested to Party conservatives that economic reform and China's "opening to the outside world" continued to contaminate the thinking of many citizens. In 1983–1984 the target had been "spiritual pollution": in 1987 "bourgeois liberalization" was the chosen label. Wu Yigong's criticism of intellectual elitism, published in a major national daily, supported the short-lived government propaganda efforts of 1987.

Tribulations of a Chinese Gentleman was one of the most successful Chinese films of 1987, earning nine million *yuan*. (Xie Jin's highly popular *Hibiscus Town* [*Furong zhen*], a Cultural Revolution melodrama, made a million more). Chen Peisi won the best actor category in the Hundred Flowers readership popularity poll. The Shanghai studio received two million *yuan* from the film, and Zhang Jianya received a two thousand *yuan* bonus for his efforts.[128]

Alone among his classmates, Zhang continued in comic vein. *Kidnapping von Karajan* (*Bangjia Kalayang*), made in 1988, was a satirical look at contemporary fashion, fads and snobbery. A group of friends in their twenties decide that classical Western music is *the* thing. They are excited to learn that the German conductor Herbert von Karajan is coming to Shanghai to conduct a concert. They hatch a scheme to kidnap von Karajan (played by a stand-in) to secure sold-out tickets and to impress everyone with their refined musical tastes. On the day, the scheme falls apart in a series of slapstick mishaps, and the friends learn a lesson in social responsibility and maturity: musical taste, and indeed any fashion, should be what you really like, not what you think will impress others.

Kidnapping von Karajan was not a success with critics or at the box office. The real von Karajan's death not long after its completion did not help. Despite its artistic shortcomings, Zhang Jianya's wit and charm were captured in the film. Like its director, the film was a true Shanghai product, with its satirical focus on contemporary urban life. Zhang continued his career into the 1990s with an action film with a sports setting and a live-action comedy based on Sanmao, a cartoon character popular in Shanghai in the 1940s and remembered with nostalgia by older generations. *San Mao Joins the Army* (*San Mao congjun ji*), filmed in black-and-white, is a remarkable effort to animate an old favorite. Perhaps its greatest success lies in the skilful use of amusing musical punctuation and effects. The film established Zhang Jianya's pre-eminence as a director of comedies, which he continued with a series on the comic adventures of an early twentieth-century fop, Mr Wang.

But by the end of the 1990s, Zhang returned to drama with the hugely successful *Crash Landing* (*Jinji pojiang*). This dramatizes the lives of the crew and some passengers on board a jet-liner with landing gear problems. As they circle the airport burning off fuel, the flight-deck crew make heroic efforts to fix the trouble while the cabin attendants try to calm an assortment of panicking passengers. Notable special effects, achieved with models and computer simulation, are as effective as anything from Hollywood and, indeed, are used with a restraint that adds to their impact in building the excitement. *Crash Landing* was one of the highest Chinese-made box-office earners in 1999–2000, in a theatre market dominated by the official, annually imported ten Hollywood titles.[129]

This mix of projects summed up well Zhang Jianya's achievement and predicament. Fifth-generation innovation was hard to sustain by the end of the 1980s; it was even harder to sustain in Shanghai. In an enterprise desperate for box-office success, he delivered well-made crowd pleasers. Their polish and cosmopolitanism were a reflection of the director himself, known by some at the film academy as "Mr Shanghai." They also reflected the city itself, as Shanghai's modernization finally took off in the mid-1990s, with dramatic results. These entertainment films may have lacked much substance, but substance was a quality near-bankrupt studios, anxious to recover investment, could ill afford.

Jiang Haiyang returned to Shanghai in 1982 with his new wife, Chen Ying, newly graduated from the film academy's sound-recording department. His father-in-law Chen Zhigu, was deputy president of the Shanghai Film Corporation. Things looked promising. Jiang was looking forward to applying some of his thinking on film to his first directorial effort. His graduation thesis, "On film plots and moods" (*Lun dianying qingjie he qingxu*), had been well received at the film academy, and was the only thesis from the directing department class among the seven class of '82 theses published in the 1983 *China Film Yearbook*.[130] In his dissertation Jiang argued that Chinese filmmakers had always been concerned with telling a story, but underrated the use of shots to express moods and evoke emotion. Literature had always formed a foundation for Chinese cinema, but literature also included poetry, which could be especially expressive. Jiang proposed that Chinese cinema be more like poetry and less like novels, by using the expressive power of images.

Despite his good connections, Jiang had to serve an apprenticeship. His first project was as continuity person on Wu Yigong's third film. Wu graduated from the Beijing Film Academy in 1960. His first film was *Night Rain on the River* (*Bashan yeyu*, 1980), made under the supervision of veteran 1930s director Wu Yonggang.[131] Jiang assisted Wu on *Sister* (*Jiejie*, 1984). Unlike the usual Shanghai urban, contemporary setting, this much overlooked film is set in Gansu, usual early fifth-generation territory. It was scripted by Ye Nan, the writer of Wu Ziniu's banned *Dove Tree*. In 1937 a Red Army nurse, a wounded teenage soldier and a young woman of the Yugu minority make their way across the desert wastes, heading east towards the Communist headquarters at Yan'an. The young man is killed and the nurse also dies. The Yugu woman alone heads east for Shaanxi toward the rising sun, determined to report her friends' heroism. In its reliance on images, with an emphasis on the earth, attempts at naturalism in the sweaty portrayal of war and suffering, and slow pace,

Sister shows similarities to *One and Eight*, despite its well-worn story. The film was released in August 1984.[132]

At this time Wu Yigong was appointed head of the Shanghai studio in an effort to promote younger leaders in Chinese enterprises. Jiang Haiyang served as assistant director on Wu's *University in Exile* (*Liuwang daxue*), about intellectuals fleeing Japanese invasion in 1937. There is an old-fashioned quality to *University in Exile* which calls to mind the careful screen adaptations from the ten years before the Cultural Revolution of twentieth-century fiction. Mao Dun's *The Lin Family Shop* (*Linjia puzi*, filmed in 1959 from an adaptation by Xia Yan), Lu Xun's *New Year's Sacrifice* (*Zhufu*, filmed in 1956), and Rou Shi's *Early Spring in February* (*Zaochun eryue*, filmed in 1963) were among the most accomplished films made between 1949 and the Cultural Revolution. Jiang Haiyang and Zhang Jianya cited these films as those they most admired from earlier Chinese filmmakers.[133]

Jiang Haiyang's debut as a director, like Wu Yigong's *University in Exile*, is an homage to an older generation. In 1986 he made *The Last Sunrise* (*Zuihou de taiyang*): the initial credits even include a dedication "to our beloved elders." The film tells the story of six retired people who form an old folks' choir to help fill their time and make a useful contribution. The choristers achieve a rather extraordinary and instant harmony at their first rehearsal, and also spend some time singing their way through the magnificent Huangshan nature reserve some distance from the city. Veteran Shanghai actor Liu Qiong plays the conductor and Jiang and his father, Jiang Jun, play father and son on screen.

Jiang Haiyang's directorial efforts to create atmosphere, in line with his graduation thesis ideas, perhaps meant that questions of story and believability did not receive enough attention. Simultaneous sound recording in many scenes adds much to the ambiance: whole city blocks were blocked off to traffic by studio personnel and police in order to ensure that the usual honking car and truck horns would not intrude onto the soundtrack. The choir's ability to move a rowdy audience to silence by a musical rendition of a poem by Mao Zedong is another unconvincing element. Although older figures in the Shanghai film world reportedly liked *The Last Sunrise*, younger filmmakers were disappointed by what they saw as its maudlin qualities. But the older studio leaders gave the film considerable publicity with several strategically placed billboards around the city.

As *The Last Sunrise* was being released, Jiang Haiyang became head of

the Second Creative Group into which Wu Yigong had organized the
studio in early 1985. Jiang's career as studio administrator was going well,
but his filmmaking efforts did not reflect this success. In his second
independent feature he tried to break new ground. *The Anonymous
Phonecall* (*Niming dianhua*) was one of China's first psychological
thrillers. The story centers on a successful scientist who believes his phone
rings constantly. Each time he picks up the receiver, there is no-one at the
other end. Deeply troubled, he eventually seeks the help of a psychologist
at a mental hospital. Through this therapy, we learn that the scientist is
deeply disturbed by a sense of guilt. During the Cultural Revolution he let
Red Guards attack a university classmate, instead of admitting his own
part in writing the report that had caused trouble. This story had
considerable resonance for many Chinese in the 1980s, for both former
Red Guards and their victims.[134]

Jiang Haiyang uses surreal sound effects and camera angles to convey
the mental disturbance of the central character. Incessant cutting to
different angles even in scenes of ordinary dialogue stemmed from the
Jiang Haiyang's concern with mood and emotion.[135] The scientist's visits
to his doctor at the mental hospital include some intriguing suggestions
that lunacy may not be confined within the walls of the institution, but
may infect society at large. Overall, *The Anonymous Phonecall* is not a
success, although its innovation in examining the private psychological
condition of a publicly successful figure should not be underestimated.

Jiang's work on his thriller coincided with the financial crisis in the
Chinese film industry that had deepened in 1987. From about 1983, as
the urban box-office began to shrink, filmmakers had began to worry
about their lack of experience in making "entertainment films" (*yule pian*,
in contrast to mainstream or propaganda films). The film academy
incorporated "entertainment films" in its research activites and curriculum
after 1985.[136] At the start of 1987 Jiang's classmate, Tian Zhuangzhuang
had argued that in China it was generally difficult to differentiate
commercial from art films. In contrast, the higher living standards in other
countries, whose production and distribution systems were different from
China's, allowed a clearer distinction between the two kinds of films.[137]

By the summer of 1988 there were even moves to encourage
independent film production by enterprising entreprenuers. This was in
response to the near bankruptcy of the state-owned studios, which were
reliant on bank loans.[138] Any newly completed film, for example, was to be
treated like a studio production and carry an established, state-owned

studio logo. After a lot of talk, most so-called independent productions at this time turned out to be studio films using outside investment money. These efforts, however, were highly circumscribed by official caution: film was still too important a medium for true independence. The idea of independent production faded after the June 4th killings in Beijing, to be revived in the following decade by sixth-generation artists. By this time critics were earnestly assessing the evolution of the Chinese entertainment film and lamenting the difficulties in achieving the success of equivalent imported films. It was a strange discussion, for the political censorship that had such power to shape film production could not be properly addressed.[139] At the end of the decade, Xie Fei, one of the class of '82's main teachers, lamented how cinema attendances in 1999 amounted to each Chinese attending just one-half of a show each year. In contrast in the early 1980s, when Jiang Haiyang and his classmates were on the eve of their careers, attendance had averaged twenty-nine annual visits to the cinema per person.[140]

His concentration on strictly urban, contemporary stories reflected Jiang Haiyang's sense of self as a true son of Shanghai. By 1987 three other directing department classmates assigned to Shanghai had left for study abroad or to work at other studios. Jiang Haiyang and Zhang Jianya, two remaining fifth-generation graduates at Shanghai, were heads of two of the three production groups. But opportunities for innovative films remained infrequent for both. In the 1990s Jiang joined the efforts of several of his classmates, including Liu Miaomiao and Hu Mei, at making television dramas, where experimentation with mood and atmosphere was perhaps more affordable. Television offered also the kinds of mass audiences which Shanghai filmmakers had always aspired to reach.

6. "Passion, Courage, Commitment": Chen Kaige's Later Films

Having established the international reputation of his generation of filmmakers, Chen Kaige went on to film a variety of subjects. Through them all, however, ran the themes of loyalty and commitment, and a fascination with history. By the turn of the twenty-first century he found himself caught between his Chinese roots and his international engagement.

In 1985, after the critical and international success of *The Yellow Earth*, Chen Kaige made his second feature *The Big Parade* (*Da yuebing*) also at the Guangxi studio. The challenge for Chen, Zhang Yimou (whose cinematography had been crucial to the artistic success of Chen's first film) and He Qun, the art director, was to prove that *The Yellow Earth* had not been an accident. Their response was a completely different film, with a contemporary setting and military subject, in which experiments with light and overexposure replace the naturalistic darkness in much of their earlier film. *The Big Parade* also offered a profoundly ambivalent discourse on youth and service in contemporary China.

The film crew set out in the early summer of 1985 for an airfield in northern Hubei province in central China. Chen and Zhang the previous year had shot *Forced Take-off* (*Qiangxing qifei*), a television documentary on the air force. They were able to use their connections with the service from this time to gain cooperation in filming *The Big Parade*. The crew spent over two months in Hubei in the summer heat. Originally Chen planned to make the film with synchronized sound recording, a considerable innovation in Chinese filmmaking which Wu Ziniu was about to achieve with his banned *Dove Tree*. But the disadvantages of working at a smaller studio became apparent when the equipment necessary for on-location recording was not available and could not be borrowed from one of the larger studios. Sound recording in the finished film, however, retains a complexity and a dialectic with the images that are central to *The Big Parade*'s impact.

Chen, his editor Zhou Xinxia, Zhang, and composers Zhao Jiping and Zhai Xiaosong spent between August and November completing the project in Nanning. It had to be submitted to the Beijing Film Bureau before the last day of the year to mark the crew's completion of their 1985 duties. The Beijing censors, however, insisted that the film be revised. They objected to some of the rough and tumble of the barracks dialogue, and wanted the film to end with an actual parade. Chen Kaige returned to Nanning in the summer of 1986 to produce a new version of *The Big Parade*. The new version was finally approved by the Film Bureau on the second to last day of 1986. His original idea had been to end the film with a shot of Tian'anmen Square empty of parading soldiers or of anyone at all, as an ironic commentary on the arduous training. The approved film ended with footage shot by Zhang Yimou of the thirty-fifth anniversary parade in Tian'anmen Square.

The Big Parade presents the story of an airborne division in training for eight months to participate in this parade on 1 October 1984. There are two main elements to the film: the highly regulated training on the parade ground, and the more relaxed, individuated lives of the soldiers in their barracks. On the parade ground everything must be perfect. The men are selected for uniformity of height and build. The slope of their rifles, fall of their shoulders, and angle of their salutes must all be standardized. Even the height of each step of their march is measured to ensure standards are shared. At one point the squad stands at attention in the summer heat for three continuous hours. Invitations to rest if they feel unwell are bravely ignored, even when several soldiers drop in a faint. Toward the end of the training an officer announces that they have each worn out four pairs of boots and each marched a total of almost ten thousand kilometers in order to fulfill their training. Not all the men make the final cut, despite their earnest efforts. The names of these soldiers are solemnly inscribed on a red flag, along with the signatures of all those who will participate in the parade.

Unlike the rather sparse psychological dimensions of *The Yellow Earth*, *The Big Parade* shows considerable depth and subtlety in its portrayal of the inner worlds of these soldiers. Six characters form the central focus of the story. Sun Fang is the training instructor, who is hard but fair in his treatment of the men. Squadron leader Li Weicheng, in his mid-thirties, feels that this is perhaps his last chance to achieve something in a long army career which has never seen combat or real danger. He is eventually obliged to withdraw because he is subject to seizures. Jiang Junbiao is a long-time comrade of instructor Sun. Jiang in fact once saved Sun's life on a battlefield, presumably at the Sino-Vietnamese border, carrying Sun to safety under fire. The men are intrigued by Sun's strictly equitable treatment of Jiang. The latter can barely sleep at night in the barracks because he binds his legs tightly at night in an effort to straighten his bow-legs. He fears they will disqualify him from participation in the Beijing parade.

Three younger men are also central to the film. Liu Guoqiang likes to give an impression of urban sophistication, even though the main street in his home town is a dirt road. Hao Xiaoyuan is an earnest young man with a stutter. After news comes that his mother has died, he sets out in a truck for the railway station more than twenty kilometers away. It seems to be the end of his chances to be in the parade. Later that day he reappears, soaked from the rain through which he has walked back from the station. His mother had said he should participate in the parade, so that not to march, as Hao announces through his stutter, would be more unfilial than not returning for her funeral. The raincoat which was one of the gifts the men had given him when he left is still unopened in his luggage. Lü Chun, the intellectual in the group, is anxiously awaiting acceptance into an officer training academy. He feels this is his last chance, having failed to pass the national university entrance examinations. When word finally comes from the training academy that he has not been selected, his newly nourished sense of dedication encourages him to go on with his part in the parade.

A marked dialectic between parade ground and barracks serves to underscore the thematic concerns of service and individual aspirations at the center of *The Big Parade*. The filming of the serried ranks of the soldiers as they train is often static, confrontational, and frequently at considerable distance. This emphasizes how the individual men are being transformed into a disciplined unit. In contrast, the framing and angles in the barracks scenes are relatively chaotic. People and bustle fill the frame as the central characters talk and interact. Even in the barracks, however, there is another dialectic, in this case between the setting and the action. When empty, the barracks are a large hall with highly formal rows of beds, lines of water canteens, and regulation folded comforters under a huge photo-mural covering most of one wall. The photo is of ranks of soldiers on parade flanked by two huge, red, four-character slogans: "March for the quintessence of the nation. March for the prestige of the armed forces." (*Zouchu guocui. Zouchu junwei*). The contrast between this formalism and the interactions of the trainees as individuals is strengthened by the voice-overs of some of the central characters as they express their own feelings and their attitudes to their squad mates.

This parade-ground and barracks contrast is reinforced by a highly experimental use of overexposed, bleached shots by Zhang Yimou. In contrast to the deliberate use of darkness, almost a trademark of fifth-generation films, in *The Yellow Earth*, *The Big Parade* uses brightness to help make its thematic points. In the first shots, as the men are going through medical inspection and outfitting at the start of their training, they step in from the glare and brightness of outside the barracks. The overexposure renders the groups of soldiers a blurred and almost indistinguishable mass. Instead of the sounds of the actual scene, the sequence is backed by the sound of marching boots. The soldiers walk out into the sunlight and again blur and merge. This transformation in the fire

Publicity shot for *The Big Parade*

of the sun emphasizes the change the soldiers will undergo on the parade ground under the unremitting discipline of instructor Sun and the other officers.

This dynamic relationship underscores the contrast in *The Big Parade* between the naturalism of the soldiers' lives and the formal, political, apparently propagandistic themes. The relationship is highly ambivalent. Squad leader Li himself asks, in a speech prior to leaving the troupe, whether each man should have marched more than nine-thousand kilometers in preparation for just ninety-six steps across the central part of Tian'anmen Square. No answer is given to Li's rhetorical question, although the soldiers proceed to their solemn flag signing. Likewise, Lü Chun had earlier brashly wondered about the point of all their training during a barracks study session. In voice-over Li Weicheng expressed his own ambivalent feelings about Lü and his youthful restlessness.

This profound ambivalence in the film is not simply an outcome of the censorship which delayed release of the film for a year. The mixed feelings about service and individual fulfilment stand as a metaphor for the fifth-generation's attitudes to China and their place in the nation. The Tian'anmen parade footage at the end of the film, incorporated at the Film Bureau's insistence, as the filmmakers frequently pointed out, contains mixed signals. At the start of the sequence the camera almost drifts in what seems, in contrast to the rest of the film, downright sloppy filming. Soon the formalism of the earlier parade scenes returns. But filming the soldiers in the massed band presenting their French horns and other instruments as the trainees had earlier practiced with rifles seems comic comment on the rifle toting. So too the slow-motion presentation of the anonymous ranks of sailors, soldiers, and even nurses in skirts seems ambiguous. The almost funereal music which accompanies these slowed-down shots adds to the effect of undercutting the solemnity and importance of the occasion.

These final effects may not be just an effort to undermine the censors' intentions, at least among perceptive or sympathetic audiences. These mixed images also reflect the ambivalence which invests the whole film. Even if the cut dialogue in the barracks scenes, which the censors felt too coarse to come from Chinese soldiers, had been kept in the final version, the impression would remain. Chen Kaige had produced an anti-nationalistic nationalist film. The final shot is of the head of a single, anonymous soldier silhouetted against a red sun. It is a reminder of the individuals who submitted consciously and proudly to training which submerged their individuality. *The Big Parade* is not simply a film about a military parade. It is about the social psychology of individuals submitting to service in a group. *The Big Parade* served as a metaphor for the fifth-generation's China.

Chen Kaige made his next film under the auspices of Wu Tianming, head of the Xi'an Film Studio. Wu Tianming sought to push the limits of cultural liberalization. The application of the experimental "management responsibility system" at the Xi'an studio allowed Wu considerable power to decide who could make films and what projects should be encouraged. As Tian Zhuangzhuang and others had already discovered, Wu allowed directors to complete projects about which other studio heads might feel disquiet, for artistic, political, or commercial reasons.[141] *King of the Children* (*Haizi wang*) was the most autobiographical to date of any of the fifth-generation films. Like Chen's other works, it was a carefully constructed presentation of philosophical issues that went beyond the subject-matter of the film itself.

Chen Kaige found his story source in a novella by the writer Ah Cheng, pen-name of Zhong Acheng. He had known Zhong since his days as an educated youth on the Xishuangbanna rubber plantations in Yunnan province. Zhong had in fact been two years senior to Chen at the Number 4 High School in Beijing. His father, Zhong Dianfei, had worked in the Party Propaganda Department until labelled a "Rightist" in 1957.[142] Ah Cheng became one of the leading new Chinese writers in the 1980s. Chen Kaige and another young writer, Chen Maiping using the pen name Wan Zhi, adapted the *King of the Children* story for the screen.[143]

The "king of the children" is "Beanpole" (*Lao ganr*, literally "Old Pole"), a teacher at a country primary school in the remote Yunnan hill country, where more than half the students, all poor and barefoot, are non-Han, minority children. The teacher is an educated youth from Beijing, who after seven years of labor, is assigned to be a village schoolmaster. He is both reluctant to leave the friends in his sent-down youth team and excited by the prospect and responsibility of being a teacher. On his first day in the classroom, an open-sided thatched shed, he instructs the children to take out their textbooks. They have none. They have spent the previous semesters laboriously copying out the contents of an old textbook which their previous teacher had copied onto the battered blackboard.

The new teacher changes the teaching methods, discarding the old notion that in merely copying characters from political texts the children are learning Chinese. He teaches the children the characters, relating his teaching to their everyday lives in this remote village. As their ability increases, the children begin to write essays about their lives, families, and aspirations. One of the boys, however, asks to be allowed to make a handwritten copy of the teacher's precious dictionary, which a commune team mate of Beanpole had given him. The son of a woodcutter, Wang Fu regards the dictionary as a talisman. It is his one connection with the world beyond his own. At the end of the film, Beanpole is dismissed for unorthodox teaching and returns to the commune. He leaves a message for his student Wang Fu: "Never copy anything again, not even the dictionary."

King of the Children was filmed with synchronized sound recording.[144] The aural ambiance this provides contributes much to the film's effect. Synchronized recording required special effort from the film crew. The location of the school set was less than two kilometers from a road. Crew members armed with two-way radios (probably illegal at the time in private hands in China, but provided by a Hong Kong friend) stopped trucks and other noisy traffic on the road. The generator for lighting was placed in a two-meter deep pit to help reduce its sound. Three of the crews' bed comforters were draped over the camera to muffle its sound. Even with these precautions, uncontrollable elements, like wind noise, made the recording process a taxing effort for recordists Tao Jing and Gu Changning of the class of '82. The attention required on the sound recording compounded the challenge Chen faced with a crew he later described in highly disparaging terms as addicted to gambling and sex. The crew was reportedly equally fed up with what they viewed as Chen's arrogance and preoccupation with his private affairs.[145]

The special sound quality to *The King of the Children* is particularly effective because of the especially static camera work in the film. Long takes prevail, often of the landscape with the children. In one shot, for example, the rounded hilltop on which the school building sits is captured in a fixed gaze. As the skies darken from the rising fog and the setting sun the class and their teacher feed a bonfire. Their voices and laughter echo in the increasing gloom. These frequently still images and the sound serve to emphasize the sense of place and of isolation in a natural setting. The cinematographer, Gu Changwei, was a classmate of Zhang Yimou at the Beijing Film Academy also from Xi'an, to whose studio he had been assigned on graduation in 1982. The acting of the school students is unforced, as is much of that of Xie Yuan, a member of the acting department in the class of '82, as the teacher. Despite the naturalistic sound design and the minimal use of music, Chen Kaige sought an overall effect of heightened artificiality. In an interview in the spring of 1987 as he began work on the editing of the raw footage in Beijing, he spoke of wanting a deliberate "staginess" in the finished film.[146] The construction seems even more deliberate than for *The Yellow Earth* and *The Big Parade*.

Nature is central in *King of the Children*, both in the images and on the sound track. Scenes in the thatched classroom are frequently accompanied by eerie sounds echoing from the surrounding hills. They seem to be the sound of bamboo and trees being cut down in the forest.[147] A deliberate contrast is drawn between the artificiality of the education these students are getting and the untamed, natural world around them which their textbook ignores. Unremarked is the fact that this forest is being cut down or burned off in an annual cycle of renewal, just as the children are the latest generation to be acculturated through their schooling. The importance of a close connection between humans and nature was something Chen had come to realize as a teenager when "sent down" to a Yunnan rubber farm.[148]

The stylized visual and aural presentation reinforces the thematic considerations of *King of the Children*. In some ways this film contemplates the impact of outside ideas on a closed community that *The Yellow Earth* first essayed. Beanpole, from a big city, brings his new ideas about teaching to the grass huts of this school in the backwoods of Yunnan. More broadly the film addresses the importance of education. When their new teacher first arrives he finds that the education the children have been getting is incomprehensible to them. In the late Cultural Revolution context, the texts they laboriously transcribe are filled with talk about "poor and lower middle peasants" and "ex-landlords." In such a backward, poor village this political posturing is irrelevant. As the teacher learns how to release the creative energies of his young charges, the experience is itself an education for him.[149] In contrast to the children in the classroom, a young cowherd appears on a couple of occasions and stares silently at the teacher. He pees on the grass for his cows to eat the saltiness. This natural knowledge and the freedom the boy perhaps enjoys are contrasted with the discipline and falseness of what happens within the open thatched walls of the classrooms. The presence of the nature boy/cowherd, Rey Chow argues, forces us to consider the purpose of the education the children are undergoing.[150] The teacher invents a new written character made up of the characters for cow and water, to indicate "cow piss." One of the last shots of the film is that invented non-character written on the blackboard. It is a final commentary on the absurdity and powerlessness of what has happened daily in front of the blackboard. The tyranny of the written word in Chinese culture is powerfully suggested by the word on the primitive blackboard, for it is both a daring encouragement to creativity and, in its meaninglessness, an admission of defeat.[151]

One aspect of this focus on education is the presentation of the Cultural Revolution experience of educated youths.[152] The naturalistic scenes at the beginning of the film and when the teacher returns to the commune contrast with the artifice in the presentation of the schoolhouse scenes. The young urban exiles have endured seven years of their adolescence and lost seven years of schooling in this remote part of the country. Their mutual trust and dependence has gotten them through this time. In compensation they have gained a different sort of education in the shared experience of being "sent down" to Yunnan. This education is in some ways a more natural experience than what they might have received in their urban high schools without a Cultural Revolution. Beanpole and his friends have regained an innocence and sense of self that a "real" education might have obliterated. The scene when Beanpole's friends visit his schoolroom and sit in awe before a class blackboard for the first time in seven years captures nicely both this innocence and loss.

But Chen's film is much more than an indictment of Maoist narrowness and rote learning. *The King of the Children* tries to teach viewers about the weight of Chinese culture even in the remote countryside. The film seeks to raise awareness of how people become part of a culture, and of the liberating and confining power of knowledge, particularly through Wang Fu's copying of the dictionary. Chen's vision is ultimately pessimistic. By the end of the film the irony of the title is apparent. Dismissed from his job, Beanpole walks through a stand of petrified, anthropomorphic tree stumps, somewhat like a spirit-way at royal tombs. The ancient grove and its human shapes suggest that the dead weight of China's history has asserted itself. The efforts of one young man cannot change a tradition far older than Mao's. In a director's note published with the English translation of the script, Chen writes of these broad concerns: "Repetition is a characteristic of Chinese traditional culture.... Man, in his preservation of himself, has developed culture, but in the end, the culture has become master of the man."[153] Of all the fifth-generation films, *King of the Children* most eloquently captured both the lives of its makers and the attitudes inherent in the 1980s "search for roots" movement reassessing the basis of Chinese culture.[154] A major element in this movement was the insistence on the margins of the Chinese pale being sources of creativity, in contrast to the deadweight of the civilizational center.

The film's autobiographical base proved an obstacle to its international reception. The first Chinese film in official competition at Cannes, *King of the Children* failed to win a major award. Conservatives in the Chinese film industry greeted the news as further evidence of the failure of fifth-generation art films to find an audience.[155] More supportive critics and Chen himself ascribed the film's failure to gain the top prize to foreign viewers' ignorance of the historical and cultural background of the story, particularly its oblique, Cultural Revolution setting. Chen's own career had become more international. He moved to New York and a fellowship at New York University in 1987 and married Hong Huang, the step-daughter of a former Chinese foreign minister, working in New York.

Chen's next completed project, after making a music video in early 1989 for the pop group Duran Duran with Gu Changwei as cinematographer, was an international production that aspired to universal significance. *Life on a String* (*Bian zou bian chang*) was shot in China in the second half of 1990 with a Chinese cast and crew. Gu Changwei was again Chen's cinematographer. Including a token presence of the China Film Co-production Corporation and assistance from the Beijing Film Studio, the production was an international effort, with funding from the United Kingdom, Germany, and Japan. Zhang Yimou, Tian Zhuangzhuang, and Wu Ziniu had already entered co-productions with Hong Kong and Japanese investors. In the case of *Life on a String*, the director himself returned from abroad for the filming. He adapted a short story by Shi Tiesheng, a Beijing writer one year older than himself. The English title of the film comes from Shi's story title (*Ming ruo qinxian*: life like a banjo string): the film's Chinese title can be translated "Walking along, singing."

As with Chen's other films, a plot summary for *Life on a String* is rather bare. Somewhere in the northwest two blind musicians make a living playing the *sanxian* (a three-stringed banjo, the Japanese *samisen*). One is seventy years old, and has inherited from his master a prescription which is kept inside the soundbox of his instrument. His late master told him that once he had played enough music to break one thousand strings, he could take out the paper and his sight would be restored. The younger is seventeen years old, called Shitou ("Stone"), an apprentice to the old man. Together they trek about the dry landscape or cross a roaring stretch of the Yellow River. The local people call the old man "the Saint," in part because of his distinctly innocent and otherworldly air, but mostly because of his service to the community. At two points in the story his singing brings clan fighting to a stop.

The Saint cleaves firmly to his calling, counting the knots in a rope that record the number of strings he has broken: 995, 996, 997…. When he has only one string to break, he decides he shall play only for himself. Seated at the top of a hill, he takes up his banjo. A passing caravan far below is shooed away. Finally, the thousandth string breaks, although, as Shitou observes to the young woman he has befriended, it probably broke in the heat of the sun on the hilltop. The Saint rushes to the druggist's store in the town, excitedly handing over the old paper from inside his instrument. Holding it up to the sunlight, the druggist cannot read anything on it. The paper is blank. Whether it was blank from the moment his old master handed it to the Saint, or whether it has faded over the time it took to break one thousand strings is never explained.

Furious, the Saint smashes the tombstone of his master. Then he goes back to the riverside inn, where the owner tells him in hushed tones: "Life is a drama. Some perform well, some don't." The old man dies, and his body is set adrift on the Yellow River. The blind Shitou, of late more interested in the girl Lanxiu than in his music, realizes his duty to his master and to their art. Lanxiu has died in a fall from a high cliff above the river. The local people accept and honor Shitou as the successor to the old man. The story has come full circle when Shitou inserts a paper into the secret drawer in his own banjo. But the paper his hand finds is not the blank prescription: it is a love note in the form of a self-portrait from the illiterate Lanxiu. Shitou, of course, only knows it as a piece of paper with talismanic powers, rather like the dictionary for Wang Fu in *King of the Children*. The final image of *Life on a String* is a kite high in the sky on the end of a string, like the lives of the artists, tossed and turned by forces beyond their control.

In a statement on the film, Chen noted a spiritual void in the lives of Chinese. He shared this attitude with many Chinese commentators, including conservative authoritarian leaders confused by the social changes associated with economic reform in the 1980s and 1990s. Chen Kaige's themes (and portentousness) are as vast as the landscape presented spectacularly by Gu Changwei's camera. The film is at its most effective in several set pieces that have a distinctly operatic flavor. In each the Saint, surrounded by respectful peasants, sings a stirring song. One of these performances occurs on a battlefield between the Li and Sun clans and brings the fighting to a halt. Another song is sung at night in a circle of flaming torches held by the silent clans people. The lyrics for these songs are the work of the director, and the music is by Qu Xiaosong, who wrote the limited musical episodes for *King of the Children*, *The Big Parade*, and Tian Zhuangzhuang's *Horse Thief*. Liu Zhongyuan, the actor who plays the Saint, is a fine amateur singer of Beijing opera.[156] His voice in the film is dubbed by Wang Di, a popular rock singer about half his age. The songs are a version of the northern Shaanxi "folksongs" (*min'ge*) that enjoyed a vogue after the popularity of *Red Sorghum*. They are an invented "folk" form that functions in counterpoint to the film's authentically early twentieth-century milieu. The Saint and Shitou may be "traditional" musicians, but the music they make definitely is not, even if it can have operatic power.

The ersatz nature of the music points to some of the film's flaws. Like the songs, the film seems to reach too far. One of Chen's lyrics is a call for humanity to triumph. The Saint sings it to stop the Suns and Lis from fighting. The original Chinese is simplicity itself, reminiscent of the repetitive conundrums of the writings of the Daoist Laozi. But in a song,

Life on a String

the words (along the lines of "man fighting, man loving, man triumphant") come close to banality.

Perhaps the international production of *Life on a String* helps account for its faults. In his director's statement and in conversation before starting the film, Chen was highly conscious of the implications of his story and themes that extend universally.[157] Assembling money from at least four countries added to the pressure on Chen to make a film to appeal across cultures. Indeed, the highly theatrical noodle shop sequences, set beside the Yellow River, in particular can to some extent be accounted for by an urge for exoticism to appeal to foreign tastes. The ending of the Saint's song of peace with a shot of geese flying in the V-shaped formation of the Chinese character for human (*ren*) is a resort to a hoary Chinese cliché, last seen most notably at the end of Bai Hua's banned *Unrequited Love* (1980).

But there are also elements of self-portraiture here. At times, the musicians are buffoons and the butts of the local people's jokes and teasing. At other times, in their passionate commitment to their calling, they are artists who link the simple folk and the universe of ideas. The respect shown the musicians by the local people suggests an attitude to "the masses" that Maoists could have held. This heroic image of the respected artist may have had personal resonance for the director, in light of his father's checkered career.

At the end of *Life on a String*, hidden at the tail of the English credits (there are no Chinese language credits in the international version), are three words: passion, courage, commitment. Chen Kaige dedicates *Life on a String* to his mother, who died in early 1989 after a lengthy illness. Chen saw these qualities as his mother's legacy to him. All of his films, from *The Yellow Earth*, through *The Big Parade* and *King of the Children* to *Life on a String*, showed a passion for understanding, courage to break new ground, and a commitment to the power of art to change his world. But to critics such as Wang Bin, *Life on a String* marked the last rite of the fifth generation, an exhaustion of the path first mapped in *The Yellow Earth*.[158]

His films after 1990 can be seen as an effort by Chen to show he was not trapped by philosophizing and fifth-generation angst at the state of China, and that he could make a commercial success. They also confirmed that the fifth generation, as a distinct "wave" in Chinese cinema, was over. All three films, like most others made for international consumption, were co-productions. Chen's producer on *Farewell, My Concubine* (*Bawang bie ji*), made in 1993, and *Temptress Moon* (*Feng yue*, 1997) was Hsu Feng, a Taiwan actress noted for her performances in the art-house martial arts films of King Hu (Hu Jinquan). Hsu's Hong Kong-based Tomson Films provided the budget for both projects.

Shooting on location in Beijing for *Farewell, My Concubine* extended from spring through fall in 1992. Gu Changwei served as director of cinematography, taking a somewhat low-key approach on set. Chen Huaikai took care of art direction for his son and was given the first credit at the end of the film. Chen senior's reputation derived from his accomplished screen adaptations of Beijing opera. In May the following year at the Cannes Film Festival *Farewell, My Concubine* shared the Palme d'Or with the New Zealand director Jane Campion's *The Piano*. Chen Kaige now had international awards to match those of Zhang Yimou, the most successful Chinese director worldwide.

The film spans the decades from the 1920s to the 1970s, presenting the changing relationship between two Beijing opera performers. Douzi ("Beanie") is handed over by his mother, a prostitute, to the head of an opera school. The young boy's friendship with another trainee, Shitou ("Stone"), offers some comfort during the rigorous training and harsh punishment meted out by the master. Douzi's soft features and gentle nature lead to his specializing in female roles, while Shitou's height and bearing make him ideal for martial roles. The young men become stars of the opera stage on the eve of the War of Resistance to Japan, taking the professional names Cheng Dieyi (Douzi) and Duan Xiaolou (Shitou). During the war they are obliged to perform for boorish Japanese army audiences. Their speciality becomes "Farewell to My Concubine," based on an historical episode in which a concubine shows her devotion by committing suicide when her lover is faced with military defeat.

Cheng Dieyi is angered when he learns that Duan Xiaolou has fallen in love with Juxian, a prostitute. When they marry, his jealousy drives him almost insane. Meanwhile, Master Yuan, a wealthy opera aficionado and scion of a minor branch of the former imperial family, becomes the patron of Cheng Dieyi. The post-war and post-Liberation years are difficult times for both actors as they are first accused of collaboration with the Japanese and then find it hard to adapt their art to the new political requirements of the Communist regime. By the start of the Cultural Revolution, the two men have drifted apart. Red Guards force Duan Xiaolou to denounce his friend and extract confessions of wrong-doing from Cheng Dieyi, who makes a public attack on his old classmate. The film ends at a point after the finish of the Cultural Revolution in 1976. The two men are in costume as beautiful maiden and handsome general in an empty amphitheater. They express regret for their past actions, then, in a final enactment of the "Farewell to My Concubine" scene, Cheng Dieyi takes his own life.

Chen Kaige, who played a minor role in Bertolucci's *The Last Emperor*, attempts a similar epic sweep in his film, based on a novel by the Hong Kong writer Lillian Lee (Lee Bik Wah). Much time is spent on the 1920s scenes in the opera school, with the beatings and abuse of the boys highlighted. In almost three hours of screen time, the film teems with characters: Master Yuan appears in the middle part as does Juxian, although the latter re-emerges in the Cultural Revolution scenes. Yuan is played by Ge You, a contemporary of Chen and one of China's most popular character actors. With a similar eye to the box-office at home and abroad, Gong Li was cast as Juxian and the role expanded to appeal to viewers. Zhang Fengyi, an acting student in Chen's class of '82, plays Duan Xiaolou. The popular Hong Kong singer Leslie Cheung (Zhang Guorong) took the role of Cheng Dieyi, drawing a wide audience of fans. But the attractions of the film perhaps centered on the prominence given cross-dressing, which, as Bonnie McDougall suggests, also serves as a metaphor for art as illusion.[159]

The relationship between Douzi/Cheng Dieyi and Shitou/Duan Xiaolou makes *Farewell, My Concubine* a homosexual love story. But Chen's treatment makes the issue somewhat opaque. Part of the problem undoubtedly stemmed from the context in which the film was made: homosexual themes were new in Chinese cinema and Chen had to win official approval from Beijing to be able to film in the city and to enable the film to be distributed in China. For Beijing censors, as perhaps for most Chinese viewers, the Beijing opera setting was the main attraction and glossed over the gay subtext, which itself is not unexpected in Chinese opera. When Shitou thrusts a pipe into Douzi's mouth, when the boy repeatedly mistakes his lines, proclaiming he is a man when he should say "I am a woman," reference to Freud is unnecessary to understand the implications. The adult Cheng Dieyi, while apparently yearning for Duan Xiaolou, becomes a both a pitiable and repulsive figure, even as the audience sympathizes with his helplessness at the hands of the evil Master Yuan. The narrative sweeps through the decades to its late 1970s denouement. Cheng Dieyi's suicide occurs off-screen and is suggested by blood splattering a painting of the famous opera scene the two men enact for the last time. The initial banning of the film in China seemed more related to its suggestion of the violence of the Cultural Revolution than to the gay subtext.

The combination of the theatricality of the opera world and the gender confusion of the central character underscores the importance of issues of performativity in the work. Cheng Dieyi must perform his preferred gender role, the artifice of Beijing opera's face make-up making visible his desire to adopt a womanly role, at least in relation with his oldest friend and fellow performer. Wendy Larson argues that what she identifies as the feminization of male characters, in this film and in *King of the Children, The Big Parade* and *The Yellow Earth*, produces males who "become the shattered victims of what was once a unified consciousness."[160] The use of a play within a play (the suicide of the loyal concubine of the noble general) gives this motif of performance even more layers and complexity, as Jerome Silbergeld makes clear in a stimulating analysis of the film as national allegory.[161]

But Duan Xiaolou, Juxian and all the people in the film must also perform in another sense, displaying their loyalty to the current power holders, be they the opera school principal, the brothel madam, Japanese generals or Communist Party propaganda workers. This point is made most forcefully in the Cultural Revolution sequence, when the opera singers and Juxian must present themselves as loyal subjects, in heart and action, of Chairman Mao. Chen Kaige's own bitter memory of publicly criticizing his own father adds a particular poignancy to this sequence. The director, like his classmates, had all been obliged to perform their correctness in thought and behavior.

With his long-coveted win at Cannes (even if it was shared), Chen Kaige had become an international director. His years in New York meant his English was now fluent. Combined with his natural confidence and a Versace suit, the effect was impressive. His next film, *Temptress Moon* was a gothic tale of incest, opium addiction and prostitution in the mid-twentieth century around an extended family in Jiangnan, the watery hinterland west of Shanghai. Leslie Cheung again starred, this time as a man who seduces middle-aged women in Shanghai in order to blackmail them. The distinguishing feature of the film suggested that fifth-generation experimentation still fascinated Chen. The camera is constantly mobile in *Temptress Moon*, sweeping and gliding throughout the rooms and gardens of the family mansion, suggesting the swirling uncertainty of an hallucination and the instability of this world. Australian-born, Hong Kong-based Chris Doyle, as director of photography, seized the opportunity to take charge of the look of the film. The result is a lavish but confusing production. Efforts at recutting and adding explanation of the characters' relationships with each other at the start of the film proved unhelpful. Despite also starring Gong Li, the most famous Chinese actress in the world, the film was an artistic and box-office flop. It was not released in China.[162]

Determined to set that experience aside, Chen Kaige turned to a subject close to his heart, the ancient Chinese history that he had devoured as a school-boy with no school to go to in the late 1960s. He selected a story from the *Historical Records* (*Shi ji*), written by Sima Qian in the first century B.C.[163] *The Emperor and the Assassin* (*Jing Ke ci Qin wang*) was a truly epic production, set in the third century B.C., when a centralized Chinese kingdom first emerged. The story, punctuated with large-scale battle scenes, is one of palace intrigue and political rivalry swirling around the first emperor of Qin, who in 221 B.C. established himself as founder of the Chinese empire. His kingdom fell in 206 B.C., to be succeeded by four centuries of Han dynasty rule. The film's ambition amounted to a combination of *King Lear* and *Richard the Third*, suggesting both the pathos and the evil of China's founding father. An allegorical reading might see distant allusions to Communist China, for Mao Zedong was often compared by his critics with the first emperor. The unexpected plot, in which the Qin emperor tries to arrange for his own assassination in order to provoke war with another kingdom, would fit well with more fevered interpretations of contemporary China's central politics. Also apparent was an urge by Chen to prove that he was fully capable of directing action scenes on a large scale.

The perfectionism that had become a Chen Kaige directorial hallmark was apparent in the making of the film. On a sound-stage in the Beijing Film Studio in December 1997, Chen took many rehearsals and several takes to get the exact expression he sought from his actors, who included Gong Li. A measure perhaps of Chen's self-image was his casting himself as the father of the first Qin emperor. His greying wig and costume added further color for the Japanese photographer working on the set to compile illustrations for an elegant coffee-table book of the production. In May 1998 Chen was busy with his editing team on an elaborate computer system set up in one of the bedrooms of his expensive, west Beijing home. A late-model Mercedes Benz, identified as being for Hsu Feng's use when she was in the city, ferried the director and his visitors about town.

The film competed in Cannes in May 2000, garnering only an art direction award. The consensus of the critics was of a film too long (at close to three hours) to engage foreign audiences. Beautiful, misty images of battalions of soldiers in spare northern landscapes are a reminder of the visual impact of *Yellow Earth*'s loess hills. But the elaboration is far from the sparseness of 1984.

In an interview in Beijing in 1993 prior to leaving for Cannes and the top prize for *Farewell, My Concubine*, Chen recalled that making *The Yellow Earth* ten years earlier now seemed like a dream and that he had still felt like a student then. After *King of the Children* he was confused and uncertain of his future direction. Would his audience be both Chinese and Westerners? He acknowledged autobiographical elements in his films and spoke of his identification with Cheng Dieyi in his most recent: "He's the soul of the film; he's part of myself."[164] In mid-2000 Chen Kaige went to Hollywood to prepare a new production, *Killing Me Softly*, with a budget of US$25 million and no Chinese setting or actors. This study of obsessive sexual attraction was a critical and box-office failure upon its release in mid-2002. The dissolution of the fifth generation, or their incorporation into an international cultural project seemed complete.

In 2001 Chen returned to China and a modest project which continued his fascination with relationships between fathers and sons, teachers and students, and art and life. *Together* (*He ni zai yiqi*) was in part funded with South Korean production money. It traces the musical and life education of Xiaochun, a thirteen-year-old with a gift for the violin. His father insists on moving to Beijing to further his musical study. The boy becomes as engrossed in the worldly young woman in the apartment upstairs as in his musical education. His first teacher in Beijing, an eccentric genius obsessed with little other than art, is succeeded by a manipulative star-maker. Chen Kaige plays this famous music professor. The result is a work that seems an exercise of a talent better suited to more ambitious projects. Leaving aside the glancing exploration of teacher-student dependence and gestures towards a contemplation of the mysteries of artistic achievement, the film appears an oblique commentary on the contemporary Chinese middle-class obsession with music lessons for the one-child "little emperor." But the music of Bruch, Richard Strauss, Liszt, Massenet and Tchaikovsky are an indication of the extent to which Chen and his contemporaries had become part of an international cultural discourse. His project in mid-2004 confirmed the incorporation. On a sound stage at the Beijing Film Studio Chen was shooting scenes from *The Promise* (*Wuji*), a fantasy historical drama in the vein of Zhang Yimou's *House of Flying Daggers* and Ang Lee's *Crouching Tiger, Hidden Dragon* (*Wohu canglong*, 2000).

7. Reds: Zhang Yimou's Films

When he turned to directing films, Zhang Yimou proved to be the most popular of his filmmaking generation: his directing debut was at the heart of a major development in youth culture in China. Internationally, Zhang secured lavish praise from Western critics and several of the most important honors ever won by Chinese films. This ability to reach broad popular audiences with serious artistic intent placed enormous pressure on Zhang Yimou. It also encouraged criticism, from a range of voices in China and abroad, that his films presented an orientalist, post-colonial Chinese imaginary for the edification and entertainment of international audiences.

The Guangxi Film Studio's *One and Eight*, *The Yellow Earth*, and *The Big Parade* established Zhang Yimou as the pre-eminent cinematographer of his generation. His election in April 1985 at the China Film Association national conference to a position on the association's 273-seat council was an indication of his distinction.[165] Even the critics who had not liked the message of *The Yellow Earth* had consistently praised its photography.

In late 1985 Wu Tianming, head of the Xi'an Film Studio, brought Zhang Yimou back to his home town. On loan from Guangxi, Zhang set to work on a new film project to be directed by Wu, who also managed to find a job in the studio library for Zhang's wife. The new project was *Old Well* (*Lao jing*), the latest in a series of Chinese "Westerns," in which the Xi'an studio had begun to specialize under Wu's regime. These were films set in the villages and barren lands of China's northwest, for which Xi'an served as gateway. *Old Well* told the story of a poor village in Shanxi province which is severely short of water. The struggle to find a productive well is presented in ways that went beyond Maoist paeans to proletarian solidarity, suggesting instead the plain humanity in these efforts to survive. A young well-digger attempts one last well, despite the death of his father and brother in the latest of a series of abortive wells.

Wu Tianming and Zhang Yimou spent months casting *Old Well*, travelling throughout China seeking suitable actors. People to play peasants were hard to find, and the part of Sun Wangquan, the young well-digger, was particularly troublesome to cast. Wu found that actors who looked the part lacked the necessary training and understanding of the character. Properly trained actors with the educational level to grasp the significance of the part and story usually looked physically unconvincing as a Shanxi well-digger.[166] Eventually Wu found his Sun

Wangquan right under his nose. Zhang Yimou, especially with his close-cropped hair and his gaunt face, looked the part. He also understood all its ramifications. In late 1986 Zhang Yimou set off to the Taihang mountain location with Wu and the crew, as both co-cinematographer and lead actor. In October 1987 he won the best actor prize at the second Tokyo International Film Festival, at the same time as *Old Well* won the Grand Prix and several other awards at the festival. Zhang's performance had domestic appeal also. He won best actor prizes in the Golden Rooster Awards and in the Hundred Flowers popularity poll.

While Wu Tianming put the finishing touches to *Old Well*, Zhang Yimou set out in the spring of 1987 to become a director. But first he had to be a farmer. He travelled to Shandong to supervise the local farmers in planting a hundred *mu* (almost seven hectares) in several fields of sorghum. Given the recent economic reforms in the countryside, sorghum was no longer an attractive crop to farmers producing cash crops for market. The Shandong farmers had to be bribed to set aside some fields for red sorghum. Once grown to about two meters in height, the crop featured prominently in Zhang Yimou's directorial debut, *Red Sorghum* (*Hong gaoliang*).

The story that Zhang had selected was drawn from two 1986 novellas by Mo Yan, a young Shandong province writer. Mo writes with great sensory power, investing the natural environment and his characters with an almost supernatural spirit. The liveliness and energy that Mo conveys in his writing appealed greatly to Zhang Yimou when he first read them in March 1986.[167] Zhang had perhaps grown weary of the intellectual coolness of *The Yellow Earth*, *King of the Children*, and other films by his film academy classmates. In August he left the location shooting for *Old Well* for Beijing, where he met with Mo Yan about filming his stories. Several studios had expressed interest in adapting them, but Mo Yan decided Zhang Yimou should have the film rights. As Zhang later recalled, his bronzed and toughened appearance, after several months on location in the Taihang mountains, may have been the key in persuading Mo Yan, who himself lived in the countryside as a self-styled peasant writer, that he was up to the task. Mo Yan remarked at their meeting that Zhang looked just like a commune production-brigade leader.[168] At this stage Maoist communes, the standard agricultural organization throughout China, had been abandoned and family farming restored.

Red Sorghum is a love story set just before and during the Japanese invasion of north China. Despite its clear historical setting, the narrative is presented as something of a fable. An off-screen voice sets out to present the story of "my grandma" and "my grandpa," as heard from his own father, the couple's son. Grandma first appears as a young woman on her way in a sedan-chair to an arranged marriage with the leprous owner of a distillery. One of the sedan carriers takes a liking to the young woman. On her way back from a visit to her parents, she is stopped by a mysterious bandit. He carries her into the wild stand of tall sorghum beside the road and has sex with her. The bandit is in fact the sedan carrier. After grandma's husband is mysteriously murdered, the sedan carrier returns to claim the young widow as his own. He wins her trust and they set up a home together. The sedan carrier thus becomes my (future) grandpa. Soon the distillery prospers, selling its red sorghum spirits far and wide, despite interference by a local bandit chief. When the Japanese army occupies the district, all the local people, bandits or distillers, suffer greatly. Grandpa leads the resistance to the Japanese. The films ends with a disastrous ambush of an enemy convoy travelling through the sorghum. Grandma perishes, but grandpa and father, a small boy, survive.

Zhang made several key changes to the script that Mo Yan and two other writers had prepared for him while he was shooting and acting in *Old Well*. Grandfather was changed from bandit to an ordinary peasant, so that his love of freedom and gusto would be more unexpected and thus have more impact. Zhang also reduced the fighting scenes in the film script to just one rather broadly presented skirmish.[169] The Japanese only appear in the last third of the film, whereas they frame Mo Yan's original stories at their beginning and end. Zhang's aim was to create an idealized world of liveliness that he felt most Chinese artists and writers had talked a lot about but had not managed to create. The Japanese atrocity sequence adds political content in part to forestall the film censors who might otherwise have asked what educational significance the film had.[170]

The visual qualities of *Red Sorghum* are extraordinary. Zhang persuaded his classmate Gu Changwei to join the crew as cinematographer after *King of the Children*. The sorghum becomes the third leading character, lending mystery and the threat of violence in episodes set in Qingshakou ("green killer's crossing"). As in Zhang's previous films, color is a central, coded element. The red of the spirits symbolizes the passions of the heroes, their life, and ultimately their deaths in the struggle to defend their homes. Zhang cast Jiang Wen, a 1984 graduate of the Central Drama Academy then on the teaching staff, to play grandpa. Jiang's versatility as an actor earned him the role, having recently played with equal effectiveness the last emperor, intellectuals, and peasants. He plays this part with the vigor and humor that Zhang sought. For the part of grandma, Zhang needed an actress who could convey a sensuality, strength and determination not often found in women on China's screens. His search stopped at the Central Drama Academy. Gong Li, a second-year student actress from Shandong province, won the part, and she and Zhang became lovers on location. The film's passionate love story, the stunning images, and a series of joyful folk-style songs combined in a directorial debut like no other. *Red Sorghum* won the Golden Bear at the Berlin International Film Festival in early 1988, the highest international award that had ever been won by a Chinese film.

Red Sorghum proved a phenomenal success at home as well. In Beijing, for example, it played for eight days in March in twenty-two cinemas, and continued in seven cinemas for five more days, previously unheard of statistics.[171] Ticket prices were three or four times higher than the usual amount, and scalpers made a killing catering to popular demand. The songs from the film, roared out heartily by Jiang Wen and the other male actors, created a fashion for so-called "northern Shaanxi folk songs" (*Shaanbei min'ge*). Zhang noted after the film's completion that he had

Shooting *Red Sorghum* with actors Gong Li and Jiang Wen

become aware of peasants' preference for opera arias over other songs during his years as an educated youth in the Shaanxi countryside. The film songs, while not arias, are inspired by the tunes and solitary voices of opera. For two of the three songs he had written the lyrics himself, in a self-conscious invention of a "folk" tradition.[172] The invention extended to other parts of the film: the bridal palanquin and the procession that starts the film were the product of Zhang's imagination.[173] Subsequently this sequence, of boisterous young men bouncing a bridal chair, became a folkloric element in performances at festivals and for tourists, just as had happened with the more authentic waist-drum dancers of *The Yellow Earth.*

By the summer of 1988, young people in Beijing and elsewhere were wont to burst into: "Little sister, go boldly forward . . ." and other songs from *Red Sorghum.* For two nights in June the 18,000-seat Capital Gymnasium was packed with youthful enthusiasts of the genre for a concert of northern Shaanxi folk-songs. Outside on the street people anxious for tickets held up as much as ten *yuan* (a considerable sum in 1988), some including a couple of *yuan* of the more prized "foreign exchange certificates" that could be exchanged for hard currency. Most of the singers at the concert were professional pop stars, but Zhang Yimou good-naturedly croaked his way through the *Red Sorghum* songs to an appreciative audience, and was joined in one by Wu Tianming, the producer of the film, who had been trained as an actor and enjoyed a crowd. There were critics of the film, mostly concerned at the crudeness of peasant culture they saw presented, but most media coverage was highly positive.[174]

The life in *Red Sorghum* is what appealed to its youthful, mostly male, enthusiasts. Having helped create a school of films that valorized the untrammelled, raw landscapes of northwest China, Zhang Yimou can be said to have applied this ethos to human relations. Grandpa and grandma approach life with a natural, instinctive passion, responding to their feelings, with no interest in thinking and no doubts. The narrative device of traditional story-telling creates a distancing effect and enriches the impact of these untutored, vigorous ancestors. For male Chinese audiences this story-telling drew upon a long cultural tradition of historical tales of chivalry and brotherhood. The episode in *Red Sorghum* in which grandpa visits the bandit chief's lair echoes episodes of individual bravery in old novels like *The Water Margin* (*Shuihu zhuan*). Grandpa uses his natural wit to earn the grudging respect of the bandit leader, but not before being presented with a whole cooked cow's head upon ordering food from the innkeeper (the bandit chief's henchman). Mo Yan's story had used a dog's head, but a cow's head, flung on the table and filmed from a low angle, was much more dramatic. Outlandish gestures like this had great appeal to young Chinese viewers. Similarly appealing was the episode in which grandpa defiantly pees into the sorghum spirits. The narrator notes that from then on the spirits had a different, wonderful taste that made it a best-seller in the district. This delight in life is what attracted Zhang Yimou to Mo Yan's stories. He deliberately blurred indications of the specific time and setting in the first two-thirds of the story to enhance the sense of a legend.[175]

One important element in the appeal of Zhang's film is male chauvinism. Grandpa is a man who lives out his sexual desires. Disguised as a bandit, he forces himself on the young woman in the wild sorghum at Green Killer's Crossing. Later, he gets roaring drunk and tries to approach the woman at her distillery, but is repelled. Having slept off his hangover, he boldly undoes his trousers to pee into a pot of newly distilled sorghum spirits. He breaks into the woman's bedroom to stake his claim as her partner. His encounter with the bandit leader is further evidence of his male self-assurance. The men who work at the distillery are a band of brothers: grandma is the only female character of any note in the film. The distillery workers sing a song to the god of spirits, playing on the number nine, which in Chinese is a homophone for the word for spirits (*jiu*). The number nine (also a homophone for the word for "a long time") occurs throughout the film: grandma's name is Jiu'er ("Ninth Child") and the distillery is at Eighteen *Li* Hill (*Shibali po*).[176] The comradely band of distillery workers has many predecessors in centuries of Chinese story-telling, a tradition from which some of the most popular novels after 1949 also drew.[177] After the Japanese have come and killed local people, grandma leads the men in a ceremonial swearing of vengeance. The killings include that of the former head of the distillery workers, skinned alive in front of the assembled Chinese as a lesson for all. While grandma remains a forceful presence, particularly in the preparations for the ambush of the enemy convoy, grandpa's archetypal masculinity was the overwhelming impression for its young male Chinese audience.

The carnivalesque qualities of the film do not, of course, preclude a political reading of *Red Sorghum*. Allegory is a common feature of pre- and post-1949 Chinese art and literature. Some foreign critics wondered if the audience popularity of the film was in part because the Japanese, who bring destruction to the natural world of the grandparents, were seen to represent the Chinese Communist Party. In this reading, grandpa stands for popular resentment against the Communist regime. At the end of the story, grandpa and father, as his young son, survive. The screen is washed in red, matching the blood of grandma and the others that has just been spilt in the abortive ambush. The narrator notes that from then on father's sight was affected, and everything he saw was bathed in red. Red is the color of revolution. This strictly political interpretation may not convince, but a broader contrast informs the film between the natural autonomy and love of life that delighted Chinese audiences with the strictures of Chinese existence even in the reformist decade of the 1980s. Grandpa's and grandma's freedom, despite the war around them, was obvious to Chinese audiences. As Zhang himself noted:

> Different people in different times and from different classes each have their views on what constitutes living a fulfilled life. But people should realize that a life which is free and unrestrained is in itself the beauty of life. We cannot again let ourselves be forced to live in any sort of artificial restrictions and conventionality.[178]

Zhang Yimou captured in his film the optimism of 1987–88 about China's future and the prospects for political reform. But he also presented a world "before the fall," in which civilizational philosophies such as Confucianism, Marxism or Communism had no place. In this world people live, not by rules imposed from outside, but by their own instincts and wit. The only rules, such as the lusty ritual offering to the God of Wine, are of these people's own making, not insisted on by outside organizations. The ruined archway that marks the limits of the distillery, seems a relic from a more ordered time, now lost. The Japanese, of course, impose their new order on this world. Before the arrival of that outside army and before (or after) the strictures of organized beliefs and expectations, the world of *Red Sorghum* offered many Chinese film-goers the idea of an irresistible haven.

Pride in *Red Sorghum*'s international success was another factor in the film's popularity in China, which extended to all levels in the national cultural apparatus and to youthful film-goers throughout the country. This pride matched the patriotism of the film's wartime scenes, where distillers, peasants, and bandits unite in resistance to the invaders. In several statements on the film, Zhang Yimou emphasized the need for Chinese to be strong and to assert their self-confidence. But for Zhang Yimou and his largely youthful audiences this was not a conventional nationalism endorsed by Party officials. Theirs was a pride in being fully human as well as Chinese.

After such a smashing critical and box-office success with *Red Sorghum*, Zhang Yimou was naturally under some pressure in preparing his next film, like Chen Kaige in similar circumstances after *The Yellow Earth*. He decided to try something completely different. In the summer of 1988 he worked on a script tentatively titled *Yinyang Man* (*Yinyang ren*), with Wang Shuo, a young writer whose innovative stories were some of the most creative and rebellious then being published in China. At least four films based on his stories were in preparation in 1988. *Yinyang Man* was about an ordinary Beijing youth who carted goods around town on the back of his three-wheeled pedicart. He takes up a traditional Chinese exercise and herbal regimen that has the unexpected side-effects of turning him increasingly into a woman. The *yin* and *yang* of the title refer to the female and male principles in early Chinese philosophy. The young hero eventually wins a contest, not as a man but as a woman. Wang Shuo and Zhang eventually abandoned the project, dissatisfied with the draft script they had produced. The film was to have been funded by a young Chinese entrepreneur who had made his money as a private businessman under Deng Xiaoping's economic reforms. By mid-1988 independent production (*duli zhipian*) was seen as a way out from the financial crisis that Chinese filmmaking was in. The aborted script seems to have been Zhang's self-mocking response to the male chauvinist elements in *Red Sorghum*.[179]

Instead, Zhang made an action thriller to fulfil his undertaking to the backer of the Wang Shuo project. *Codename Cougar* (*Daihao "Meizhoubao,"* a.k.a. *The Puma Action*) was not a film in which Zhang or his co-director Yang Fengliang had any pride. Yang, a young employee of the Xi'an Film Studio and sometime actor, had been Zhang's assistant director on *Red Sorghum*. In the film, a flight between Taipei and Seoul is hijacked by a terrorist group, the Asian Black Commandos. The plane is forced to land on the Chinese mainland, precipitating an international crisis in which the governments in Taipei and Beijing are obliged to conduct secret face-to-face negotiations. The main action of the film is the rescue operation for the plane's passengers, mounted by an elite band of Chinese military commandos. Gong Li plays one of the flight attendants.

Zhang knew that the political dimension of the story would earn him credit from the film authorities in Beijing who had begun to express doubts about supporting independent productions, but would be pleased at a story bringing the two sides of the Taiwan Straits together.

Codename Cougar has a certain interest as an entertainment film when compared with the usually incompetent examples of the genre that limped from the studios in search of a blockbuster in the late 1980s. To economize on sets, actors, and shooting, Zhang adopted a journalistic narration that covers much ground with an off-screen voice and frequent montages of still photographs outlining reactions and planning in Taipei, Hong Kong, and Beijing. But overall the film was a sideroad in Zhang Yimou's directorial development, though its broad political alignment with Beijing's official view of the world may have been a harbinger of films, or criticisms, to come.

Zhang's next film project was a remarkable continuation and yet change from his achievement in *Red Sorghum*. Just as he had captured the optimistic spirit of 1987–88 in his debut film, so in *Judou* Zhang Yimou spoke for a contemporary, now post-Tian'anmen China. A study in oppression and helplessness, *Judou* won a nomination for the best foreign-language film in the 1991 U.S. Academy Awards. It was the first Chinese film to be nominated, and only the second film from Asia outside of Japan to compete for an Oscar.[180]

Many of the themes in *Judou* had been explored in earlier fifth-generation films. As in *The Yellow Earth*, the position of women is a major concern. But, as in the earlier work, marriage is a metaphor for a broader social restriction that includes men as well as women. Judou is a young woman trapped in an arranged marriage to Yang Jinshan, a much older man, somewhere in central China in the 1920s. Her husband, the childless and impotent owner of a cloth dyeing works, abuses Judou nightly. This is his third marriage: his previous wives had died from his abuse. Yang Tianqing, his adopted nephew, helps with the dyeing. One day Judou discovers that the young man has been peering at her when she bathes. She deliberately lets Tianqing see the wounds inflicted by her husband, and the two become lovers, furtively conducting their affair under her husband's nose. When Judou becomes pregnant by Tianqing, his uncle claims paternity of the son. An accident at the works turns Yang Jinshan into a paraplegic. Unable to move and sitting in a modified barrel which serves as a wheelchair, he watches in helpless humiliation as Judou and Tianqing conduct their affair in open defiance of him. The townspeople, however, begin to gossip about the couple. When Judou becomes pregnant again and aborts the pregnancy, she loses her ability to bear children. Eventually their son, a silent brute of a child, watches Yang Jinshan's death in a vat of dye. Eight years later, the boy exacts a terrible revenge on his own father. When Judou and Tianqing almost suffocate in a storage dungeon, Tianbai rescues his mother but kills Tianqing by tossing him into the same dye vat in which Yang Jinshan had drowned. In her grief, Judou takes a torch to the home and dyeing works. A huge fire consumes all.

The tone of *Judou* is profoundly pessimistic. All the characters are trapped by a centuries-old system of oppression. The Yang clan gathers to assert the power of the ancestors as the clan elders select a name for the child, who is named Tianbai ("sky-white"), in unconscious linkage to his real father, Tianqing ("sky-blue"). The Yang family ancestral hall and altar figure throughout the narrative. The home and dyeing works are part of the same courtyard, whose high walls and huge doors form a jail for the people who live and work within them. Even the town outside the Yang home is presented as a series of narrow allies and high, confining walls. Rarely do the characters venture into a more open setting. Judou and Tianqing find places to make love in the countryside. But the funeral procession of Yang Jinshan is also conducted through these more open spaces, sealing the fate of Judou and Tianqing. No motivation is offered for their son's vengeance. The suggestion seems to be that fate and the system in which all the characters find themselves are responsible for what happens.

The phallocentrism seen in *Red Sorghum* figures also in *Judou*. The story by Liu Heng from which the film script was drawn was titled "Fuxi, fuxi." Fuxi is a Chinese ancestral, first-male figure from ancient, legendary times. Liu's original story covered the period from the 1920s to the Cultural Revolution. In adapting the story with Zhang Yimou, Liu limited the narrative to the 1920s. Impotence is the immediate cause of Judou's suffering in her marriage, for she cannot bear a son by Yang Jinshan to carry the ancestral line. Judou's husband and his nephew compete for sexual power over her. Judou herself seduces Tianqing and is more determined than her lover, who hesitates at crucial moments in the battle with his uncle. But ultimately her son, a living symbol of Yang Jinshan's failed phallus and a silent, cropped headed presence in the ancestral home, asserts his clan duty and, in an Oedipal outburst, destroys his errant parents.

The contrast between Yang Tianqing and grandpa in *Red Sorghum* is striking. Grandpa was assertive, in command, living by his strength and wits: Tianqing is helpless most of the time. He starts in abject servitude to his uncle, sneaking furtive glances at his new mistress as she washes. Even when he becomes her lover, he remains rather timid. Judou is the aggressor and stronger partner, pushing him to taunt her crippled husband about their affair and its offspring. Although Judou herself tries to resist her oppression, her last act of setting fire to the home and dyeing works is another act of desperation, rather than of defiance. In response to the change in mood between 1988 and 1989, *Judou* has no heroes.

Zhang Yimou, his collaborating director Yang Fengliang, and cinematographers Gu Changwei and Yang Lun, give this gothic tale the visual power it needs to convince audiences. The original story was not set in a dyeing works. Zhang's change of setting allows for ravishing images of long ribbons of colored cloth in rich reds, blues, and yellows. The crew bought 750 meters of the cloth to hang in the dyeing factory. The factory itself and its machinery was an invention of the art directors Cao Jiuping and Xia Rujin. Technicolor shooting brings out the dazzling colors of the cloth lit by the sun. At one point sexual ecstasy is suggested by a shot of a long length of cloth dropping rapidly into a vat of red dye. But the cloth also serves to bind the lovers and Yang Jinshan to their fate. When Tianqing is drowned by his son, his body is covered by a similar long red cloth dropping into the vat.[181]

Zhang Yimou chose an actor whose shaved head and general demeanour resemble himself to play Tianqing. This similarity introduces a personal subtext to *Judou* that refers to the real-life relationship between Gong Li, who plays Judou, and Zhang Yimou. Zhang and Gong had been lovers since the shooting of *Red Sorghum*. Zhang's wife, Xiao Hua, back at the Xi'an Film Studio library, refused to contemplate a divorce, and presented her opinions of Zhang Yimou in a lengthy, serialized memoir of their lives together that caused a sensation among the readers of China's tabloid press.[182] The public then had the opportunity of seeing Zhang Yimou and Gong Li playing historical lovers in *A Terracotta Warrior* (*Qin yong*), a Hong Kong-China co-production shot after the completion of *Judou*. Zhang played a warrior from the third century B.C. who becomes one of the army of clay statues buried in the tomb of Qin Shihuangdi, the first emperor of China. The warrior and his lover from Qin times, played by Gong Li, come to life in the 1930s to go through a series of comic misadventures. Both Zhang and Gong acquitted themselves nicely as comic actors, but most viewers probably watched for the parallels between the historical story and the real lives of the two leads.

When *Judou* won the Academy Award nomination in 1991, fifth-generation filmmaking seemed to have achieved a signal honor. Instead of delight, however, the reaction from some authorities in Beijing to the announcement was one of horror. Formal requests were made to withdraw the film, on the grounds that *Judou* did not qualify for nomination because it had not been released domestically. *Judou* had in fact been banned in China. The flap over the Academy Award nomination rehearsed internationally the reasons for the film's banning at home. Some voices in Beijing suggested to the Academy that the film had in fact been shown on a college campus to a paying audience and thus met the nomination criterion. The Academy decided that the nomination should stand, but the award went to a Swiss production, *Journey of Hope*.

The real problem for *Judou* (at the Oscars and in being banned in China) was *Red Sorghum*'s success. Some senior figures in the film and propaganda hierarchy in Beijing viewed the Academy Award nomination with alarm: should *Judou* win the award, it would be difficult to avoid full release of the film in China. *Red Sorghum*'s massive popularity in 1988 would ensure huge numbers for Zhang Yimou and Gong Li's latest collaboration. But whereas *Red Sorghum* had been an optimistic, life-affirming story, the tone and message of *Judou* were utterly different. The sombre outlook of *Judou* owed most to the changes after the suppression of the Beijing demonstrations in June 1989. Some leaders in Beijing seem to have believed that *Judou* would remind Chinese audiences of those unhappy events. Those Beijing leaders who sought its withdrawal from the Academy Awards probably also hoped that foreign audiences might not be reminded of June 4th by *Judou*. The Chinese authorities' ignorance of the effect that their interference might have in galvanizing foreign opinion in defence of the film was a product of their long practice of ignoring public opinion in their own country. In the United States, however, senators, writers, artists, and journalists signed petitions and made speeches demanding that *Judou* be allowed to compete for an Academy Award and Zhang Yimou be permitted to attend the award ceremony.

Since *Judou* had been officially nominated in the first place, in contrast to the usual Chinese practice which had been to nominate the most unlikely, usually mediocre or highly culture-bound products of the studios, it clearly had friends in high places in Beijing. The nomination and then attempted withdrawal was further indication of the deep divisions in the Chinese cultural apparatus and national leadership. The Party that ordered the People's Liberation Army to fire on protesters in Beijing in June 1989 was profoundly divided even as those orders were given. After June, the divisions were papered over but clearly persisted, in cultural policy as elsewhere in Chinese public life.

In *Judou*'s favor was it being a co-production with Tokuma, a Japanese company, for even if a co-production was banned in China, foreign audiences might see it. Foreign producers could also provide the finances that the generally bankrupt studios could not find. Particularly after June 4th, Chinese filmmakers of the fifth and earlier generations actively sought foreign producers. *Judou* proved a comparative box-office success in North America and Europe, undoubtedly helped by the Oscar nomination. Particularly after June 4th, an historical setting like *Judou*'s, safely distant from contemporary times, was another way to try to ensure domestic release, although no guarantee of success.

Ever sensitive to the political climate, Zhang Yimou chose to make his next film another costume drama co-production, this time with Taiwan. The project thus had a political significance in building cultural relations between Taipei and Beijing that might protect the film from the Chinese censors and their political masters. *Raise the Red Lantern* (*Da hong denglong gao gao gua*) was shot in the fall and winter of 1990, before the Academy Award fiasco over *Judou*. The executive producer was Hou Hsiao-hsien (Hou Xiaoxian), one of the younger filmmakers on Taiwan who had created a cinematic New Wave on the island at about the time Zhang and his fifth generation were doing the same on the other side of the Taiwan Straits. Ch'iu Fu-sheng (Qiu Fusheng), producer of Hou's award-winning *A City of Sadness* (*Beiqing chengshi*, 1989), served as producer for *Raise the Red Lantern*.

Like *Judou*, the new film starred Gong Li as a young woman trapped in an arranged marriage in the 1920s. Songlian is a nineteen-year-old college student who is obliged to give up her studies after the death of her father. Unable to endure her stepmother's abuse, becoming the fourth wife (or third concubine) of the master of the Chen clan offers Songlian a way out. Chen Zuoqian is fifty and Yiru, his first wife, has a son who is older than Songlian. Yiru has lost her youthful beauty and rarely ventures out of her courtyard in the Chen family mansion. Zhuoyun, the second wife, is clever and seems to welcome Songlian. The third wife, Meishan, is a former opera actress and is conducting a secret affair with the family doctor. Each wife lives in her own quarters around one of four courtyards in the Chen mansion. Red lanterns are hung above the door of each wife's chambers. They are lit in the evening according to which wife with whom Chen Zuoqian chooses to spend the night. Chen likes to make love by the red glow of lanterns. The wife chosen for the evening is given a foot massage by servants, and the evening stillness is punctuated by the "clack, clack, clack" of the wooden massage hammers.

The narrative revolves around Songlian's engagement in the domestic intrigues and jealousies between the wives. Being the newest, most attractive mistress in the household is a heavy burden, as she must juggle her relations with the other women. When she discovers that Zhuoyun, despite her apparent friendliness, has been secretly plotting against her, Songlian resolves to have her revenge. She is horrified when, through a casual remark by her, Meishan's affair with the doctor is exposed. Wandering in the mansion, Songlian discovers an isolated, roof-top pavilion that contains a horrible secret. Determined to win favor, Songlian announces that she is pregnant. A delighted Chen Zuoqian orders that the red lanterns be lit in her courtyard until further notice. Then her servant, an ally of Zhuoyun, exposes Songlian's scheme. Chen Zuoqian orders that her red lantern be replaced by a black one, as a symbol of her permanent demotion. One day her misery is relieved by the sound of a flute being played on the rooftop by Feipu, Chen's son, who has returned from the city. Songlian is filled with hope. But these are soon dashed, as she is brutally expelled from the household.

As in *Judou*, Zhang Yimou explores here the complexities of oppression. Chen Zuoqian is complete master of his household. He is filmed consistently at great distance or from behind, so that the audience never sees his face properly. Such obliqueness makes even more fearsome the menace and destruction he can wreak. Oppression is a more complicated concept in *Raise the Red Lantern* than in *Judou*. The relations between the four women are fraught with jealousies, sensitivity to slights, and their perceptions of their own proper roles in the household of Chen Zuoqian. They are collaborators in the oppression of others and of themselves. This deeper exploration of the psychology of his characters and their relationships marked a further step in Zhang Yimou's filmmaking.

The formalistic visual impact typical of Zhang's films is repeated in *Raise the Red Lantern*. In his first film, the sorghum had become a major visual element; in his second, the lengths of cloth featured prominently. In this film, the Chen mansion is more than the setting for the narrative. Its walls, doorways, courtyards and roofs are filmed with a formalism and stasis that reinforces their function of separating and confining the people within them. The nightly raising of the red lanterns is carefully documented, punctuating the story with its ritual. Zhao Fei, a class of '82 classmate and photographer of Tian Zhuangzhuang's *Horse Thief*, photographed *Red Lantern* along with Yang Lun. The set is a Qing dynasty mansion near Taiyuan, the capital of Shanxi province, preserved as a historical museum.

In a setting that epitomized China's history, Zhang's exploration of the meanings of oppression take on broader significance. Su Tong's novella "Wives and Concubines," from which the author produced a script for Zhang Yimou, had appeared in an issue of the literary journal *Harvest* (*Shouhuo*) published in June 1989. The events of the democracy movement and the aftermath of June 4th were proof of the destructiveness of an apparent Chinese capacity for jealousies, treachery, and a concern for "face." *Raise the Red Lantern* is as much about collaboration in oppression as about the withering of the human spirit under an oppressive system. Assessments of the student movement in China and abroad focused particularly on the failure of the protesters and their supporters to achieve unity of purpose and effort and on the relative ease with which the old men in power asserted their control.

Refused release in China, the film proved an international success, winning the Silver Lion and several critics' prizes at the 1991 Venice International Film Festival. The following year *Raise the Red Lantern* was nominated for a foreign-language Academy Award, being considered a Hong Kong production, as Ch'iu Fu-sheng had established a production company in the colony because Taiwan law forbade direct investment in China. An Italian comedy beat Zhang's film for the 1992 Academy Award. For a filmmaker who sees himself and his art as firmly rooted in Chinese culture, the ability to speak to a world audience was a remarkable achievement. Indicating the extent to which cultural relaxation had returned after June 4th, *Raise the Red Lantern* and *Judou* were both released in China in the autumn of 1992 and proved big successes at the box office.[183]

Zhang Yimou's next film, completed in the early summer of 1992, was both a departure and a continuation of his established interests. *The Story of Qiuju* (*Qiuju da guansi*) eschewed the formalism of *Judou* and *Raise the Red Lantern*, adopting a naturalism unprecedented in Chinese cinema. The new film was a comedy, although Gong Li again starred as a strong-willed woman. She plays Qiuju, a northern Shaanxi peasant whose husband is kicked in the groin by the village head. The film follows Qiuju's efforts to seek redress for the abuse of her husband, who had accused the village head of only producing "hens," meaning daughters. A visibly pregnant Qiuju and her sister-in-law go from the local police station to the prosecutor's office in town and then on to court in the city, where she is unsuccessful in convincing the judges to support her case. When Qiuju goes into life-threatening labor, the village head helps save her and the baby, a son. The village is celebrating the birth, when the police arrive to take the chief away, as a re-assessment has been made of the seriousness of the kicking case.

Zhang Yimou explored a new way of filming in shooting the film in the winter of 1991–92. Using the 16 mm format allowed flexibility not possible in 35 mm. More than half the film was shot with a hidden camera and crew on the streets of towns and cities, so that most of the people on screen were unaware that they were being filmed. As he was editing the work in a Beijing apartment owned by the left-wing Sil-Metropole film company based in Hong Kong, Zhang described the procedure. The cast and crew would scout sites, camera angles and movements one night. The next night the camera and crew would be hidden before dawn. Shooting often had to wait until well into the morning, when the light was sufficient. To enhance the naturalism of hidden shooting, Zhang used synchronized sound recording: remote microphones were secreted on the actors' clothing. Gong Li and the non-professional playing her sister-in-law wear headscarves against the winter chill and to hide the earphones through which Zhang Yimou, from his own hiding place, instructed them to move or repeat a take.[184] Limited use of folk music from Shaanxi includes a theme associated with the pregnant Qiuju, who waddles around as a country bumpkin in the big city. The effect was a milestone in Chinese film history: compared to decades of previous screen peasants, Qiuju came closest to the real thing.

Unlike Zhang's previous two films, his *Story of Qiuju* was immediately approved in China, where it joined the other two in distribution in the autumn of 1992. The cultural authorities apparently liked the film's suggestion that the legal system provided a means of redress to even an ordinary peasant. For his part, Zhang wanted to ensure that this film would win approval, having been frustrated at not reaching his domestic audience in timely fashion with the two earlier films. Some critics felt that the ending of the film was too accommodating of official views. Countering this is the strong subtext of Qiuju's own sense of justice: the legal system may work, but it is Qiuju's own determination and refusal to quit that rights the wrong.

For someone who had initially been refused admission to film school and almost asked to leave halfway through his degree, Zhang Yimou's achievement was remarkable. The top prizes at Berlin and Venice and two consecutive nominations for an Academy Award made Zhang the most successful filmmaker of his generation or any other in China. Unlike several members of his film academy class of '82 (most notably Chen Kaige), Zhang never thought of working outside of China. He saw himself and his art as rooted in the yellow earth of the northwest. As Chen Kaige observed in a widely recognized essay on his friend, Zhang is a "son of Qin," the ancient state (headquartered near Zhang's native Xi'an) that formed the core of the first Chinese empire.[185]

In the second half of the 1990s, Zhang continued to make films in the twin veins explored in the *Raise the Red Lantern* and *The Story of Qiuju*. *To Live* (*Huozhe*) essayed life in China from late 1940s to the end of the Cultural Revolution in the late 1970s. To manage such an epic topic Zhang focused on one family and its efforts to survive the onslaught of political campaigns. Xu Fugui, the scion of a wealthy family, loses his fortune gambling and ends up, largely by accident, entertaining troops during the Civil War of the 1940s with the puppets he had won on a bet. Having secured a piece of paper which certifies he fought with (that is, entertained) the Communist army, he and his wife Jiazhen (played by Gong Li) set about living their lives and raising a family without causing any trouble to their neighbors.

Campaigns like the Great Leap Forward are both threats to their quiet existence but also opportunities to prove their dedication to the Communist government. Their younger child, a boy called Youqing, learns rhymes from his father about a prosperous future under the leadership of the Communist Party. After one exhausting night helping with the smelting of iron, Fugui insists that his young son go to school. The boy falls asleep under a wall on the way to school and is crushed when a vehicle crashes into the wall. Fugui's daughter, Fengxia is married to a factory worker during the Cultural Revolution. Their wedding presents include Chairman Mao's collected works. Later, when Fengxia has complications during the birth of her first child, Fugui finds an old gynaecologist who had been condemned by the inexperienced, young nurses who are panicking during Fengxia's delivery. To strengthen the old man and to show his appreciation, Fugui feeds him steamed bread and water. On the prisoner's empty stomach, the bread expands and renders helpless the only person with the skills to save his daughter's life. By the end of the film, Fugui's grandson is learning the nursery rhymes his late uncle, Youqing, had also learned. His grandfather promises that in the future the family will have not only chickens, like those they are keeping in his old, now empty puppet box, but horses, cars and planes. There is no mention of the Communist Party in this latest rhyme, for this is after Deng Xiaoping has launched economic reform.

Such a narrative, punctuated with deaths and suffering, could easily slip into melodrama. Zhang avoided this by using a strong thread of black humor throughout the film. The civil war enters Fugui's world when a bayonet suddenly punctures his shadow puppet screen close by his face. His furtive peeing in the street is suddenly interrupted by gun shots, but they are not directed at him, instead at the man who had taken all his wealth in a bet and was now accused of being a big landlord. The death of Fengxia in confinement is the most extraordinary mix of tragedy and bathos, with the old gynaecologist rolling about helpless, stuffed full of food.

Throughout the film the concentration on the family brings momentous historical events down to a personal level. Fugui and his wife live in two realms: a public one, in which they are under constant pressure to prove or perform their commitment to the revolution, and a private world, where, usually over meals at a round table, the family can relax a little and stop performing. Even the final credits in the film contribute to Zhang's themes. As the family enjoys a meal, the credits roll not upwards but across the bottom of the screen, rather as a Chinese scroll painting is "read." This movement suggests a continuing cycle, like that of death and birth in the film's narration. *To Live* was Zhang Yimou's most overtly political film, at least in dealing directly with post-1949 Chinese history. Like Tian Zhuangzhuang's *Blue Kite*, which covered similar ground, *To Live* was banned in China.

Shanghai Triad (*Yao a yao, yao dao waipo qiao*, literally "Shake, Shake, Shake Along to Grandma's Bridge," 1995) was Zhang's last film with Gong Li. She plays Xiaojinbao ("Bijou"), a night-club singer in 1930s Shanghai, who is caught up in internecine gang warfare. In Shanghai, mirrors and reflections constantly remind viewers of the artificiality and deceit of this decadent world. When the action moves to the safe haven of an island in the Yangzi River far from Shanghai, the country idyll is no protection from urban treachery. Told through the eyes of a boy who becomes Xiaojinbao's servant, the narration ends with an upside-down shot as the boy is strung up on a mast at the island. The film was a bitter-sweet experience for Zhang. His partnership with its star had come to an end. The script, partly his own work, was not satisfactory, but production funding was available from French investors. At a time when there were grumblings from the Beijing film authorities about excessive reliance on co-productions, Zhang chose to go ahead and make the film. He feared the uncertainty of not knowing when he might next be able to direct, should Beijing ban foreign co-productions.[186]

The result was one of Zhang's lesser works, though one that added fuel to suggestions that Zhang made films that met Western audience's expectations about the exotic otherness of China. Gong Li, though far from a standard classical Chinese beauty (she seems too strong and self-assured for that), was taken by Western observers as an icon of Zhang's orientalist program to formalize and mystify the cruel exoticism of his China. Sheldon Hsiao-peng Lu sees Zhang engaged in presenting China as a Third World allegory, submitting, as the archetypical Third World

Zhang Yimou shooting *Shanghai Triad*

filmmaker, to a capitalist and orientalist gaze. Foreign production monies and the transnational nature of film production and distribution apparently have made Zhang a kind of sideshow entertainer in a globalized carnival.[187] Zhang Yimou's interest, as a former painter and still photographer, in surface and display suggests an ironic bind to Rey Chow. He is caught between the orientalist gaze of the West and the surveillance of the Chinese state. In response, Chow argues, Zhang has produced a new kind of orientalism: "The Oriental's orientalism ... self-subalternizing, self-exoticizing visual gestures ... a demonstration—the display of a tactic."[188]

Discussions on Zhang's alleged orientalism had appeal also in China, to many Chinese post-modern critics and to conservative observers, resentful of Zhang's international success. A writer in the first group was Wang Yichuan, an associate professor in the Chinese department at Beijing Normal University, who made a career of writing about "the Zhang Yimou myth" (*Zhang Yimou shenhua*). Wang's elaborations went beyond suggestions of orientalism to elaborate a complex schema involving China, the West, identity and "the traditional father."[189] It was all too much for Zhang Yimou, who has consistently insisted since the 1980s that, despite his international success, his target audience in all his films is Chinese.[190] It is noteworthy that while other fifth-generation directors, such as Chen Kaige and Peng Xiaolian, have spent years abroad and have become fluent in English, Zhang is largely monolingual and makes his home in Beijing.

As if to expunge the memory of *Shanghai Triad*, Zhang Yimou turned again to a contemporary setting and a story by Shu Ping, *Keep Cool* (*You hua, hao hao shuo*, more precisely "If you have something to say, say it nicely," 1996). Working again with Jiang Wen, his male star in *Red Sorghum* and with Li Baotian, his alter-ego in *Judou*, Zhang even appears on screen himself. The result is a romp through contemporary Beijing with a group of down-and-out workers. Filmed with a highly mobile camera and rapid editing, the work had an MTV quality that did not appeal to Zhang's followers at home or abroad, even while some applauded his invention. Some regarded this curiosity as an effort by Zhang (now well into his forties) to emulate the hip style of younger filmmakers, including some who had inevitably been labelled sixth-generation directors.

With two films made virtually back-to-to back in 1998–99 Zhang re-established his international award winning and the style he had found in

The Story of Qiuju. *Not One Less* (*Yige dou buneng shao*, literally "Every Last One," 1999) and *The Road Home* (*Wode fuqin muqin*, literally "My Father and Mother," 1999) were both set in the countryside. The former gained international attention when the Cannes Film Festival announced that it was too much a propaganda film for the Chinese government to compete in May 1999. It went on to win at the Venice International Film Festival a few months later.

Not One Less tells the story of a village youngster who, at age twelve, is drafted into becoming the local school teacher, when the adult teacher suddenly leaves. Zhang Yimou achieved a remarkable authenticity by using an entirely amateur cast and filming in an actual run-down school house in a remote part of Hebei province. The young teacher goes to the city, somewhat in the manner of Qiuju, in her search for one of her students. When she appears on the local TV channel, she is in tears of nervousness and frustration. The film ends with a call for urban Chinese to support charitable work in poor areas of the country. This direct plea apparently offended the sensibilities of the Cannes programmers. It does little to diminish the power of the film as social document. This commitment in a sense made *Not One Less* seem like the last of the truly fifth-generation films, coming a full fifteen years after *The Yellow Earth* and ten years after June 4th.

The Road Home showed that even master filmmakers can lose their judgement. The story is framed by a black-and-white narrative of the return to his home village of the son of the former school teacher there. His father has just died in a nearby town and his mother is determined that his body be carried back to the village along the road that figured so much in their lives. The flashbacks are in color and show what the road meant to the parents. As the symphonic music swells, the mother as a young woman runs back and forth along or beside the road, hoping to steal a glimpse of the handsome young teacher. The girl is played by Zhang Ziyi, who had become Zhang Yimou's new muse.[191] Vivaciousness and pigtails can become annoying to even the most indulgent viewer. The film is an empty celebration of the sunny days of yore, despite the cloud of a suggestion that political problems in the Anti-Rightist campaign of 1957 have detained the school teacher in the city.[192] Contemporary life, in contrast, is grey and cold (father dies in winter). The good people of the village rally round and supply the teams of men to carry the late teacher's body along the road back to his home. Zhang spoke of setting out to make a love story as unlike that of Hollywood's *Titanic* as possible.[193] But simplicity and concentration on small things can seem empty when there is not much more apparent in a text.

Despite its emptiness, the film won an award at the Berlin Festival in 2000, twelve years after the triumph there of *Red Sorghum*. By 2000 Zhang had achieved celebrity status in China and abroad. In 1997 in Italy and again in 1998 on the fringes of the Forbidden City in Beijing he had been commissioned to direct international stage productions of Puccini's orientalist opera *Turandot*, attended by wealthy socialites from around the world. The contrast with the poverty and plainness of the world of *Not One Less* could not be greater, though Zhang went from completing one to starting filming on the other while living a relatively public life as a media celebrity. Side work including filming publicity for Beijing's bid for the 2008 Olympic Games.

Hero (*Yingxiong*, 2001) was Zhang's second film in the new millennium. First came *Happy Times* (*Xingfu shiguang*, 2000), a modest, urban story of a blind girl and a middle-aged worker trying to survive in times of economic and social change, made in the realist mode of *Not One Less*. Zhang's greater investment of resources, time and reputation was spent on *Hero*. As his life had changed, so the context in which his films were released internationally had also been transformed. The success in North America and other Western nations of Ang Lee's *Crouching Tiger, Hidden Dragon* had excited many Chinese and other East Asian directors. Clearly designed as an international blockbuster in the mold of Ang Lee's work, the new film re-captured the formalist imagery of Zhang's early works, to a musical score by Tan Dun, who had also been Lee's composer.

Hero follows the confrontation between Wu Ming and the Qin state warrior-king, central also in Chen Kaige's *The Emperor and the Assassin*. Wu Ming, a man of the rival Zhao kingdom, intends to assassinate the Qin leader. In the course of preparing to attack his intended target, Wu Ming is forced to acknowledge that his personal vendetta is not in the interests of society. But Qin law requires that he be killed, which is done with waves of arrows fired by his enemy's massed troops. He is honored with a state funeral. The imagery is stunning, reminiscent of the late work of Kurosawa Akira. But, like the latter's *Ran* and *Dreams*, viewers may be inclined to consider the images shot in the northwestern deserts and in a huge palace set as somewhat empty. This vacuity of the content of *Hero* suggests that the thrust of the work is to endorse the kind of authoritarian leadership tradition that the first emperor established for China. The film ends with a picture of the Great Wall and a statement that the Qin leader went on to found the first Chinese state in 221 B.C. For a filmmaker who had grown up as the son of an "anti-revolutionary," the change in attitude and implied status that *Hero* suggested was startling. There could be no better evidence of the end of the fifth generation as a significant group of Chinese artists. In 2004 Zhang confirmed this with the sheer commercialism of another historical costume drama, *House of Flying Daggers* (*Shimian maifu*, literally "Ambushed on Ten Sides"), starring three East Asian pop idols.[194] The work encapsulated the changes in Chinese public life in the twenty years since *The Yellow Earth*.

8. Beyond the Fifth Generation

There were no generations commonly spoken of in the Chinese film enterprise until this distinctive group started to make its mark on the industry with *One and Eight* and *The Yellow Earth*. The invention of a "fifth generation," attributed sometimes to Ni Zhen of the film academy, implied predecessors and so other generations had to be more specifically identified.[195] Differentiation of their immediate predecessors was easy, as the fourth generation of Chinese filmmakers had already been identified as a group which shared a high degree of career frustration.

They were caught between two stronger currents. On one side were their own predecessors, many of whom could lay claim directly to the pre-1949 Shanghai cinema tradition. Even those who had only received their film training in the 1950s from Soviet-trained teachers could at least take some credit for helping to create China's new socialist cinema. Although socialist realism in its Stalinist version was never fully adopted, a film tradition fitfully emerged in the 1950s that combined the Shanghai legacy with the political direction of art first fully articulated at Yan'an.[196] On the other side was this distinctive group of younger directors, cinematographers and others making unexpectedly new-style films.

Most of the fourth generation artists were 1960s graduates from the Beijing Film Academy and the film training courses run at the Shanghai and Changchun studios at that time. Having entered professional filmmaking upon graduation, many had to wait close to twenty years for an opportunity to direct a film. The natural and man-made disasters associated with Mao Zedong's Great Leap Forward in 1958 caused a scaling down in film production in the early 1960s and closing of many provincial-level studios set up during the Great Leap. Film production slowed further after 1964, as political campaigns foreshadowed the Cultural Revolution. Feature filmmaking stopped from the start of the Cultural Revolution in 1966, although studio staff remained on duty (and collecting pay packets) until about 1969, when many artists were sent to the countryside and to other work units.

When film production (apart from documentaries) resumed in the early 1970s, the fourth-generation filmmakers had opportunities to practice on the film versions of the "model performances." The range of officially sanctioned cultural activities expanded after 1972 and the "model films" then made provided further occasions for younger filmmakers to apply their training. The new studio leaders trusted these post-1949 artists to follow instructions more carefully than their older, more established colleagues. The restrictions imposed by the cultural authorities, however, prevented much artistic fulfilment or originality in these 1970s works.

The late 1970s and early 1980s were a period of transition in Chinese art and literature.[197] Much writing and filming was devoted to an assessment of the Cultural Revolution and the influence of those "ten years of catastrophe." Fourth-generation filmmakers at last had fuller opportunities to display their talents and outlooks. Directors such as Teng Wenji, Yan Xueshu, Zhang Nuanxin and Wu Tianming made thoughtful examinations of Chinese life after the ten years had interrupted their careers. In retrospect, however, much of their work looked more like the continuation of an artistic and political tradition of film realism than a new beginning.[198] Just as they were getting into their stride, often with film adaptations of the post-Cultural Revolution "scar literature" about suffering during those years, along came the fifth generation to redefine Chinese cinema. The response from the more able fourth-generation directors was a reinvigoration of their own work. Indeed, as Huang Jianzhong, one of the most able of the fourth-generation artists later observed, both fifth and fourth generations came into their own almost simultaneously in the space of six or seven years.[199]

Zhang Nuanxin, who taught the class of '82 at the Beijing Film Academy, shows the impact of the class's films in her 1985 work, *Sacrificed Youth*. Her film also reflected the ambiguity of feelings about the Cultural Revolution years which the fourth and fifth generations to some extent shared. The narrator of the film is a woman who was sent down in the late 1960s from a Beijing high school to an isolated village in a Dai minority region in Yunnan province. As in the case of Hu Mei's *Army Nurse*, this off-screen narration helps make *Sacrificed Youth* a somewhat subjective work. Li Chun, the heroine, slowly becomes aware of the centrality in Dai life of beauty, nature and instinct. In contrast, her Han Chinese world is modern, pretentious and inhibited.[200] While some of her Beijing friends in neighboring villages feel exiled and unhappy, Li Chun is awakened to her own youth and an awareness of her own body. She recognizes that her parents and her own generation have been sacrificed to a political ideology that has destroyed their humanity. As she recalls at the end of the film, the Cultural Revolution was a time of great pain, and yet only through that experience has she gained a greater understanding of the world and herself.

Zhang Nuanxin's representation of the Dai minority marked a

Sacrificed Youth

departure from the usual mode of expression in the "happy, dancing natives" genre of the 1950s and 1960s. But comparison with the work of Tian Zhuangzhuang helps highlight the limitations of the fourth generation's work. Although Zhang uses an understated naturalism in *Sacrificed Youth*, the audience still confronts the minority culture through a Han intermediary, Li Chun.[201] The nostalgic framing of the presentation compounds the lyricism and emphasis on soft beauty in the film. Zhang's two cinematographers, Mu Deyuan and Deng Wei, were members of the class of '82. In contrast, Tian Zhuangzhuang's *On the Hunting Ground* and *Horse Thief* refuse to offer explanation or orientation. Their settings among northern and northwestern minorities help reinforce Tian's decision not to give audiences any help: these are cultures surviving in a harsh landscape, not the tropical lushness of the far southwest. The younger filmmakers did not necessarily feel obliged to spell everything out for audiences, unlike most Chinese film artists (and certainly their political managers) since 1949.

Huang Jianzhong was a fourth-generation director much stimulated by the innovation of the younger artists. In 1964, upon graduation from the film academy, Huang had been assigned to the Beijing Film Studio where he worked first as a log-keeper. After 1969 he spent nearly four years at a May Seventh Cadre School, working in the fields at the peak of his youth and creativity. Returning to the Beijing studio in 1973, he served as assistant director on a 1976 Gang of Four tribute to educational reform, *Breaking with Old Ideas* (*Juelie*). He worked in the same capacity in 1980 on *Xiao Hua*, a sentimental story of an orphaned young woman in the 1940s civil war and one of the most popular films of the immediate post-Cultural Revolution period.[202] With a fresh pictorialism reminiscent of fifth-generation work, Huang presented in his 1985 *A Good Woman* (*Liangjia funü*) the sexual frustrations of a peasant woman married to a child husband in the 1940s. The appearance in the film of a wildly bearded artist and a mad woman who live in the mountains was a somewhat excessive product of a directorial imagination just beginning to flourish.

Questions for the Living (*Sizhe dui shengzhe de fangwen*, 1986) was Huang's exploration of the relationships between individuals and society and was based on a controversial news story of the time. Some toughs rough up an inoffensive man on a city bus while none of the other passengers makes any effort to help. The thugs produce knives and kill the man, but the passengers still prefer not to become involved. The victim returns from the dead to elicit from some of the passengers their individual rationalizations for not offering help.

Questions for the Living was an essay on the previously taboo question of alienation in Chinese society. It also could be read as an allegory on the excesses of Cultural Revolution, during which most citizens kept a low profile. What gave Huang's film its particular zest was his inter-cutting between the contemporary world and a surreal landscape, littered with half-excavated (or half-buried) terracotta figures associated with the burial mound of China's first emperor, Qin Shihuangdi. The landscape is also peopled by the victim (a set designer for a theatre company), his girlfriend (who is an actress), a group of fur-clad primitive humans from the Stone Age and a swarm of naked, prepubescent boys. One of the primitives, muddy breasts bared, beats a huge Bronze Age drum. The setting recalls Tian Zhuangzhuang's fascination with "pre-civilized" societies. Again these are humans before the Fall engendered by literacy and strict codes of social behavior. The dead hero, his girlfriend and the others wander through this landscape, debating the morality of the incident on the bus with some of the passengers and with the murderer. Huang's effort at filmic philosophizing ultimately confuses, but the attempt deserves credit.

At the film academy the class of '82 earned a reputation for disrespect toward older filmmakers. One of their favorite targets was the director Teng Wenji, who represented for the class the limitations of the Chinese cinema they were determined to transform. The students even once passed a solemn resolution proclaiming: "Down with Teng Wenji!"[203] Undeterred, Teng used two of that class of '82 cinematographers and an art director who had been assigned to his Xi'an Film Studio to make *At the Beach* (*Haitan*), a film which answered much of the criticism with its innovation in style and content.

Gu Changwei and Zhi Lei give the seashore which is the focus of the film an almost religious quality, using the sun shimmering on the water or through mist to good effect. Fishermen have been deriving their livelihood and raising their families by the seashore for generations. Now the expansion of the city and its industries has begun to transform their lives. A petrochemical works lures young people with the offer of regular employment and urban worker status. The older villagers see the works as a threat to their fishing and the closed community (in which backwardness is symbolized by a village idiot). The elderly pray to the spirits of the fish, while their sons and daughters work for bonuses at the chemical plant. Teng Wenji brings out these tensions with lyrical imagery and a novel musical score by Tan Dun.

Even such a hackneyed topic as the biography of the founder of modern China made use of stylistic innovation. Ding Yinnan at the Pearl River Film Studio borrowed heavily from the fifth-generation visual repertoire in *Sun Yat-sen* (*Sun Zhongshan*), completed in 1986 to commemorate the 120th anniversary of the man who became the first (provisional) president of the Republic of China in 1912. Surprisingly, the film is more than a hagiographic tale. A 1966 graduate of the Beijing Film Academy, Ding had made several films which suggested the interest in his characters' psychologies that he brought to the Sun Yat-sen project. The subject matter and the occasion of the film somewhat inhibit this aspect, but the work is of consistent visual interest. A confrontational camera, for example, in the manner of *The Black-Cannon Incident* (*Hei pao shijian*), helps enliven the many scenes of revolutionaries meeting to plot the overthrow of the Qing dynasty.

The fourth-generation filmmaker most respected by the class of '82 was Wu Tianming. As head of the Xi'an Film Studio from the mid-

1980s until June 4th, Wu did more to encourage the new filmmakers than any other older colleague. Chen Kaige's *King of the Children*, Tian Zhuangzhuang's *Horse Thief* and Zhang Yimou's *Red Sorghum*, for example, all owed their existence to Wu Tianming's support and encouragement. The film that emerged from his co-operation with Zhang Yimou combined elements typical of the two generations of filmmakers. At first glance, another contribution to a hoary genre of rural revolution films, *Old Well* reflects instead the changes in Chinese life wrought by the Cultural Revolution and its aftermath. There is little here of the Communist Party and revolution. Wu, a trained film actor, also appears in the film as the county Party secretary who attends a young well-digger's funeral. In older films in this genre, the visitor would have seized the occasion to make a bombastic speech about supporting the revolution and remembering the deceased hero. Wu's Party secretary says not a word. His concern for the local people is expressed by a glance toward the bereaved mother and by his silent dismissal, with a wave of his hand, of two zealots who want to accuse the dead man of encouraging an obscene performance by a blind itinerant musician.

This treatment of the Party and the psychological dimensions of *Old Well* were less a product of fifth-generation influence than a reflection of changes in the 1980s common to all filmmakers. The very existence of these elements in the film, however, was a consequence of the transformation of Chinese filmmaking for which the emergence of the fifth generation was in part responsible. Zhang Yimou's hand in *Old Well* is apparent in much of the shooting. His trademark still camera, first seen in *One and Eight* and *The Yellow Earth*, presents the stasis that has held the village in the grip of the stone mountains for centuries. Even action scenes, such as when two groups of villagers fight over the rights to an ancient well, are presented with a detached camera style that lends them great power.

Wu Tianming's emphasis on the circle of the well-hole within the almost square proportions of the screen image, using two motifs of pre-Confucian vintage, draws attention to his thematic concerns. *Old Well*, Wu noted, presents the ancient ability of the Chinese to persist against adversity. These sentiments were shared by Zhang and the other former educated youths of his generation.

Xie Jin, at sixty-three, the pre-eminent third-generation artist, also responded to the challenge. His immensely popular 1986 melodrama, *Hibiscus Town* (*Furong zhen*), included a number of stylistic features that can be ascribed to an urge to prove that he too could handle these as skilfully as the younger artists. Its story of a small-town bean curd seller from the late 1950s until after the Cultural Revolution, however, attempted an epic quality that was untypical of fifth-generation work in the 1980s.

Xie Jin's limitations in responding to the challenge of the fifth generation stemmed from a fundamental difference in their approaches to film art. One of the younger directors pointed out the difference shortly after *Hibiscus Town* went into release in early 1987. Stretching his arms out, the director characterized Xie's approach to his subjects as taking a small event and giving it wider and wider significance, leaving the reality of the original events far behind. In contrast, Zhang Jianya suggested, the fifth generation took a subject and went increasingly into its nuances, giving it significance through depth rather than through lending it obvious epic qualities.[204]

The stylistic innovation and the outlook that Xie Jin was responding to was not confined to the Beijing Film Academy class of 1982. Several other filmmakers active in the 1980s shared their backgrounds and outlooks with that class. These other artists were born in the 1950s, had had their education disrupted and redirected during the Cultural Revolution, entered the film industry in the 1980s and produced innovative work. Prominent among them were Huang Jianxin and Zhou Xiaowen in Xi'an and Zhang Zeming in Guangzhou. The trajectories of their careers from the mid-1980s to the 1990s followed closely those of the other fifth-generation directors, from usually stern-faced examinations of the condition of China to efforts to achieve commercial success.

Huang Jianxin made the first fifth-generation comedy, *The Black-Cannon Incident*, China's first film satire in almost thirty years. Huang was thirty-one when he made his first feature in 1985 at his home studio in Xi'an. His own history fit the pattern of the fifth generation.[205] At the start of the Cultural Revolution Huang was still in elementary school. Classes were cancelled and his class encouraged to regard themselves as Little Red Guards, organizing neighborhood grandmothers to parade in the streets to denounce enemies of the revolution. In 1970, at age sixteen, he was sent to an air force base in Wuwei in Gansu province, where he serviced MIG fighters and also became a photo-journalist. After six years, as part of the nationwide demobilization of young soldiers that also released Chen Kaige and Tian Zhuangzhuang, Huang was assigned to *Health News* (*Weisheng bao*) back in Xi'an. He worked as a still photographer on the magazine and also made some crude 16 mm short films. In 1977 he joined a non-degree, journalism class in the Chinese department of Northwestern University, the leading university in the region.

When his studies ended a year and a half later, Huang Jianxin passed an examination to enter the Xi'an Film Studio as an editor in its script department. He already had some connection with the film industry: his father was head of the Xi'an Film Corporation, in charge of film distribution in the city. Huang and another young recruit at the Xi'an studio established a monthly magazine, *Western Film* (*Xibu dianying*) to publicize the studio's new works. Like other Chinese studios, Xi'an was beginning to gear up for full restoration of production after more than a dozen years of interruption. In these circumstances, Huang's talents were better used in actual production. He transferred to the directing department and worked as a log-keeper on several films before being promoted to the position of assistant director.

In June 1983 Huang was one of about forty-five candidates who participated in a nationwide examination to join an advanced training class at the Beijing Film Academy. Ten students were selected, seven from film studios and three from television stations. Huang went to Beijing in September, where the Zhuxinzhuang campus housed a short-term class of filmmakers from national minorities as well as Huang's group. A new, four-year degree class had not yet enrolled to succeed the class of '82. Huang did well at the academy, earning a high assessment from his teachers. How much he could learn there was sometimes unclear. He later recalled that at the end of a course on rhythm in films lasting several months, the teacher simply said: "It doesn't matter what I say about rhythm. You have to be born with it (*Na shi tiansheng de*)."[206]

Returning to Xi'an in the spring of 1985, Huang found a script in the studio by the Ningxia writer, Li Wei, based on a short story by Zhang Xianliang. The story idea appealed to him, and after rewriting about half of it, he started shooting *The Black-Cannon Incident* in July. As with the early fifth-generation films in Guangxi and Changsha, this was a young crew: the average age was twenty-seven. Wu Tianming, the studio head, helped find money from a West German producer to underwrite the production and provide one of the main actors.

The "black cannon" of the title is the name of a Chinese chess piece. Zhao Shuxin, an engineer, is sentimentally attached to his old chess set. When he returns from a trip and discovers this piece missing, he sends a cryptic telegram to a friend to look for it. Suspicious minds in the post office and at his work unit conclude that the telegram looks like a spy message in code. Zhao is prevented from serving in his usual capacity as interpreter for Hans Schmidt, a German expert who arrives to help install a massive new piece of equipment imported from his firm in Europe. The substitute interpreter, more used to guiding German tourists around museums and temples, botches his assignment, causing a major problem with the equipment. Zhao is brought back to the job and is ultimately cleared of suspicion.

In terms of its impact on audiences at home and abroad, *The Black-Cannon Incident* can be considered the urban equivalent of *The Yellow Earth*, although, unlike Chen Kaige's film, it was an immediate domestic success. As a satire, Huang's film had few predecessors. The only previous efforts at satire emerged briefly in 1956–57, during the Hundred Flowers period of relative political relaxation. Most of these satires were banned, and Lü Ban, the veteran filmmaker responsible for several of them, never made another film for the rest of his life (he died in 1976).[207] Perhaps only the boldness and resolution of Huang's fifth generation made this new effort at satire possible.

The German element in *The Black-Cannon Incident* reflected the extraordinary internationalization of Chinese urban life in the 1980s. China's cities were more open to cultural, social and economic contact with foreign cultures than at any time since the first half of the twentieth-century. The portrayal of the relationships between the German engineer and his Chinese colleagues, especially Zhao Shuxin, is the most believable of such film accounts. Hans Schmidt is neither hero nor villain, but a tough, hard-drinking professional, while Zhao represents a new kind of heroism in Chinese cinema: morally right, but confused and picked upon; socialist Chinese cinema's first anti-hero. Indeed, all the characters in the film share a characteristic Huang Jianxin described as inspired by Beijing opera. All the characters were "painted faces" (*lianpu*), with fixed natures and attitudes and do not change in the course of the film.[208]

Huang Jianxin's directing was similarly innovative. Objects and people are filmed full-on, sometimes with telephoto limiting of depth, from the first shots of Zhao's efforts to send a telegram to retrieve his missing chess piece to the final shots. The scenes of the works' committee meetings are striking. Huang decided to use an exaggeratedly simplified set, with a white cloth-covered table, white chairs, walls and curtains. The actors all wear white shirts. Art director Lu Yichuan's final, witty touch was the huge clock face which fills the wall behind the head of the table.

The color scheme of the film adds much to its impact. Red stands for neither revolution nor its older Chinese association with good fortune, but is the color of warning lights, signifying anxiety.[209]

One of the most intriguing features of *The Black-Cannon Incident* is the presentation of Zhou Yuzhen, the deputy secretary of the works' Party committee. Although her rigidity and suspicions when confronted with engineer Zhao's telegram are satirized, she comes across as a figure deserving sympathy. A dedicated Communist, she has problems keeping up with the times: her own children are abandoning the ideals that have guided her life. In some ways she represents the confusion of many of China's leaders faced with rapid economic and social change in the 1980s.

In an interview shortly after completing *The Black-Cannon Incident*, Huang Jianxin expressed admiration for a number of Western European directors, including Fassbinder, Wenders and Buñuel, whose work he had seen at the film academy.[210] Their films may have influenced Huang's tendency to find the absurd in everyday life. This was a vein he continued to mine throughout the 1980s and 1990s. As he noted in a later interview, his resolutely urban settings contrasted with the "root-seeking" rural locations of films like *Red Sorghum* and *King of the Children*. "On the question of China's cultural roots," he noted in 1994, "I'm inclined to the view that a culture's roots are in the here and now, in every individual."[211] His second film, *Dislocation* (*Cuo wei*), took further absurdist liberties with Zhao Shuxin, now a corporation head who invents a stand-in, look-alike robot.

In the summer of 1988 Huang made a film more closely connected to Chinese reality. One of several films made around that time that were adapted from short stories by Wang Shuo, *Samsara* (*Lunhui*, a.k.a. "Transmigration") presents the shiftless life and meaningless death of a typical product of the decade of economic reform. Shi Ba, the orphaned son of high Party cadres, has used his parents' connections to set himself up as an entrepreneur, wheeling and dealing on the fringes of the legitimate economy. A deal with some gangsters turns sour and Shi Ba is knee-capped. Sobered by this excruciating experience, he marries a ballet dancer but his life remains purposeless. Overcome by feelings of alienation from all around him, he leaps from the balcony of his apartment. The screen goes black, then a baby's cry is heard. A title announces that Shi Ba's son was born six months later. The cycle (*samsara* in Sanskrit) continues.

That summer was a high point in post-Cultural Revolution optimism for many Chinese, but corruption and the abuses of economic liberalization were becoming a matter of popular discontent, fuelled by unfamiliar, double-digit price inflation. Like his fifth-generation colleagues, Huang Jianxin captured on film the spirit of 1988.[212] A sequence in *Samsara* filmed in Tian'anmen Square took on a terrible irony the next summer. Shi Ba and two women friends try to tease the soldiers

Samsara

who raise the national flag and stand guard under it. Huang Jianxin seems to be reminding his audience that despite all the economic opportunism and abuse that Shi Ba represents, the apparatus of the state remains ready to assert itself.[213]

Zhang Zeming, born in 1951 in Guangzhou, was perhaps the only self-taught major film artist in the fifth generation. His senior high school studies were interrupted by the start of the Cultural Revolution, and in 1968 he was part of a large group sent to state farms in Wanning on the mountainous southeast coast of Hainan island. He returned to Guangzhou from the tropical island in 1978, two years after the arrest of the Gang of Four which marked the end of the Cultural Revolution. Having failed to pass the Beijing Film Academy entrance exams in the spring of 1978, Zhang was assigned to the Pearl River Film Studio. His father had worked as an actor at the studio before moving on to stage drama. His mother had directed documentary films, then was assigned to library work. Zhang's parents had known Jiang Haiyang's parents before 1949.

Zhang Zeming after 1978 worked from the bottom up, first as a production assistant and later as a camera assistant on such films as the lyrical *Longing for Home* (*Xiang qing*).[214] In 1981 he was promoted to continuity, working on *Three-Family Alley* (*San jia xiang*) and the patriotic political biography *Liao Zhongkai*. In 1983 Zhang again failed to gain acceptance by the Beijing Film Academy in the advanced training class that Huang Jianxin had joined. As word spread of the New Wave films like *One and Eight* and *The Candidate* from the hands of young filmmakers, the studio leadership in Guangzhou seems to have regretted their earlier decision not to take any of the film academy's 1982 graduates. Looking around for youthful artists with potential in their own studio, they found Zhang Zeming, trying his hand at script writing. He was encouraged to complete his film script, titled *Swansong* (*Juexiang*), and, after some debate, granted permission to direct it. Zhang Zeming's crew, with an average age of twenty-seven, was the Pearl River Film Studio's equivalent of the Youth Filming Groups in other studios. For most of the crew it was their first independent work on a production.

Zhang Zeming's debut film had an intensely personal quality that set it apart from other fifth-generation works, with the exception of Hu Mei's *Army Nurse*. *Swansong* is a quiet study of the generation gap and the private consequences of public decisions. The story centers on Ou Laoshu, a veteran Cantonese opera musician and composer. During the Cultural

Revolution years he was forced to abandon his traditional work and produce instead tedious "revolutionary" pieces. He kept, however, the original scores of his mentor. He dreams of working with an old friend who moved to Hong Kong to publish a comprehensive collection of Cantonese musical scores. Ou's son, Guanzai, returns home. When his father was publicly criticized at the start of the Cultural Revolution, Guanzai was shocked to learn of his decadent past and had left home. Before leaving his father, the boy had trained in classical music to succeed Ou. Now in the 1980s, he sits at a chicken stall in the free market, occasionally strumming a Western guitar. Guanzai wants nothing to do with his father, partly because he blames his embarrassing pre-1949 background (including opium smoking) for his own misfortunes. He also feels his father was responsible for his mother walking out on the family. Only after his father's death and reunion with his mother and half-sister does Guanzai really come to realize that his father was the only person who understood him.

In adapting for the screen a story written by a contemporary who had also spent time as an educated youth in Hainan, Zhang Zeming found room to add much of himself to the film. The evocation of the old-style back alleys of Guangzhou and of the folk culture that used to inhabit them is haunting. Unfortunately the language standardization that applied to all Chinese films since 1949 denied *Swansong*'s audiences the greater authenticity that a Cantonese-language soundtrack would lend it. Zhang makes full use of the fifth-generation hallmark of using naturalistic lighting in scenes in the old musician's home and on the quiet streets. The acting by Kong Xianzhu as Ou Laoshu avoids histrionics, combining great dignity and a deftness of touch rare for most Chinese film actors.

Swansong is not without flaws, particularly in the second half as the story turns to the return of Guanzai's mother and half-sister. The half-sister, a conservatory graduate, takes one of Ou Laoshu's compositions and, without acknowledging its origins, performs it as a Western-style piano concerto. The climactic concert is a forced note, out of harmony with the earlier lyricism.[215] *Swansong* won the cinematography and art direction prizes at the 1986 Golden Rooster awards, China's highest film honors. Zhang Zeming went on to make *Sun Showers* (*Taiyang yu*) in 1987. A modern story of friendship among urban youth, the film's tone and theme of alienation anticipated Huang Jianxin's *Samsara*. In 1988 Zhang married an English woman and went abroad to live.

Zhou Xiaowen was the most commercially successful of the fifth-generation directors, with the exception of Zhang Yimou. His series of "frenzy" films (they all had *fengkuang* in the title) made in the late 1980s proved highly attractive to urban audiences looking for thrilling tales of contemporary life. But his first film, directed with Fang Fang in 1986, was in a distinctly fifth-generation vein. *In Their Prime* (*Tamen zheng nianqing*) even shared its 1979 Vietnam border war setting with Wu Ziniu's banned *Dove Tree*.

Thirty-two when he co-directed the film, Zhou Xiaowen had entered the army, in which his father was an officer, in 1969 upon finishing high school in Beijing. After three years in the ranks, Zhou was allowed to take examinations to enter the May Seventh Art University in Zhuxinzhuang. He was a member of the second class at this Cultural Revolution academy: the first to enter by exam, not simply by virtue of being classified as worker-peasant-soldier students, though that status still helped secure admission. Zhou graduated from the cinematography department in 1975 and was assigned to the Xi'an Film Studio. Just before starting work on *In Their Prime*, he served as assistant director to Yan Xueshu on *In the Wild Mountains* (*Ye shan*).[216]

Fang Fang (originally Guo Fangfang) was thirty-four when she co-directed *In Their Prime*, immediately after finishing in 1986 a two-year course in directing at the Beijing Film Academy. She had completed junior high in 1969 and spent three years in the countryside before joining the Xi'an studio in 1971. After eight years in the studio's developing laboratory, Fang Fang became a log-keeper by passing a special studio examination. She had risen to assistant director rank and worked on a production before successfully taking the exam for the film academy's advanced training class. Most of her eleven classmates had also come from similar backgrounds.

With a crew whose average age was twenty-seven, Fang and Zhou spent forty days shooting on a blasted cliff-face near the Yunnan province border with Vietnam. Seven of the nine main actors in these war scenes were soldiers. The woman who plays a Vietnamese guerrilla had been discovered by a director's assistant on the street in a nearby town. Off the set, the actress was a planned parenthood worker. Synchronized sound recording proved impossible, as one of Xi'an's two recorders was being used by Wu Tianming in making *Old Well* and the other was with Chen Kaige, elsewhere in Yunnan on location with *King of the Children*.

In Their Prime was based on a script from the August First studio, revised by the directors. The film's army origins are striking, as it is an indictment of the experience of war. Labelling their film as "anti-war" troubled the two directors in an interview shortly after completing *In Their Prime*. "War is not something to praise, we can all agree," Zhou noted. The label, the directors felt, did not do justice to the full range of the film. Their focus was on the relations between war and people's lives and feelings. *Dove Tree* had been banned a year earlier for exploring similar ground. *In Their Prime* slipped through Film Bureau approval on 27 December 1986, in the lull between the nationwide student demonstrations for democratic reform in late 1986 and the consequent dismissal of Hu Yaobang from his Party Secretary position and the expulsion of several major intellectual figures from Party membership early in 1987.

Most of *In Their Prime* centers on a platoon of nine men trapped by enemy fire in a cave. They go for days without adequate water or fresh supplies, cut off from the rest of their unit. The naturalism of these cramped, sweaty scenes is underscored by a counterpoint with scenes from civilian life set in Beijing and filmed in deliberately expressionist style. The relationship of the two places is unclear until the end of the film: the Beijing scenes could be flashbacks or flash-forwards, but turn out to be the former. Images in the Beijing sequences serve the directors' thematic concerns. A beheaded doll on a kindergarten floor refers to the abortion planned by an officer's widow and also emphasizes the vulnerability of the soldiers trapped in the cave. In a military museum, the widow voices her confusion over whether to have his baby. The imposing cannons, tanks and aircraft of earlier campaigns fill the frame in confrontational shots as the soundtrack becomes increasingly unclear. The woman's uncertainty over whether to have an abortion turns into an hysterical garble. As she and her late husband's deputy leave the museum, a shot from above shows a huge statue of Mao Zedong gazing down on them with helpless benevolence. In the next shot the couple stand in the middle of Chang'an Avenue, central Beijing's main east-west thoroughfare, trapped by night-time traffic. The continued mixed-up sound and the sign "safety island," where they remain, emphasize the urban alienation that the men on the front are in effect fighting to protect.

The presentation of the Vietnamese enemy in *In Their Prime* reflects the humanism that the Beijing censors had found so offensive in *Dove Tree*. One Vietnamese soldier, who ties up the youngest Chinese soldier and cuts at his chest before being shot, is barely more than a terrified child. A Vietnamese guerrilla carries a baby on her back. The Chinese soldier who suddenly encounters her on the cliff only shoots her when she seems to throw a grenade at him as he goes to walk away. Her death off-screen is suggested by the sound of her baby crying. The scene cuts immediately to the Beijing hospital where the deputy company commander, leader of the men on the cliff, has accompanied the wife of the martyred officer to the abortion clinic. Hearing babies crying, he decides that the child of his dead comrade should be born, and drags the widow from the hospital. Later the Vietnamese are allowed to pick up their dead at the base of the cliff during a lull in the fighting. The Chinese soldiers, in digging a grave for a dead Vietnamese on the cliff, had earlier discovered older Vietnamese remains. Men have been fighting here for generations.

In the final sequence of *In Their Prime* the now six-month pregnant widow of the fallen officer has arrived at the front after a long journey. She has brought cartons of her husband's favorite cigarettes to put on his grave. She and the deputy commander spend a long time searching for the right grave among the hundreds on a hillside covered with serried rows of tombstones. The hill is filmed with telephoto lens and at a full-on angle to emphasize the weight of the deaths that the graves represent. The image

In Their Prime

fades to a black screen, the flames usually associated with revolutionary martyrdom then fill the frame and a children's a cappella choir sings: "Close our eyes, open our hearts. Let our souls soar into the blue sky."

Zhou Xiaowen and Fang Fang reported that, although they expected audiences to start leaving the theatre during the flames sequence, people were so moved that they remained in their seats until the song ended. *In Their Prime*'s certification to be shown abroad was withdrawn in 1987. The army leadership, reportedly fearful that the film would affect recruiting, insisted that the Film Bureau ban the film. Zhou Xiaowen made some cuts in order to appease the objectors, but the Film Bureau appears to have been intimidated and the film was not released in China.

Zhou Xiaowen then went on to direct highly successful commercial films, that beneath their action and excitement, contained some sharp social commentary. *Desperation* (*Zuihou de fengkuang*, literally "The Last Frenzy," 1987) follows a police detective's obsession with catching a criminal whose single-mindedness is matched by the policeman's own. In *Obsession* (*Fengkuang de daijia*, literally "The Price of Frenzy," 1988) a young woman searches obsessively for the man who raped her sister. Again the distinctions between criminal and innocent are deliberately blurred. In both films Zhou Xiaowen was a pioneer in showing how a fifth-generation sensibility could be channelled into highly commercial films. In 1990 he completed a non-commercial, art film titled *Black Mountain Road* (*Hei shan lu*), about a small group living on their wits in a ruined church near the Burmese border during the war with Japan. In its brutalism of subject matter and attitude, the film was reminiscent of *One and Eight* from seven years earlier.

A 1986 film by a young director at the Emei Film Studio in Sichuan province showed how much the fifth generation's innovation extended to other filmmakers in that decade. *Visions from a Jail Cell* (*Moku zhong de huanxiang*) was the first feature by Wang Jixing, a thirty-seven-year-old writer from the 1984–86 advanced training class at the Beijing Film Academy. The film explores the mind of a small boy, a six-year-old "political prisoner," born and raised in a Nationalist jail in the 1940s. Learning about the world outside the prison from a newly arrived little girl, he fantasizes about what life is like on the outside. Knowing no other world, he imagines the school is headed by the chief jailer and that play in the school yard is like the tedium of prison-yard exercise sessions. The boy's visions sour when an authority figure who resembles the chief warder intervenes. One day the boy seems to have been granted his wish to visit the world outside. It is more beautiful than he had imagined, with children clad in clean white gowns singing a heavenly chorus. But the dream comes to a sudden, violent conclusion.

Despite the staginess of the writing and rapid visual and thematic exhaustion of the notion of the real world's resemblance to a big jail, *Visions from a Jail Cell* was a remarkable film. Standard fifth-generation techniques in framing and composition are applied to the fantasy sequences. The political significance extends far beyond the historical setting. The metaphor of life seen from inside a jail was one of the boldest suggestions of political dissent ever to reach China's screens. Its achievement served as a gauge as the political climate grew colder after events in Tian'anmen Square in June 1989.

Conclusion:
Generating the New

—ɯ—

This study has presented an account not only of a group of filmmakers who fundamentally changed Chinese cinema, but also of changes in Chinese society from the Cultural Revolution through the 1990s. From the point of view of a film enterprise that served over one billion people, the history of this group and the artistic revolution they lead was of great importance. But the men and women introduced in these pages are as much of interest for what they tell us about the transformation of Chinese society in the last third of the twentieth-century.

Central to the fifth generation was their individual and collective experiences in the Cultural Revolution. As the histories of some key members of the group indicate, the disruption of family life, the ending of formal education and the sending out into society that happened after 1966 were crucial in the development of most of the members of the Beijing Film Academy class of '82. Individual stories differ, but the broad experience was shared with a whole cohort of other Chinese. The political and cultural upheaval of the 1960s and 1970s helped create the conditions for the questioning of previous orthodoxies by all thinking Chinese. Even the leaders of the nation started wondering about their established ways of organizing China. One result was the economic reforms promulgated under Deng Xiaoping after 1978. The most pertinent questioning of past practices, however, came from younger Chinese. Their exposure, during the Cultural Revolution, to parts of Chinese society was unprecedented in modern Chinese history, except during the war against Japan. Through most of the preceding centuries Chinese scholars had usually managed to keep a distance from less educated people. This was one of Mao Zedong's obsessions when he called on educated adolescents in 1966 to discard old patterns of thought, overthrow representatives of the scholarly elite and destroy vestiges of the old culture.

The youthful intellectuals who were sent from the high schools to the countryside or to urban factories learned different kinds of lessons in the state-owned farms, in poorly constructed housing built for them by reluctant farmers obliged to accept them, in the workshops of factories or in army barracks. A high proportion of these educated youths responded to this "education" with resentment and withdrawal. Others, often with backgrounds in which respect for learning was well established, made use of their banishment from the classrooms to learn about society in ways impossible behind a school desk. Some took to self-learning of foreign languages or other specialities. With the benefit of not receiving a proper Chinese education, most had time to think about China and their place in it.

The years they spent at the Beijing Film Academy between 1978 and 1982 provided these artists with the means to express their new thinking. For those who had not even completed high school, it was their last chance at a formal education. Just as important was the public intellectual openness and curiosity possible during those years. The Democracy Wall ferment was a symptom of the re-examination of the political history of the previous three decades being conducted at all levels in society, which the film academy students could not ignore. Another important element in their film-school experience was the interaction between the students themselves. Several emphasized later how much they learned from each other rather than from their instructors. Also of vital significance was the exposure the class of '82 was given to international cinema. Earlier filmmakers had never enjoyed this range of access to foreign films, not even the creators of the Shanghai film legacy in the 1930s. After 1978 access included a range of non-Marxist aesthetic and other theories. Charting the influence on the students of reading Freud and viewing Buñuel and Tarkovsky is difficult. The students spoke years later, however, of the stimulation, no matter how brief or fragmentary, of novel ideas and movies. Other educated young Chinese in a range of fields were equally stimulated by China's opening up to new ideas, theories and ways of talking about the world. Their response included new kinds of poetry, fiction, painting, theatre, performance art, dance and music.

Their film academy teachers knew that the class of '82 was different from previous students. Through a number of films, represented most dramatically on the international scene by *The Yellow Earth*, the freshness of this group's art and attitudes became obvious. The innovation seen in the finest films from the 1930s and 1940s (and subsumed by socialist artistic strictures after 1949) returned to Chinese cinema, but the changes in the 1980s had unique features. For almost the first time since at least 1949 and perhaps since the 1930s a group of filmmakers emerged whose primary means of expression was film art. They did not see film primarily as a means to promote social reform, political transformation or to strengthen the nation. They were not interested in making respectful and moving adaptations of great literature, which might bring this writing to the enjoyment of a wider audience. The young film graduates in the 1980s wanted simply to make great films.

A common characteristic was their rejection of the falseness typical of much of their predecessors' work. In this they again were reflecting wider attitudes among younger artists in the 1980s. Audiences and older artists had voiced disquiet with the false for decades, but the new filmmakers were equipped to do something about the problem. Their experience suggested that the falsity lay not simply in highly politicized scripts and their stage-inspired filming. The distance between most older film artists and social reality was fundamental to the shortcomings of Chinese cinema prior to the emergence of the new generation. Given this gap, Party cultural leaders could claim a direct understanding of mass political and artistic audiences and command what should be produced for them. In centuries past emperors, chaffing at bureaucratic restrictions, had also been wont to claim a special connection with their subjects. Previous filmmakers had no means to dispute what Party leaders concluded were the masses' needs and wants. The fifth-generation veterans of the Cultural Revolution had their own firm notions of what the masses were like, having spent years living and working alongside ordinary citizens. Many realized, indeed, that the very expression "the masses" had little meaning, given the variety of people they had encountered in their somewhat forced growing up in the previous two decades.

One startling innovation on the part of this new generation was the notion that mass audiences could be differentiated, and some films appeal to more intellectual tastes. Here again the diversity of avant-garde art and literature that emerged from roots in the 1970s also paralleled developments in film. The new films relied less on dialogue to convey their meanings than on images. These were often raw or harsh views of the margins of society or of the landscapes of the birthplace of Chinese civilization. The major change was the way these films invited audiences to think about what they were seeing, rather than addressing them as if in a classroom. Many Chinese had already become inured to this kind of paternalistic posturing that had enfeebled political as well as artistic audiences.

The result was a fundamental change in thinking about what it meant to be Chinese. In literature, art and drama young artists in the 1980s injected a high degree of innovation and vigor into all areas of cultural practice. Much of the new works and thinking had started in the 1970s, even in the later years of the Cultural Revolution, as informal underground groups of poets and other intellectuals began to dabble in the excitement and risk of experimentation. They did this at a time when most officially sanctioned art and writing had fallen into mind-numbing patterns. One of the sources of the new artistic impetus was the so-called "opening up" of China which was part of the economic liberalization introduced after 1978. Influences, both direct and indirect, from international exposure encouraged a critical re-examination of being Chinese. As Huang Jianxin, a fifth-generation director by age and experience, pointed out in 1998: "Reform and opening up gave us a new space for creativity. History (or we could say, the Cultural Revolution) gave us good time in which to be free of control and free to grow up."[1]

The group that appeared in filmmaking was only one of the most highly visible of a whole generation which entered Chinese public life in the 1980s. The films made in the middle of that decade joined a so-called "cultural fever" (*wenhua re*, literally "culture hot"), in which Chinese civilization was placed under examination. Some writers and artists lead an effort to "search for the roots" of Chinese culture, finding it not in the settled, cultivated areas of eastern central China, but on the margins. In the regions where ancient cultures and kingdoms had been conquered by a centralizing Chinese state, writers thought they found aboriginal cultural spirits that challenged the centuries-old orthodoxy. Folk art was more vital and considered more authentic than the polished, somewhat lifeless and predictable art of the cultural heartland, after centuries of Confucian and lately Marxist accretion.[2]

Zhang Yimou's *Red Sorghum* (1987) was a highly significant film, for it served as a marker for several of these trends. In presenting a world of natural, unfettered instincts ungoverned by organized religion, political ideology or established power holders, *Red Sorghum* brought this "cultural fever" to a mass audience. But it also marked the apogee of the fifth-generation enterprise and the beginning of the dissipation of that effort in the face of new, more commercial pressures.[3]

Like all films made in the Chinese industry after 1949, the work of the fifth generation had to negotiate the obstacles of Film Bureau approval and politicians' interest at all levels of the Party apparatus. Until the 1980s, film was invested with all the expectations, on the part both of audiences and of managers, that television enjoyed in Western societies. This increased the attention given to film. The rapid expansion of television as a medium of entertainment and education that coincided with the emergence of the fifth generation may have diminished some of the official importance ascribed to film. But this change did not mean that the censors were less vigilant. The fate of the films of the fifth-generation was as dependent as others' works on the changing currents of cultural and political thaw in the 1980s.

After the pulling back from the centrally endorsed liberalization of the Democracy Wall criticisms, the fitful attacks on Bai Hua's *Unrequited Love* in 1981 appeared to mark a return to the old, pre-1978 habits of singling out representative films or other artistic works for public criticism.[4] This tendency seemed confirmed by the campaign between the fall of 1983 and the spring the following year against the pernicious "spiritual pollution" (*jingshen wuran*) attributed to ideas from abroad. The failure of this half-hearted campaign hinted that looser control of film and other media might prevail. The fifth National Congress of Writers and Artists in December 1984–January 1985 heard some of the boldest calls for artistic autonomy that had been voiced by artists or officials since the Hundred Flowers discourse of 1956. But limits remained. Large-scale demonstrations by students in many cities in late 1986 drew attention to the increasing disjunction between recent economic liberalization and continuing political restriction. The rising expectations voiced in these urban protests were quickly met with the cold blast of yet another official campaign criticizing "bourgeois liberalization." The spring warmth of a cultural thaw returned with the thirteenth Communist Party Congress in 1987. But the contest between the most conservative figures and the reformers in the political leadership remained unresolved.

The relative relaxation of 1988 proved exhilarating for many Chinese students and intellectuals. Again Zhang Yimou's *Red Sorghum* served as a symbol of the optimism of the time. Across Chinese cities young men were apt to burst into a song from the film, expressing a joy in life uninhibited by rules and manners. But building up were economic pressures, including a growing public disquiet at official corruption and alarm at inflation, that set the scene for protests in the spring of 1989 in Beijing's Tian'anmen Square and elsewhere.

Any artists working in these changing circumstances had problems and the fifth-generation filmmakers were particularly vulnerable. In the studios, studio leaders read the cultural thermometer and practised self-censorship at the script stage before much money had been expended on a project. Adjustments, both large and small, could begin to undermine or weaken the scriptwriter's and director's intentions before any film footage was exposed. Once a new film was finished, the studio management again tried to ensure that what they sent up for higher-level inspection would not bring trouble down on their heads. Local organs, particularly of the Party, often had a say in the production from the studios. As in centuries past, local officials feared provoking the wrath of the central authorities in Beijing. Further adjustments to the finished film could be demanded by the central Film Bureau before the movie could be released.

The criteria for interference in artistic intent were different in China, but the system operated in effect along lines familiar to filmmakers elsewhere. In Hollywood or Hong Kong the criteria usually involved the box office and producers' caution at spending money on projects that would not find audiences. Film is an expensive and risky business everywhere. Fifth-generation directors recognized that the relative neglect of box-office returns in China (at least until the late 1980s) allowed them to make films that could never be produced abroad in a strictly commercial industry.[5] This freedom from commercial pressure that the new filmmakers experienced in the mid-1980s was a major factor in allowing a space for the emergence of these new-style Chinese films. From the perspective of the early twenty-first century, they were utopian times.

Finding an audience for innovative films produced in this system in the 1980s was not easy. The release of fifth-generation films coincided with a slump in Chinese cinema attendances, which alarmed both filmmakers and their managers. The rapid acceleration of television set ownership made entertainment at home easier to come by.[6] Imported programing and foreign films in theatres also attracted more popular interest than the Chinese product. This broadening of the range of recreational options available to the public helped empty the cinemas showing Chinese films. By one estimate, film audiences declined from 29.3 billion in 1979 to 16.85 billion in 1989.[7] By the mid-1990s, the Hollywood dominance of cinema in China, last seen in the late 1940s (when it was replaced by Soviet dominance), returned. Each year ten Hollywood titles were imported and monopolized audiences at the expense of the local product.[8]

The problems of finding an audience were particularly severe in the 1980s for films by the fifth generation. These often difficult, challenging works needed to cultivate a new audience, but experiments with designating "art-house" cinemas in the mid-1980s in Shanghai and some other cities were short-lived. Some of the stylistic features of the new films were unattractive, especially the natural lighting and downright gloom (in rejection of the usual glossy brightness of mainstream Chinese films). Many people first saw these new-style films on television. Even with ideal transmission and reception conditions, the murk on a television screen could render the films incomprehensible and obliterate their cinematographic nuance. Here again *Red Sorghum* was a marker of ways in which fifth-generation filmmaking could find a mass audience. It was a signal taken up by Chen Kaige in *Farewell, My Concubine* and further developed by Zhang Yimou in the first half of the 1990s.

By the end of the 1980s the most vital talents from the class of '82 and their counterparts were in their middle and late thirties. A younger group of filmmakers was about to graduate from film school and had already been identified (though rather meaninglessly) as the "sixth generation." These younger people were better equipped to contribute to the youth culture that was emerging as the Cultural Revolution years became a distant memory and consumerism engaged the energies of people who had once been labelled "the masses." As they produced more films, the difference in artistic temperaments and political and social outlooks that had always existed among the classmates of '82 perhaps became more important than the similarities. The label "fifth generation" began to lose its utility.[9] By the turn of the twenty-first century the kinds of obsessions about China, its identity, its cultural roots and shortcomings, that lay at the heart of the fifth-generation enterprise seemed old-fashioned and even irrelevant. Globalization and nationalist responses to those impulses changed the context and manifestations utterly. The northern Shaanxi waist-drum dancers, first screened in *The Yellow Earth*, could be brought out to provide local color for entertainment that was as much global as Chinese.

In the fall of 1980, while in the first semester of his third year at film school, Chen Kaige was cautious, predicting that it would take ten years for his generation to make an impact: "When we reach middle age, there'll be some hope that the system will have changed enough to allow worthwhile films."[10] Four years later his first film, *The Yellow Earth* had an impact not even Chen could have foreseen.

Events centering on Tian'anmen Square in the spring of 1989 served to remind the fifth generation as much as anyone else in China of how far times had changed. The students who claimed possession of the square and bravely turned it into something resembling an enormous political carnival were barely out of their teenage years. For them the fifth generation's obsession with ideology, with Chineseness and with the Cultural Revolution seemed positively quaint. But the spring protests in 1989 were only possible through the transformation of Chinese unofficial, public discourse that the fifth generation had helped push through.

On the morning of June 4th, 1989 the main streets of Beijing were in ruins. For film artists, political strictures became more confining and further complicated the problems produced by the commercial pressures of falling box-office receipts. Stories set safely in the past and co-productions with foreign investors were ways around these political and commercial pressures. The artistic integrity and accomplishment of films like Zhang Yimou's *Judou* and Tian Zhuangzhuang's *The Blue Kite* suggested that all was not lost. Within three years of the Beijing incident, in the midst of rapid economic growth, artistic activity reached a level of innovation and boldness that approached that of 1988. The cultural climate, however, remained highly changeable throughout the 1990s.

By this time the relative coherence of the fifth generation had faded. Having reached middle age, individual members of the class of '82 made up the central corps in Chinese filmmaking. They had more choice in what they made, whether films or television dramas, could command higher budgets and could expect more international co-production opportunities than any other film professionals. But they did so as individuals, who could call upon a distinguished heritage, rather than as a group.[11] This history has tried to show how the New Wave which this group produced could not have happened in Chinese cinema until the mid-1980s. But the fifth-generation innovation flourished for only a few years, then was overtaken by broader changes in China. It was a passing phenomenon whose success required its obliteration by it being adopted and adapted by others. Some of the filmmakers who had created the New Wave still had long careers ahead of them. And for the first time in Chinese history, the world was watching.

Notes

—ɯ—

Introduction

1. The first generation had been active in the 1920s and even earlier, when Chinese began to make feature films. The second generation had been responsible for the politically charged artistic achievements of the 1930s. The main corps of new China's fimmakers in the 1950s were the third generation. The fourth had started in the film industry in the 1960s, had their careers interrupted by the Cultural Revolution, and become active again in the late 1970s. Some scholars attribute the first use of the term "fifth generation" to Ni Zhen, a professor at the Beijing Film Academy since 1980, though he demurs: see Ni Zhen, *Memoirs from the Beijing Film Academy: The Genesis of China's Fifth Generation* (translated by Chris Berry), Durham: Duke University Press, 2002, pp. 188–190.

Part One

1. The limitations of these histories that make up the group biography are obvious. For the most part, my main source has been the person who told each story. Most information comes from interviews and informal interactions over a number of years. I did not use a tape recorder, as a good deal of these memories have an intimacy, personal and political, that a recording machine might not have elicited. In interviews, I took notes in English and Chinese. I may of course have misheard some things. On other occasions, a detailed daily journal afforded an opportunity to record information gained in informal settings.

2. Unlike the collective biography presented here, Ni Zhen's 2003 book (*Memoirs from the Beijing Film Academy*, first published in Japanese in 1995 and in Chinese in 2002) provides biographical information on these filmmakers in a somewhat free-form, less systematic and often less detailed manner.

3. Edgar Snow wrote about these young soldiers in his influential 1937 report from Yan'an: *Red Star Over China*, Harmondsworth: Penguin Books, 1972 revised edition, pp. 369–375.

4. The information on Hu Mei that follows is largely based on two interviews in Beijing, 19 May and 24 May 1986.

5. The information on Chen Kaige in this chapter is from conversations with Chen over twenty years, since first interviewing him in Beijing in November 1980, when he was halfway through film school. Further detail can be found in his

autobiographical *Shaonian Kaige* (Growing Paeans or Songs of Childhood, also literally Young Kaige), Taipei: Yuanliu Publishing Corporation, 1991 and from Bonnie S. McDougall, *The Yellow Earth: A Film by Chen Kaige*, Hong Kong: The Chinese University Press, 1991. A version of the autobiography appeared on the mainland (Beijing: Renmin wenxue chubanshe) in 2001.

6. An interview with Tian Zhuangzhuang in Beijing on 8 June 1988 provided most of the material on his life in this chapter.

7. Much of this biography is drawn from an interview with Peng Xiaolian, Beijing, 3 June 1988. In mid-2000 Peng Xiaolian published a prize-winning account of her parents, *Tamen de suiyue* (Their times), Shanghai: Shanghai wenyi chubanshe.

8. A long interview with Liu Miaomiao in Beijing on 10 May 1986 is the main source on her life for this chapter.

9. Interviews with Zhang Yimou in April 1985 (Hong Kong), December 1985 (Honolulu), 27 April 1986 (Xi'an) and 11 April 1988 (Hong Kong), as well as conversations since provided much of the material for his life in this chapter.

10. Much of this biography is from an interview with Zhang Li in Beijing, 4 June 1988.

11. This biography is drawn from interviews with Zhang Jianya in Shanghai, 16 May 1986, 20 March 1987, and 2 July 1988.

12. This biography is drawn mainly from an interview with Jiang Haiyang in Shanghai, 15 May 1986.

13. Most of this biography of Wu is drawn from interviews in Beijing, 12 May 1986, and Fuzhou, 5 July 1988. It has been checked against a brief account in Hua Jun, *Diwudai* (The fifth generation), Beijing: Baijia chubanshe, 1988, pp. 136–137. See also Liu Weihong, "Yu Wu Ziniu tan Wu Ziniu" (Wu Ziniu on Wu Ziniu), *Dangdai dianying* (Contemporary cinema), 1988, No. 4 (August), pp. 109–110.

14. See Jasper Becker, *Hungry Ghosts: Mao's Secret Famine*, New York: The Free Press, 1996.

15. The extent to which this episode affected Wu Ziniu came through in a 5 July 1988 interview. For four years at the Beijing Film Academy, Wu says, he never told a soul about his older sister's experience: *Dangdai dianying*, 1988, No. 4 (August), p. 110.

16. An episode in the novel provided the basis for the Cultural Revolution model opera *Taking Tiger Mountain by Strategy* (*Zhiqu Weihushan*). On the novel and opera, see Robert E. Hegel, "Making the Past Serve the Present in Fiction and Drama: From the Yan'an Forum to the Cultural Revolution," in Bonnie S. McDougall, ed., *Popular Chinese Literature and Performing Arts in the People's Republic of China, 1949–1979*, Berkeley: University of California Press, 1984, pp. 197–223, especially pp. 214–223.

17. For a pioneering study of the "sent down" youth, see Thomas P. Bernstein, *Up*

to the Mountains and Down to the Villages: The Transfer of Youth from Urban to Rural China, New Haven: Yale University Press, 1977. See also two excellent, detailed histories: Ding Xuanzhuang, *Zhongguo zhiqing shi: Chu lang (1953–1968)* (A history of China's sent-down youth: The first wave), Beijing: Zhongguo shehui kexueyuan chubanshe, 1998 and Liu Xiaomeng, *Zhongguo zhiqing shi: Da chao (1966–1980)* (A history of China's sent-down youth: The great wave), Beijing: Zhongguo shehui kexueyuan chubanshe, 1998. The latter provides the relevant statistics on pp. 180–184.

18. His mother returned to Xi'an in 1976. Zhang's father was only able to return to the city in 1980, when his "counter revolutionary" label was removed.

19. Hua Jun, p. 23.

20. Hua Jun, pp. 24–25.

21. Hua Jun, pp. 26–27.

22. On the importance of such connections, see Zhai Xuewei, *Mianzi, renqing, guanxi wang* (Face, feelings, networks), Zhengzhou: Henan renmin chubanshe, 1994, especially pp. 266–278, and Andrew Kipnis, *Producing* Guanxi: *Sentiment, Self, and Subculture in a North China Village*, Durham: Duke University Press, 1997.

23. Tian Fang and Yu Lan had meanwhile returned from rural detention to the Beijing Film Studio in October 1972 to lead a small executive staff in commencing feature film production for the first time in six years. Tian Fang's health had deteriorated in detention and at the cadre school. He died in August 1974 at age sixty-three, his name still blackened by Red Guard accusations.

24. See Liu Xiaomeng, p. 180.

25. See Paul Clark, *Chinese Cinema: Culture and Politics since 1949*, Cambridge: Cambridge University Press, 1987, p. 144.

26. For perspective on this apparently tiny income, we should note that one cent (*fen*) in those days could buy three hen's eggs in the countryside.

27. Interview with Zhang Yimou, Hong Kong, 11 April 1988. See also Chen Kaige, "Qinguo ren: Ji Zhang Yimou" (A man of Qin: On Zhang Yimou), *Dangdai dianying*, 1985, No. 4 (September), p. 103.

28. Chen Kaige, "Qinguo ren," p. 103.

29. Qu Wei, "Zoufang Xiying" (A Visit to the Xi'an Film Studio), *Beijing dianying xueyuan xuebao* (Journal of the Beijing Film Academy), 1988, No. 1 (January), p. 183.

30. Zhang and she were married in 1982, the year he graduated from the Beijing Film Academy. Chen Kaige, "Qinguo ren," p. 103.

31. Hua Jun claims Wu Ziniu studied for a little over two years, from early 1972 to spring 1974, p. 30.

32. This extra study is reported in Hua Jun, p. 34.

33. Hua Jun, p. 35.

34. See Clark, *Chinese Cinema*, Chapter V.
35. In other periods since 1949 frustrated actors had complained publicly about their unemployment: see Clark, *Chinese Cinema*, p. 73.
36. Playing Zhang Jianya's wife in the film was Pan Hong, who in the 1980s became one of China's best known screen actresses: interview with Zhang Jianya, Shanghai, 2 July 1988.
37. See *Zhongguo yishu yingpian bianmu, 1949–1979* (Chinese art film catalogue), Beijing: Zhongguo dianying chubanshe, 1982, pp. 1074 and 1194 respectively.
38. Interview with Zhang Li, Beijing, 4 June 1988.
39. *Zhonghua renmin gongheguo dianying shiye sanshiwunian, 1949–1984* (Thirty-five years of the film industry of the People's Republic of China), Beijing: Zhongguo dianying chubanshe, 1985, p. 215.
40. For a description of this Jiangxi drama form, see *Zhongguo da baike quanshu: Xiqu quyi* (Great China encyclopedia: Opera and musical theatre), Beijing: Zhongguo da baike quanshu chubanshe, 1983, p. 146.
41. I lived in Beijing as a student with Chinese room-mates from October 1974 until July 1976 and observed the public-private mix first-hand.
42. Spoken plays (*huaju*) only began to be performed in China in the 1910s, though they had Western, missionary-inspired antecedents. Stage drama for most Chinese until the late twentieth century meant performances with songs and musical accompaniment.
43. Interview with Tian Zhuangzhuang, Beijing, 8 June 1988. Among his other appearances in folktales, Sun Wukong was the hero of *Journey to the West* (*Xiyou ji*), one of China's earliest vernacular novels.
44. The industrial, regimented nature of life in Dazhai was apparent when I visited Dazhai in June 1975.
45. The academy had been reformed in 1970 as part of the May Seventh Art University on a new, rural campus, with initial film specialties in sound recording and lighting: Clark, *Chinese Cinema*, pp. 142 and 204 note 66. After 1976 short-term film training courses had been conducted on the campus, now dedicated to the film school.
46. Zhang Jianya cited this number in an interview, Shanghai, 16 May 1986. For a wide-ranging account of the examination process, see Ni Zhen, *Memoirs of the Beijing Film Academy*, pp. 8–50.
47. Hua Jun, p. 36.
48. Chen Kaige described the exam process in detail in a long interview with me in Beijing, 21 November 1980.
49 . He told this to an army art student audience in late 1999: "Zhang Yimou de 'mou yi shuo'" (Zhang Yimou on art), *Zhongguo wenyi jia* (Chinese writers and artists), 2000, No. 1 (January), p. 21.
50. Interview with film academy cinematography professor Zheng Guo'en, Beijing, 9 June 1988.

Part Two

1. I follow American convention in calling them the "class of '82." Chinese usage is to refer to them as the "class of '78."

2. For a contemporary account of these developments, see Roger Garside, *Coming Alive: China after Mao*, New York: New American Library, 1981, pp. 182 ff.

3. For an account of this Shanghai legacy and its attempted transformation in the 1950s, see Clark, *Chinese Cinema*, Chapters I and II.

4. See the chapter on the Beijing Film Academy in *Zhonghua renmin gongheguo dianying shiye sanshiwunian, 1949–1984*, pp. 378–386.

5. May 7, 1966 was the date of a widely publicized letter from Mao to the army commander Lin Biao in which Mao wrote of the need to train peasants in military affairs, politics, and culture.

6. Interview with Zheng Guo'en, Beijing, 9 June 1988.

7. See Paul Clark, "The film industry in the 1970s," in Bonnie McDougall, ed., *Popular Chinese Literature and Performing Arts*, pp. 177–196.

8. Ni Zhen, *Memoirs from the Beijing Film Academy*, pp. 51–147, covers the ground of this chapter in greater detail and with some diversions.

9. Interview with Chen Kaige, then a third-year student, Beijing, 21 November 1980.

10. Interview with Chen, 21 November 1980.

11. *Zhonghua renmin gongheguo dianying shiye sanshiwunian, 1949–1984*, p. 380.

12. A "Resolution on Certain Questions in the History of Our Party Since the Founding of the People's Republic of China" was later adopted by the Sixth Plenary Session of the Eleventh Central Committee of the Chinese Communist Party on 27 June 1981 in an effort to fix the official version of Party history from its founding in 1921 to 1981.

13. Later, when she was thinking in 1984 of applying to study in the U.S.A., Peng altered the English version of her transcript so that "Party history" now read "history" and a pass was recorded: interview with Peng Xiaolian, Beijing, 3 June 1988.

14. Interview with Chen, 21 November 1980. As he became more famous, Chen appears to have elaborated some aspects of his life, reportedly suggesting, for example, that he had tried opium while in Yunnan province as an educated youth.

15. Xie Fei, "Xin shiqi: Nan yi wanghuai de niandai" (The new age: Unforgettable decades), *Dangdai dianying*, 1998, No. 6 (November), p. 46.

16. Interview with Jiang Haiyang, then in his third year at film school, Shanghai, 2 December 1980; also visit to the Zhuxinzhuang campus of the Beijing Film Academy, 5 November 1980; interview with Chen Kaige, 21 November 1980.

17. On the film, see Mira Liehm and Antonin J. Liehm, *The Most Important Art: Soviet and Eastern European Film After 1945*, Berkeley: University of California Press, 1977, p. 320.

18. Visit to Beijing Film Academy at Zhuxinzhuang campus, 5 November 1980.

19. Interview with Chen Kaige, 21 November 1980. At that stage the academy itself had only just begun planning to build its own teaching film collection, soon made easier by the advent of small-format videotapes.

20. Interview with Zhang Yimou, Beijing, 11 May 1986.

21. Interview with Zhang, 11 May 1986.

22. Interview with Jiang Haiyang, Shanghai, 15 May 1986.

23. Interview with Zhang Li, Beijing, 4 June 1988. One of these paintings, "Father" (*Fuqin*) by Luo Zhongli, a huge photorealist portrait of a weather-beaten peasant, achieved iconic status in representing the move to a new kind of art. For a discussion of these developments, see Maria Galikowski, *Art and Politics in China, 1949–1984*, Hong Kong: The Chinese University Press, 1998, pp. 175–246. Ni Zhen provides a useful overview of these changes in art: *Memoirs from the Beijing Film Academy*, pp. 88–93.

24. Interview with Zhang Yimou, 11 May 1986.

25. Visit to the Zhuxinzhuang campus, 5 November 1980.

26. In 1980 there were roughly 9 million television sets in China. Twelve years later, there were close to 200 million sets.

27. The drama was *A Summer Experience* (*Xiatian de jingli*), produced for a private company: interview with Tian Zhuangzhuang, Beijing, 8 June 1988.

28. Interview with Zhang Yimou, Beijing, 11 May 1986.

29. Interview with Peng Xiaolian, Shanghai, 1 July 1988.

30. Interview with Zhang Yimou, 11 May 1986.

31. Xie Fei led the students in making the black-and-white film, though he remade the film in color as sole director the following year. Xie Fei, "'Women de tianye' daoyan chanshu" (Director's statement on *Our Fields*), in *Zhongguo dianying daoyan de yishu shijie congshu: Xie Fei ji* (The artistic world of Chinese film directors: Xie Fei volume), Beijing: Zhongguo dianying chubanshe, 1998, pp. 191–199.

32. The third-year films also included *The Last Camera Shot* (*Zuihou de jingtou*), which I have not seen: interview with Zhang Yimou, 11 May 1986.

33. Similarly writers of fiction in the "literature of the wounded" (*shanghen wenxue*) that was popular for several years starting in late 1977 also frequently used flashback narration in depicting the "wounds" suffered by characters during the Cultural Revolution.

34. The standard account of this genre is E. Perry Link, Jr., *Mandarin Ducks and Butterflies: Popular Fiction in Early Twentieth-Century Chinese Cities*, Berkeley: University of California Press, 1981.

35. The story bears a resemblance to eminent third-generation director Xie Jin's *The Herdsman* (*Muma ren*), made in 1982. In Xie's film a teacher who was sent to the Inner Mongolian steppes decides to stay there, rejecting the chance to join his wealthy father abroad.

36. Interview with Zheng Guo'en, Beijing, 9 June 1988.
37. Interview with Peng Xiaolian, Shanghai, 1 July 1988; see also a story about the film in the mass circulation *Dazhong dianying* (Popular cinema), 1983, No. 3 (March), p. 8.
38. Interview with Zhang Jianya, Shanghai, 1 July 1988.
39. He went on to co-star in Chen Kaige's *Farewell, My Concubine* (1993).
40. Parts of the theses are reprinted in *1983 Zhongguo dianying nianjian* (Film yearbook), Beijing: Zhongguo dianying chubanshe, 1984, pp. 407–439.
41. *1983 Zhongguo dianying nianjian*, p. 440.
42. *1983 Zhongguo dianying nianjian*, p. 405.
43. Shen Yun, "Liu Miaomiao fangtan lu" (Record of an interview with Liu Miaomiao), *Dangdai dianying*, 1994, No. 6 (December), p. 56.
44. Twenty-eight graduated from the directing department, thirty-two from acting, twenty-six from cinematography, forty from art design, and twenty-seven from sound recording: *1983 Zhongguo dianying nianjian*, p. 440.
45. In conversations in the autumn of 1980 with the class of '82 at the Central Arts and Crafts Academy, it became apparent that the style leaders among Beijing students at the time were their contemporaries from the film academy and the Central Art Academy. A *Dazhong dianying* report on the class of '82 at the film academy is so vague and stereotyped it might have been written without visiting the campus: *Dazhong dianying*, 1979, No. 11 (November), pp. 20–21.
46. Interview with Jiang Haiyang, Shanghai, 15 May 1986.
47. Liu Weihong, "Yu Wu Ziniu tan Wu Ziniu," *Dangdai dianying*, 1988, No. 4 (August), p. 108.
48. Interview with Jiang, 15 May 1986.
49. Interview with Zhang Yimou, Beijing, 11 May 1986.
50. Interview with Wu Ziniu and Ye Nan, Beijing, 11 May 1986.
51. Interview with Zhang Yimou, Beijing, 11 May 1986.
52. Interview with Peng Xiaolian, Beijing, 3 June 1988.
53. Interview with Zhang Li and Liu Miaomiao, Beijing, 4 June 1988.
54. Interview with film academy professor Ni Zhen, Beijing, 22 May 1986.
55. Interview with Wu Ziniu and Ye Nan, Beijing, 11 May 1986.
56. Conversation with directing professor Xie Fei, Beijing, 25 May 1986; conversations in the fall of 1980 at the Central Arts and Crafts Academy with students of that school's class of '82 also bore this out.
57. *Renmin ribao* (People's daily), 8 October 1980, p. 5; an edited English translation is in *Chinese Literature*, January 1981, pp. 107–111. There was of course no mention of this at the memorial meeting for Zhao, chaired by Zhou Yang, which I attended on 27 October 1980 at the People's Art Theatre in Beijing.
58. Interview with Jiang Haiyang, Shanghai, 15 May 1986.

59. Interview with Jiang Haiyang, 15 May 1986; interview with Zhang Yimou, Beijing, 11 May 1986; interview with Wu Ziniu and Ye Nan, 11 May 1986.
60. Interview with Zhang Yimou, Beijing, 11 May 1986.
61. Interview with Tian Zhuangzhuang, Beijing, 8 June 1988.
62. Interview with Ni Zhen, 22 May 1986. Ni had joined the academy faculty in 1980. There were about 500 faculty and staff at the academy in 1980, a typically high proportion of teachers and support staff compared to student numbers in those years in Chinese universities: interview with Chen Kaige, Beijing, 21 November 1980; interview with Jiang Haiyang, Shanghai, 2 December 1980; visit to Beijing Film Academy, 5 November 1980.
63. Interview with Xie Xiaojing, Beijing, 11 July 1988.
64. Interview with Zheng Guo'en, 9 June 1988.
65. Interview with Zhang Yimou, 11 May 1986.
66. Interview with Zhang, 11 May 1986; interview with Zhang Li, 4 June 1988.
67. *Zhongguo wenyi jia*, 2000, No. 1 (January), p. 21.
68. Zheng Guo'en, "Xin shiqi dianying chuangzuo pian yi" (Idle recollections of film creation in the new age), *Dangdai dianying*, 1998, No. 6 (November), p. 61.
69. Interview with Zhang Yimou, 11 May 1986.
70. Interview with Ni Zhen, 22 May 1986. He makes this point also in his *Memoirs from the Beijing Film Academy*.

Part Three

1. *1984 Zhongguo dianying nianjian*, p. 581; *1985 Zhongguo dianying nianjian*, p. 464. Both these films will be discussed in the chapters on their director's works.
2. Details of the origins of the Guangxi studio are from *Zhonghua renmin gongheguo dianying shiye sanshiwunian, 1949–1984*, pp. 208–214. Part of the reason for comparatively low productivity at the major studios was the annual allocation by the Film Bureau of film title quotas to each studio as part of a national plan.
3. Interview with Zheng Guo'en, Beijing Film Academy, 9 June 1988.
4. Much of this background is from "Ouge Zhonghua minzu de haoran zhengqi: Zhang Junzhao tan yingpian 'Yige he bage' de chuangzuo gousi" (In praise of the Chinese people's mighty spirit: Zhang Junzhao on the creative conception of the film *One and Eight*) in *Dianying yishu cankao ziliao* (Reference Materials on film art), 1985, No. 6 (April), pp. 3–7.
5. A list of the sixty-three changes made in the original version of the film, provided by the film crew, together with the censors' rationale for each change, can be found in *Dianying yishu cankao ziliao*, 1985, No. 6 (29 April), pp. 44–52. This is a *neibu* ("internal") publication, although it has wide circulation. A large number of the changes involved not showing Communist soldiers swearing.

6. This coincidence was pointed out by Ni Zhen, professor at the Beijing Film Academy, in an interview there on 22 May 1986.

7. "Chunzhen niandai: Xin shiqi dianying chuangzuo huigu" (A pure age: Recalling filmmaking in the new age), *Dangdai dianying*, 1998, No. 6 (November), p. 50.

8. Zhang Yimou and Xiao Feng, "'Yige he bage' sheying chanshu" (Explanation of the cinematography of *One and Eight*), in *Dianying yishu cankao ziliao*, 1985, No. 6 (29 April), pp. 29–37, 43. The quote is from p. 32. This article was considered of such interest that it was reproduced in *Beijing dianying xueyuan xuebao*, 1985, No. 1 (June), pp. 123–131.

9. He Qun, "Tansuo de jiqing: Xin shiqi dianying chuangzuo huigu" (The fervor of exploration: Recalling filmmaking in the new age), *Dangdai dianying*, 1998, No. 6 (November), p. 55.

10. *Dianying yishu cankao ziliao*, 1985, No. 6 (April), p. 5.

11. These details of pre-production are told best by Bonnie S. McDougall in *The Yellow Earth*, pp. 26–32.

12. All three statements bore the original title of the film, "Silence on the Ancient Plain" (*Guyuan wu sheng*). He Qun's statement is reproduced in Chen Kaiyan, ed., *Huashuo "Huang tudi"* (Talking about *The Yellow Earth*), Beijing: Zhongguo dianying chubanshe, 1986, pp. 298–300. Chen and Zhang's are in typescript, dated 4 April 1984 and 31 March 1984 respectively, in my possession.

13. Chen statement, 4 April 1984, p. 2.

14. Ni Zhen, "Classical Chinese Painting and Cinematographic Signification," in Linda C. Ehrlich and David Desser, eds., *Cinematic Landscapes: Observations on the Visual Arts and Cinema of China and Japan*, Austin: University of Texas Press, 1994, pp. 73–75.

15. Chris Berry and Mary Farquhar, "Post-socialist Strategies: An Analysis of *Yellow Earth* and *Black Cannon Incident*," in Erhlich and Desser, pp. 81–117, especially pp. 95–100.

16. See Zhang Yimou's March 1984 statement, p. 2. In a summary of his experience shooting the film, Zhang made reference to the Chang'an School of traditional painting as an inspiration for his framing in *The Yellow Earth*: see "Wo pai 'Huang tudi': Zhang Yimou tan 'Huang tudi' sheying tihui" (Shooting *The Yellow Earth*: Zhang Yimou talks about his experience filming *The Yellow Earth*), in Chen Kaiyan, pp. 292–293.

17. Jerome Silbergeld, *China into Film: Frames of Reference in Contemporary Chinese Cinema*, London: Reaktion Books, 1999, pp. 15–52, especially p. 50. The concept of suggestion of meaning rather than direct representation (*xieyi*) is stressed by Berry and Farquhar, p. 97.

18. A similarity or concession to mainstream films is Cuiqiao's exaggerated drawing in of breath in shock upon seeing how old her husband is for the first time on

her wedding night. Young women in Chinese films seem prone to breathless gasps like this, in what may well be a male filmmakers' fantasy.

19. Esther C. M. Yau, "*Yellow Earth*: Western Analysis and a Non-Western Text," *Film Quarterly*, Vol. 41, No. 2 (1987–1988), pp. 22–33, reprinted in Chris Berry, ed., *Perspectives on Chinese Cinema*, London: British Film Institute, 1991, pp. 62–79.

20. Mary Farquhar, "The 'Hidden' Gender in *Yellow Earth*," *Screen*, Vol. 32, No. 2 (1992), pp. 154–164, reprinted in Harry H. Kuoshu, *Celluloid China: Cinematic Encounters with Culture and Society*, Carbondale: Southern Illinois University Press, 2002, pp. 220–232.

21. Rey Chow, *Primitive Passions: Visuality, Sexuality, Ethnography, and Contemporary Chinese Cinema*, New York: Columbia University Press, 1995, pp. 92, 106–107.

22. For a typical objection, see Xia Yan's statement to the fifth Golden Rooster Awards committee, reprinted in Chen Kaiyan, pp. 4–6. There is an irony in one of the founders of left-wing filmmaking in Shanghai in the 1930s finding so upsetting a film which suggested a new course for Chinese cinema.

23. McDougall makes this point (*The Yellow Earth*, p. 27) and gives a masterly summary of the critics' charges against the film (pp. 69–82), drawing chiefly on the collection of writings on *The Yellow Earth* edited by Chen Kaiyan, Chen Kaige's sister: *Huashuo "Huang tudi."*

24. For a late-1984 outline of some of these problems by one of China's then leading film critics, see Shao Mujun, "Chinese Film Amidst the Tide of Reform," *East-West Film Journal*, Vol. 1, No. 1 (December 1986), pp. 59–68.

25. An average mainstream film at this time had 100 or more copies struck for domestic distribution.

26. "Huaizhe shenzhi de chizi zhi ai: Chen Kaige tan 'Huang tudi' daoyan tihui" (Cherishing a sincere and pure love: Chen Kaige on the director's understanding of *The Yellow Earth*), in Chen Kaiyan, pp. 264–265. This had first appeared in *Dianying yishu cankao ziliao*, 1984, No. 15 (December), pp. 2–27. It was an interview with Luo Xueying, herself an early supporter of the fifth generation.

27. He Qun, "Tansuo de jiqing" (The enthusiasm of experimentation), *Dangdai dianying*, 1998, No. 6 (November), p. 56.

28. See *Zhonghua renmin gongheguo dianying shiye sanshiwunian, 1949–1984*, pp. 215–216.

29. Interview with Zhang Li, Beijing, 4 June 1988.

30. *The Candidate* also won a prize from the Hunan Culture Bureau. Both Zhang Li and Wu later described Chen Lu's co-directing credit as meaningless: interview with Zhang, 4 June 1988 and with Wu, 5 July 1988.

31. Interview with Wu, 5 July 1988.

32. Interview with Wu Ziniu, Beijing, 11 May 1986. The studio gave Wu a bonus

of 80,000 *yuan* to buy an apartment in Beijing, where his wife worked as a symphony orchestra harpist: interview with Wu, 5 July 1988.

33. The answer print was placed in the underground storage vault in Lintong, near Xi'an, of the Beijing-based China Film Archive: interview with Wu, 5 July 1988.

34. Ye Nan's scripts, including *Naval Battle of 1894 (Jiawu fengyun)*, were in a largely socialist realist vein: see Clark, *Chinese Cinema*, pp. 114–115. For a discussion of the *Unrequited Love* controversy, see Clark, *Chinese Cinema*, pp. 167–172.

35. This account of the making of *Dove Tree* relies chiefly on a joint interview with Wu Ziniu and Ye Nan, Beijing, 11 May 1986 and an interview with cinematographer Zhang Li, Beijing, 10 May 1986.

36. Interview with Wu, 5 July 1988.

37. Interview with Zhang, 10 May 1986.

38. Interview with Zhang, 10 May 1986.

39. Reported in Hua Jun, p. 147.

40. Interview with Wu Ziniu, Beijing, 9 April 1987.

41. Wu Ziniu acknowledged this in an interview when he was waiting for approval of his film: Beijing, 9 April 1987.

42. Interview with Wu, 5 July 1988.

43. Interview with Wu, 5 July 1988.

44. On the question of nationalism in fifth-generation films, see Paul Clark "Reinventing China: The Fifth-Generation Filmmakers," *Modern Chinese Literature*, Vol. 5, No. 1 (Spring 1989), pp. 121–136, especially pp. 133–134.

45. Interview with Wu Ziniu, Beijing, 8 June 1990.

46. Sima died in 1968, at age fifty-two, under Red Guard harassment.

47. Interviews with Wu Ziniu, Fuzhou, 5, 6, and 7 July 1988.

48. Translated from an unsourced director's statement in Chinese in the *13th Hong Kong International Film Festival* (1989) program, p. 77.

49. Interview with Wu, 8 June 1990.

50. From a publicity folder for the film collected from Wu Ziniu in June 1990.

51. See *2000 Zhongguo dianying nianjian* (Film yearbook), Beijing: Zhongguo dianying chubanshe, 2002, pp. 65–66.

52. See *2001 Zhongguo dianying nianjian* (Film yearbook), Beijing: Zhongguo dianying chubanshe, 2003, p. 72.

53. In this context it is worth noting that the modern Chinese expression for "happy ending" (*da tuanjie*) literally means "great unity."

54. See Clark, *Chinese Cinema*, pp. 95–101, and Paul Clark, "Ethnic Minorities in Chinese Films: Cinema and the Exotic," *East-West Film Journal*, Vol. 1, No. 2 (June 1987), pp. 15–31.

55. Interview with Tian Zhuangzhuang, Beijing, 8 June 1988; similar views are reported in Hua Jun, pp. 102, 104.

56. Quoted in Hua, p. 105.

57. Ding Qiao, "Jinyibu duanzheng chuangzuo zhidao sixiang, fanrong shehuizhuyi dianying chuangzuo" (Further correct creative guidance, and make prosperous socialist film creation), reprinted in *1986 Zhongguo dianying nianjian* (Film yearbook), Beijing: Zhongguo dianying chubanshe, 1988, pp. 3–5.

58. Much of this account is based on an interview with Tian Zhuangzhuang, Xi'an, 27 April 1986, almost two months before the film was given final approval for distribution.

59. Interview with Tian, 27 April 1986.

60. Tian Zhuangzhuang, "Hui xiang caoyuan: 'Liechang zhasa,' 'Dao ma zei' paishe huigu" (Recalling the grasslands: Looking back on the making of *On the Hunting Ground* and *Horse Thief*), *Dangdai dianying*, 1998, No. 6 (November), pp. 53–55, especially p. 54.

61. Quoted by Hua, p. 108. Hua Jun goes on to suggest that few viewers ever realized these intentions from seeing the film.

62. Dru C. Gladney reached a similar conclusion, arguing the films were "a shift away from national narrative toward cultural critique": "Tian Zhuangzhuang, the Fifth Generation, and the Minority Film in China," *Public Culture*, Vol. 8, No. 1 (Fall 1995), pp. 161–175, reprinted in Kuoshu, pp. 200–212. The quote is from p. 200.

63. In contrast, *Horse Thief* did rather well in Europe, being one of the top earning foreign films in Great Britain in the year of its release there. The Tibetan setting had instant appeal.

64. The interview is translated by Chris Berry, ed., *Perspectives on Chinese Cinema*, London: British Film Institute, 1991, pp. 127–130.

65. The interview as published ends thus:
    Reporter: Is anything we've said off limits? Will you mind if I just write this interview up?
    Tian: Nothing's off limits. Do your worst! (Berry, *Perspectives*, p. 130).
    In an interview with me in Beijing on 8 June 1988, Tian suggested that, when he started shooting *Horse Thief*, he was convinced it would have commercial appeal. Only abroad had he been proved right.

66. The film was received with relative indifference by Chinese critics and audiences: see Hua, p. 113. This was perhaps because there was little to cite from the film as further evidence of Tian's alleged arrogance towards audiences.

67. "'Yaogun qingnian' dui guanzhong shuo" (*Rock 'n' Roll Kids* speaks to its audience), *Dazhong dianying*, 1989, No. 3 (March), p. 18.

68. Conversations with Tian Zhuangzhuang and BFA graduate Zhang Tielin, Beijing, 11 July 1988. Several of the dancers Tian was directing were from the air force song and dance troupe, an indication of the pervasive nature of the new youth subcultures.

69. *Rock 'n' Roll Kids* was one of the five biggest vote getters for favorite film in the

annual Hundred Flowers readership poll conducted by *Dazhong dianying* in the spring of 1989: *Dazhong dianying*, 1989, No. 9 (September), p. 2.

70. Interview with Tian Zhuangzhuang, 27 April 1986; conversation with Tian, Beijing, 10 April 1987; conversation with Tian, Beijing, 10 June 1990.

71. *Special Operating Room* is listed as a 1992 film co-production between the Xiaoxiang studio and a Hong Kong company in *1993 Zhongguo dianying nianjian* (Film yearbook), Beijing: Zhongguo dianying chubanshe, 1995, p. 64.

72. Liu Xiaoqing, who was accused of tax evasion in 1988 and was in prison in 2002 for the offence, was alleged to have considerable financial resources (including a house in France). Some of these also went toward the film project, in which she starred.

73. Chen Ken, "Wo fang Tian Zhuangzhuang" (A visit with Tian Zhuangzhuang), *Dazhong dianying*, 1988, No. 2 (February), p. 20. Tian went on to note that the pity was that so few Chinese could understand and appreciate the films.

74. Conversation with Tian, 10 June 1990.

75. The other two are Zhang Yimou's *To Live* (1994) and, in part, Chen Kaige's *Farewell, My Concubine* (1993), both discussed below.

76. Some viewers have observed the inconsistency of the boy narrator apparently knowing more than the boy on screen would have known. This does not undermine the impact of the narrative device.

77. Conversation with Tian Zhuangzhuang, Beijing, 9 December 1995.

78. For a brief introduction of the new group, see Harry H. Kuoshu, "*Beijing Bastard*, the Sixth Generation Directors, and 'Generation-X' in China," *Asian Cinema*, Vol. 10, No. 2 (Spring/Summer 1999), pp. 18–28 and Correction in *Asian Cinema*, Vol. 12, No. 1 (Spring/Summer 2001), p. 2.

79. It is formally listed as a 1997 production in *1998–1999 Zhongguo dianying nianjian* (Film yearbook), Beijing: Zhongguo dianying chubanshe, 2001, pp. 112–113.

80. Fei's film is characterized as a "negative" or "passive" (*xiaoji*) work in the standard mainland history of pre-1949 filmmaking, Cheng Jihua and others, *Zhongguo dianying fazhan shi* (History of the development of Chinese film), Beijing: Zhongguo dianying chubanshe, 1963, 1980 second edition, Vol. 2, pp. 269–272. The revival of interest in his work was led by Hong Kong and Taiwan critics. See Gao Xiaomei, ed., *Xiaocheng zhi chun de dianying meixue: Xiang Fei Mu zhijing* (The film aesthetics of *Spring in a Small Town*: A tribute to Fei Mu), Taipei: Guojia dianying ziliaoguan, 1996 and Huang Ailing, ed., *Shiren daoyan: Fei Mu* (Fei Mu, poet director), Hong Kong: Hong Kong Film Critics Society, 1998. See also the respected mainland film historian Li Shaobai's pioneering article: "Zhongguo xiandai dianying de qianqu: Lun Fei Mu he 'Xiaocheng zhi chun' de lishi yiyi" (A pioneer of modern Chinese film: On the historical significance of Fei Mu and *Spring in a Small Town*), *Dianying yishu* (Film art), 1996, Nos. 5 and 6 (October and November), reprinted in *1997 Zhongguo*

dianying nianjian (Film yearbook), Beijing: Zhongguo dianying chubanshe, 1999, pp. 246–259.

81. These views were expressed in production notes and publicity materials (which include a lengthy interview of the director by the actor Jiang Wen) accompanying the film, and in a documentary film made about the production.

82. Dai Jinhua, "Gender and Narrative: Women in Contemporary Chinese Film," in Jing Wang and Tani E. Barlow, eds., *Cinema and Desire: Feminist Marxism and Cultural Politics in the Work of Dai Jinhua*, London: Verso, 2002, p. 133.

83. See, for example, the report on a May 1986 conference on the issue organized by the *Dangdai dianying* editors, reprinted in *1987 Dianying nianjian* (Film yearbook), Beijing: Zhongguo dianying chubanshe, 1988, pp. 8:45–48.

84. Six members of the class of '82 were sent to the army studio, including four from the directing department. Two of these later transferred to the Beijing and Shenzhen studios.

85. Interview with Hu Mei, Beijing, 19 May 1986.

86. The short story is available in Ding Xiaoqi, *Maidenhome* (translated by Chris Berry), Dunedin: Otago University Press, 1993, pp. 1–49. The film script was written by Ding and Kang Liwen, also a friend of Hu Mei.

87. Li had been sent to the Mongolian steppe in 1968. He and fifteen Beijing high-school classmates, all fifteen-year-olds, had been given a choice of Shanxi province or Inner Mongolia. When a recruiter showed them photos of horses on the plains, they all chose the green Mongolian grasslands: short interview with Li Xiaojun, Beijing, 11 July 1988.

88. Hu Mei used this metaphor in an interview, Beijing, 19 May 1986.

89. Similar views were expressed at a formal China Film Association round-table discussion on the film attended by Hu Mei, Li Xiaojun, and myself, Beijing, 10 May 1986.

90. Interview with Hu, 19 May 1986.

91. Silbergeld, pp. 156–170; the quote is from p. 158.

92. Interview with Hu, 19 May 1986. In a later interview with Chris Berry, Hu Mei noted: "I think women have one very important characteristic, and that is that they like talking to themselves, fantasizing and remembering a lot. Especially Chinese women. They internalize a lot." (Chris Berry, "Chinese 'Women's Cinema' Dossier," *Camera obscura*, No. 18 [1988], p. 34.)

93. For a discussion of this term, see Chris Berry, "Chinese 'Women's Cinema' Dossier: Introduction," *Camera obscura*, No. 18 (1988), pp. 5–7.

94. Zhang's film will be briefly discussed below, in "Beyond the Fifth Generation."

95. Interview with Hu Mei, Beijing, 24 May 1986.

96. Interview with Hu Mei, Beijing, 21 September 1987.

97. The family apartment on the screen was decorated with some of Su Zhou's own paintings, which normally hung in the couple's two-room apartment in the Beijing military barracks where Hu Mei had grown up.

98. Interview with Hu Mei, Beijing, 27 May 1990.

99. See Jing Ronghua, ed., *Hu Mei yu 'Yongzheng wangchao'* (Hu Mei and *The Yongzheng Emperor*), Chengdu: Sichuan renmin chubanshe, 1999. Some Chinese critics saw the series as an allegorical eulogy of the present Beijing regime.

100. On He Xin, see Geremie R. Barmé, *In the Red: On Contemporary Chinese Culture*, New York: Columbia University Press, 1999, pp. 38–39 and passim.

101. Perhaps disconcerted by the gothic and camp elements in the film, the official, pre-1949 film history dwells on the film's reliance on *Phantom of the Opera* and its failure to be progressive enough: see Cheng Jihua and others, *Zhongguo dianying fazhan shi*, Vol. 1, pp. 490–491.

102. Interview with Peng Xiaolian, Kaua'i, Hawaii, 8 December 1988. Yang was convinced that the film, with his lurid elaborations, would be popular among contemporary audiences: interview with Yang Yanjin, Shanghai, 14 May 1986.

103. As an in-joke, Bu Lan's father in a photograph at home is in fact Wu Yigong, head of the Shanghai Film Studio, pictured visiting Disney World.

104. These books include John King Fairbank's classic *The United States and China*.

105. Quoted in the catalogue of the First Chinese Film Exhibition, Beijing, September 1987, p. 10. For a somewhat nostalgic view of 1930s modernism, see Leo Ou-fan Lee, *Shanghai Modern*, Cambridge, MA: Harvard University Press, 1999.

106. For some of the prizes won by the film, see *1987 Dianying nianjian*, p. 2:13. The public was less impressed: the film did not secure a Hundred Flowers prize from film magazine readers.

107. Interview with Chris Berry, in *Camera obscura*, No. 18 (1988), p. 28.

108. Interview with Peng Xiaolian, Shanghai, 1 July 1988. Peng even makes a Hitchcockian appearance in the film. While the older woman laments the seduction by a young construction worker of the youngest woman, Peng and a friend walk by, momentarily disturbed by the shouting.

109. See *2001 Zhongguo dianying nianjian*, pp. 83–84.

110. One of the film's scriptwriters was Kong Du, a teacher at the Beijing Film Academy: interview with Liu Miaomiao, Beijing, 4 June 1988.

111. Interview with Liu, Beijing, 10 May 1986.

112. Interview with Liu Miaomiao, Beijing, 7 June 1988.

113. Quoted in Zuo Shula, "Yige he bage: 'Mati sheng sui' paishe wenjian lu" (One and eight: A record of filming *The Sound of Hoofbeats*), *Dazhong dianying*, 1987, No. 10 (October), p. 12.

114. Liu Miaomiao, "Xianhua 'cong ying sheng ya'" (Digressions on "a life in film"), *Dangdai dianying*, 1994, No. 6 (December), p. 64.

115. Interview with Liu, 7 June 1988.

116. *Dangdai dianying*, 1994, No. 6 (December), pp. 64–65.

117. Liu showed her delight in this late recognition, compared to many of her classmates, in a 1994 interview: Shen Yun, "Liu Miaomiao fangtan lu" (Record

of a conversation with Liu Miaomiao), *Dangdai dianying*, 1994, No. 6 (December), pp. 56–62.

118. Chen Baoguang, "Liu Miaomiao: Qi ren ru qi zuo" (Liu Miaomiao: A person like her works), *Dangdai dianying*, 1994, No. 6 (December), p. 71. In the mid-1990s Liu Miaomiao had something akin to a nervous breakdown, from which she recovered.

119. This point is made by Shen Yun, p. 57.

120. Hu Ying, "Beyond the Glow of the Red Lantern: Or, What Does It Mean to Talk about Women's Cinema in China?", in Diana Robin and Ira Jaffe, eds., *Redirecting the Gaze: Gender, Theory, and Cinema in the Third World*, Albany: State University of New York Press, 1999, p. 278.

121. Dai Jinhua, p. 134.

122. For more on the film, see Clark, *Chinese Cinema*, pp. 177–179.

123. Interview with Zhang Jianya, Shanghai, 14 May 1986.

124. Interview with Zhang, 2 July 1988.

125. Zhang found this notion rather engaging when I suggested it to him in mid-1986, even repeating it in an interview in *New Chinese Cinema*, a documentary completed by Tony Rayns in 1987.

126. Wu Yigong, "Yao zuo yi ge re'ai renmin de dianying yishujia" (We must become film artists who deeply love the people), *Guangming ribao* (Guangming daily), 30 April 1987, p. 5. The article is translated by Chris Berry, in Berry, *Perspectives on Chinese Cinema*, pp. 133–139. The translation accompanies Berry's insightful analysis in "Market Forces: China's 'Fifth-Generation' Faces the Bottom Line," pp. 114–125.

127. Wu Yigong, in Berry translation, p. 137.

128. These figures come from an interview with Zhang, 2 July 1988.

129. Interview with Zhang Jianya, Shanghai, 6 July 2000. See *2000 Zhongguo dianying nianjian*, pp. 46–50 for a discussion of the film between Zhang and Ni Zhen, reproduced from the film academy journal.

130. *1983 Zhongguo dianying nianjian*, pp. 407–414.

131. Wu Yonggang's most remarkable film from the 1930s was a milestone. *The Goddess (Shen nü*, 1935), starring Ruan Lingyu, was one of the first films in world cinema to present prostitution in a non-judgemental fashion.

132. For a contemporary critical discussion of Wu Yigong's films, including *Sister*, see Ji Ren, "Lun Wu Yigong de dianying yishu tansuo" (On Wu Yigong's explorations in film art), *Dianying yishu*, 1985, No. 9 (September), pp. 18–24.

133. Joint interview with Jiang Haiyang and Zhang Jianya, Shanghai, 14 May 1986. On these May Fourth literature adaptations, see Clark, *Chinese Cinema*, pp. 109–113.

134. For a discussion of guilt and Cultural Revolution memories, see Anne F. Thurston, *Enemies of the People: The Ordeal of the Intellectuals in China's Great Cultural Revolution*, Cambridge, MA: Harvard University Press, 1988.

135. See also Jiang Haiyang, "Yong yishu ganjue qu gouzhu 'Niming dianhua'" (Using artistic sensation to construct "The Anonymous Phonecall"), *Yishu shijie* (Artistic world), 1988, No. 3, p. 5.

136. See Ni Zhen, *Tansuo de yinmu* (The exploratory silver screen), Beijing: Zhongguo dianying chubanshe, 1994, pp. 110, 232–242. Shao Mujun provided an early discussion in English in "Chinese Film amidst the Tide of Reform," *East-West Film Journal*, Vol. 1, No. 1 (December 1986), pp. 59–68.

137. "Duihua: Yule pian" (Conversation: Entertainment films), *Dangdai dianying*, 1987, No. 3 (May), pp. 31–37. Interestingly, neither Tian nor critic Rao Shuguang mention *On the Hunting Ground* or *Horse Thief* in their published conversation here.

138. For a relatively frank discussion of the crisis, see Lin Lisheng, "Jiushi niandai Zhongguo dianying de jingji biangeng he yishu fenye" (Economic change and artistic differentiation in Chinese cinema in the 1990s), reproduced in *1997 Zhongguo dianying nianjian*, pp. 201–205.

139. One such discussion is in Ni Zhen, ed., *Gaige yu Zhongguo dianying* (Reform and Chinese cinema), Beijing: Zhongguo dianying chubanshe, 1994, pp. 149–190.

140. See *2001 Zhongguo dianying nianjian* (Film yearbook), Beijing: Zhongguo dianying chubanshe, 2003, p. 211.

141. Liu Binyan, China's foremost journalist and later exile, created a fascinating portrait of Wu and his regime at the Xi'an studio in 1986: "Mei shang yinmu de gushi: Ji Xi'an dianying zhipian chang changzhang, daoyan Wu Tianming" (A story that has not reached the screen: On Wu Tianming, head and a director of the Xi'an Film Studio), *Renmin ribao*, 7 and 8 August 1986, p. 8.

142. Zhong Dianfei's mistake had been an article in a December 1956 issue of the *Literary Gazette* (*Wenyi bao*). The piece, titled "Gongs and drums at the movies," had criticized the artistic and box-office failures of Chinese cinema: see Clark, *Chinese Cinema*, pp. 74–75, 77–78.

143. The screenplay is available in an English translation by Bonnie S. McDougall, in Chen Kaige and Tony Rayns, *King of the Children & The New Chinese Cinema*, London: Faber and Faber, 1989. *King of the Children* is one of three "king" novellas by Ah Cheng. The others are *The Chess King* (*Qi wang*), which has also been adapted to film, and *King of the Trees* (*Shu wang*): see Bonnie S. McDougall (trans.), *Three Kings: Three Stories from Today's China*, London: Collins Harvill, 1990.

144. Synchronized sound recording had been attempted before Chen and Wu Ziniu used it. Li Jun, a third-generation director, used it in parts of his *Anxious to Return* (*Gui xin si jian*, 1979) and in all sound-stage shooting of *Xu Mao and His Daughters* (*Xu Mao he ta de nüermen*, 1981): *Dazhong dianying*, 1988, No. 8 (August), p. 31.

145. Interview with Chen Kaige, Beijing, 30 March 1987. Bonnie S. McDougall visited the shooting location and reported considerable tension among the crew.

146. Interview with Chen Kaige, Beijing, 2 April 1987.

147. The Daoist qualities of the film, including its treatment of human beings in nature, are outlined in An Jingfu, "The Pain of a Half Taoist: Taoist Principles, Chinese Landscape Painting, and *King of the Children*," in Ehrlich and Desser, pp. 117–125.

148. Chen noted this in a lengthy and candid interview with Luo Xueying upon completion of the film: "Sikao rensheng, shenshi ziwo: Chen Kaige tan 'Haiziwang' chuangzuo tihui' (Reflecting on life, examining oneself: Chen Kaige on the experience of making *King of the Children*), *Dianying yishu cankao ziliao*, 1987, No. 8 (October), pp. 17–18.

149. In the same interview with Luo Xueying, Chen contrasted his own highly structured primary and early secondary education with Beanpole's efforts: *Dianying yishu cankao ziliao*, 1987, No. 8 (October), p. 11.

150. Rey Chow, pp. 125–128.

151. Jerome Silbergeld points out the use and abuse of the written language as a feature of Chinese avant-garde art of the 1980s: *China into Film*, pp. 267–268.

152. Xudong Zhang associates this aspect with what he suggests somewhat unconvincingly as the "utopianism" of the film: *Chinese Modernism in the Era of Reforms: Cultural Fever, Avant-garde Fiction, and the New Chinese Cinema*, Durham: Duke University Press, 1997, pp. 301–304.

153. Chen and Rayns, *King of the Children*, p. 62.

154. Wu Ziniu, in a 1988 interview, made this point about the film being an expression of the "search for roots" pessimism about Chinese culture: Liu Weihong, *Dangdai dianying*, 1988, No. 4 (August), p. 105.

155. The China Film Corporation, the central organization then in charge of all film distribution in China and of Chinese film exports, had hoped the film would have foreign appeal. The corporation had supplied one half of the 700,000 *yuan* budget, enabling the Xi'an studio to go forward with the project: *Dianying yishu cankao ziliao*, 1987, No. 8 (October), p. 5. French critics at Cannes gave the film the "Golden Alarm Clock" award for the most sleep-inducing movie, a joke seized upon by some conservative Chinese critics.

156. I discovered this at a well-lubricated dinner at the Fujian Film Studio with the cast and crew of Wu Ziniu's *The Joyous Heroes* in July 1988. Liu also played the old man in Wu's *The Mill*.

157. Conversation with Chen Kaige, Beijing, 26 May 1990.

158. Wang Bin, "Di wu dai dianying: Shuailuo yu zaisheng" (Fifth-generation films: Decline and rebirth), *Wenyi zhengming* (Literature and art contention), 1993, No. 1 (January), p. 52.

159. Bonnie S. McDougall, "Cross-dressing in Modern Chinese Fiction, Drama and Film: Reflections on Chen Kaige's *Farewell My Concubine*," in McDougall,

Fictional Authors, Imaginary Audiences: Modern Chinese Literature in the Twentieth Century, Hong Kong: The Chinese University Press, 2003, pp. 115–131.

160. Wendy Larson, "The Concubine and the Figure of History: Chen Kaige's *Farewell, My Concubine*," in Sheldon Hsiao-peng Lu, ed., *Transnational Chinese Cinemas: Identity, Nationhood, Gender*, Honolulu: University of Hawai'i Press, 1997, p. 338.

161. Silbergeld, pp. 96–120, especially pp. 113–119.

162. Yang Yuanying, Preface to *90 niandai de "di wu dai"* (The "fifth generation" in the 1990s), Beijing: Beijing guangbo xueyuan chubanshe, 2000, reprinted in *Dangdai dianying*, 2000, No. 4 (July), p. 92.

163. Chen had had this story in mind for many years. He mentioned it in a piece on *King of the Children* written for *Dangdai dianying*: Chen Kaige, "You 'Haizi wang' de chuangzuo suo xiangdao de" (Thoughts arising from the making of *King of the Children*), *Dangdai dianying*, 1987, No. 4 (August), p. 99.

164. Interview with the British critic Tony Rayns, at which I assisted, Beijing, 27 April 1993.

165. For a list of council members, see *1986 Zhongguo dianying nianjian*, pp. 216–217. Wu Ziniu, fresh from his success with *The Candidate*, was the only other fifth-generation filmmaker elected to the council.

166. Interview with Wu Tianming during the testing of actors, Xi'an, 30 April 1986.

167. Interview with Zhang Yimou, Hong Kong, 13 April 1988.

168. "Zansong shengming, chongshang chuangzao: Zhang Yimou tan 'Hong gaoliang' chuangzuo tihui" (Extolling life, upholding creativity: Zhang Yimou talks about his experience making *Red Sorghum*), interview with Luo Xueying, *Dianying yishu cankao ziliao*, 1988, No. 4 (February), p. 15.

169. Interview with Zhang, 13 April 1988.

170. Zhang Yimou interview, *Dianying yishu cankao ziliao*, 1988, No. 4 (February), pp. 16–17, 23.

171. Zheng Dongtian, "The Winds of Change," *China Screen* (in English), 1988, No. 3 (September), p. 24.

172. Interview with Zhang, 13 April 1988. See also Zhang Yimou interview, *Dianying yishu cankao ziliao*, 1988, No. 4 (February), pp. 32, 35–37.

173. Zhang Yimou, "Chang yi zhi shengming de zan'ge" (Sing a song of praise for life), *Dangdai dianying*, 1988, No. 2 (March), p. 82.

174. See, for example, "D.W.", "'Hong gaoliang' shi chouhua Zhongguoren de yingpian" (*Red Sorghum* is a film which makes Chinese look ugly), *Zhongguo dianying bao* (China film news), 5 May 1988, p. 2. For a summary (and rejection) of critical views, see Li Houji, "Chou yu mei you?!: 'Hong gaoliang' guan hou" (Ugly or beautiful: On watching *Red Sorghum*), *Tianjin ribao* (*Tianjin daily*), 15 August 1988, p. 5. Typical praise can be found in Wang

Xiaobu, "'Hong gaoliang' de guanzhong" (*Red Sorghum*'s audiences), *Zhongguo dianying bao*, 5 May 1988, p. 2.

175. Zhang Yimou interview, *Dianying yishu cankao ziliao*, 1988, No. 4 (February), pp. 23–24.

176. According to the author Mo Yan, the original film script was called "Nine-nine Green Murderer's Crossing" (*Jiu jiu Qingshakou*), after the name of the wild sorghum fields, before being changed to *Red Sorghum*: Mo Yan, "Gaoliang di li de Jiang Wen" (Jiang Wen in the land of sorghum), *Huaxia jiyi* (China memories), 1998, No. 9 (September), p. 20.

177. *Tracks in the Snowy Forest* (*Linhai xueyuan*, published in 1956), for example, which in turn formed the source for *Taking Tiger Mountain by Strategy* (*Zhiqu Weihushan*), one of the "revolutionary modern Peking operas" propagated by the Cultural Revolution group led by Jiang Qing.

178. Zhang Yimou interview, *Dianying yishu cankao ziliao*, 1988, No. 4 (February), p. 18.

179. This account of the project is based on several extensive conversations with Zhang Yimou in Beijing in June 1988.

180. The first non-Japanese Asian film was *Salaam Bombay* at the 1990 awards. The U.S. print of the film was titled *Ju Dou*. The two Chinese characters are the protagonist's given names and are usually rendered as one word in standard romanization.

181. For a discussion of the use of color in the film and Chinese aesthetic principles, see Jenny Kwok Wah Lau, "*Judou*: An Experiment in Color and Portraiture in Chinese Cinema," in Ehrlich and Desser, pp. 127–145. Lau elsewhere has discussed the Chineseness of the film, focusing on concepts of *yin* (excessive eroticism) and *xiao* (filial piety): Jenny Kwok Wah Lau, "*Judou*: A Hermeneutical Reading of Cross-cultural Cinema," *Film Quarterly*, Vol. 45, No. 2 (1991), pp. 2–10.

182. In the summer of 1990, in the midst of discussions in Beijing with the Taiwan producer of his next film, Zhang was greatly distracted by what he saw as Xiao Hua's obstinacy.

183. Many urban Chinese had seen both films already on videotapes originating in Hong Kong and Taiwan and circulated unofficially in China. About 250 prints of each film were struck, indicating big box-office appeal.

184. Interview with Zhang Yimou, Beijing, 27 April 1992.

185. Chen Kaige, "Qinguo ren: Ji Zhang Yimou" (A son of Qin: on Zhang Yimou), *Dangdai dianying*, 1985, No. 4 (July), pp. 101–107. This is reprinted in China Film Association, ed., *Lun Zhang Yimou* (On Zhang Yimou), Beijing: Zhongguo dianying chubanshe, 1994, pp. 281–292.

186. Conversation with Zhang Yimou, Honolulu, 4 November 1995.

187. Sheldon Hsiao-peng Lu, "National Cinema, Cultural Critique, Transnational Capital: The Films of Zhang Yimou," in Sheldon Lu, ed., pp. 105–136.

188. Rey Chow, *Primitive Passions*, p. 171.

189. See, among other writings, Wang Yichuan, "Zhang Yimou shenhua yu chao yuyan zhanlüe" (The Zhang Yimou myth and ultra-fable strategies), *Tianjin shehui kexue* (Tianjin social science), 1993, September, pp. 78–85; Wang Yichuan, "Wo xing de hai shi ta xing de 'Zhongguo'?: Zhang Yimou yingpian de yuanshi qingdiao chanshi" (Mine or his "China"? An interpretation of the primitive sentiment in Zhang Yimou's films), *Zhongguo wenhua yanjiu* (China cultural research), 1994, Winter, pp. 67–72; Wang Yichuan, "Zhang Yimou shenhua: Zhongjie ji qi yiyi" (The Zhang Yimou myth: The end and its significance), *Wenyi yanjiu* (Literature and art research), 1997, No. 5 (September), pp. 68–79; Wang Yichuan, *Zhang Yimou shenhua de zhongjie: Shenmei yu wenhua shiye zhong de Zhang Yimou dianying* (The end of the Zhang Yimou myth: Zhang Yimou's films in aesthetic and cultural perspective), Zhengzhou: Henan renmin chubanshe, 1998. A chapter by Wang is included in one of the more serious collections of Chinese writings on Zhang: *Lun Zhang Yimou* (On Zhang Yimou), Beijing: Zhongguo dianying chubanshe, 1994.

190. See an interview with Zhang Yimou by Beijing Film Academy professor Huang Shixian, "Yi 'xiao' bo 'da'," jianshou yi fang jingtu" (Using the "small" to combat the "large": Sticking to the Pure Land [of China]), *Dianying yishu*, 2000, No. 1 (January), pp. 10–17, especially p. 14.

191. I judged this over a goose-head meal in a Guizhou-style restaurant in Beijing with Zhang and Zhang, 27 July 1999. Zhang Ziyi went on to star with a part of greater substance in Ang Lee's *Crouching Tiger, Hidden Dragon*.

192. In an interview soon after completing the film, Zhang Yimou noted that the novel from which it was drawn, *Remembrance* (*Jinian*), had followed the father's political troubles from the 1950s until the present. Zhang decided that the time of first romance between the parents allowed for what he wanted from the film: *Dianying yishu*, 2000, No. 1 (January), p. 11.

193. Zhang interview, *Dianying yishu*, 2000, No. 1 (January), p. 12. *Titanic* had dominated the Chinese box-office in 1998: see, for example, despite its numerous errors, Ying Zhu, *Chinese Cinema in the Era of Reform: The Ingenuity of the System*, Westport: Praeger, 2003, p. 144.

194. In his defence, Zhang argued that this was the only kind of film he was able to make in the current cultural climate: conversation with Zhang Yimou, Beijing, 23 June 2004.

195. See, for example, Wang Yichuan, "'Wu dai qi' Zhongguo dianying" (A period without generations in Chinese film), *Dangdai dianying*, 1994, No. 5 (September), pp. 20–27, especially p. 20.

196. See Clark, *Chinese Cinema*, especially Chapter IV, pp. 94–118.

197. For a recent account of those times in literature, see Perry Link, *The Uses of Literature: Life in the Socialist Chinese Literary System*, Princeton: Princeton University Press, 2000.

198. See Clark, *Chinese Cinema*, Chapter V, pp. 125–148 on the Cultural Revolution, and pp. 160–167 on the films of the late 1970s and early 1980s.

199. Huang Jianzhong, "Feng ji tian gao: Dianying xin shiqi, wo de shijiao" (Strong winds and high skies: The new age in film, my point of view), *Dangdai dianying*, 1998, No. 6 (November), p. 53.

200. For a brief discussion of the presentation of non-Han peoples in the film, see Esther C. M. Yau, "Is China the End of Hermeneutics?; or, Political and Cultural Usage of Non-Han Women in Mainland Chinese Films," *Discourse*, 11, 2 (1989), 114–136.

201. This point is also noted by Jerome Silbergeld, pp. 81–84.

202. Interview with Huang Jianzhong, Beijing, 21 April 1986: conversation with Huang Jianzhong, Beijing, 6 July 2002.

203. Interview with Zhang Jianya, Shanghai, 16 May 1986.

204. Interview with Zhang Jianya, Shanghai, 20 March 1987. *Hibiscus Town* is discussed by Nick Browne in "Society and Subjectivity: On the Political Economy of Chinese Melodrama," in Nick Browne, Vivian Sobchak and Paul Pickowicz, eds., *New Chinese Cinemas: Forms, Identities, Politics*, New York: Cambridge University Press, 1994, pp. 40–56. Jerome Silbergeld offers a masterful and lengthy analysis, pp. 188–233.

205. The following biographical details are drawn largely from an interview with Huang Jianxin, Beijing, 5 June 1988, supplemented with a briefer interview in Beijing on 19 August 2000.

206. Chai Xiaofeng, "Huang Jianxin fangtan lu" (Record of an interview with Huang Jianxin), *Dangdai dianying*, 1994, No. 2 (March), p. 43.

207. For a discussion of Lü Ban and the fate of his comedies, see Clark, *Chinese Cinema*, pp. 72, 73–74, 77.

208. Chai Xiaofeng, *Dangdai dianying*, 1994, No. 2 (March), p. 40.

209. The visual effects of the film are discussed in Chris Berry and Mary Ann Farquhar, "Post-Socialist Strategies: An Analysis of *Yellow Earth* and *Black Cannon Incident*," in Ehrlich and Desser, pp. 100–110.

210. Interview with Huang Jianxin, Xi'an, 26 April 1986.

211. Chai Xiaofeng, *Dangdai dianying*, 1994, No. 2 (March), p. 37.

212. See also Huang Jianxin, "'Lunhui' daoyan chanshu" (*Samsara* director's explanation), in Zhang Zilian and Zhu Zi, eds., *Huang Jianxin zuopin ji* (Collected works of Huang Jianxin), Xi'an: Huayue chubanshe, 1989, pp. 204–206. Jerome Silbergeld notes the modernism of *Samsara*, in contrast to typical fifth-generation rural settings, pp. 86–88.

213. The Tian'anmen Square sequence was not in the original story. In a conversation on location for *Samsara*, Huang thought that the subject-matter of the film would be gone in a few years. The Wang Shuo story was already two years old. Huang had hoped to film it before making *Dislocation*. Zhao Fei, a member of the class of '78, was cinematographer on *Samsara*: conversation with

Huang and Zhao, Beijing, 5 June 1988. In May 1990 Huang went to Australia on a scholarship. He returned to China in 1992 and specialized in comedies on contemporary life.

214. For a brief discussion of the film, see Clark, *Chinese Cinema*, p. 164.

215. See Zhang Zeming, "Di yi bu de changshi: 'Juexiang' yishu zongjie" (A first attempt: Summing up the art of *Swansong*), in *1986 Zhongguo dianying nianjian*, pp. 4:64–67.

216. The biographical outlines for Zhou and Fang Fang are from a joint interview, Beijing, 6 April 1987. Details on the productions come from this interview and from interviews with Zhou in Xi'an (17 June 1988) and Beijing (8 June 1990).

Conclusion

1. Huang Jianxin, "Duanxiang" (Random thoughts), *Dangdai dianying*, 1998, No. 6 (November), p. 58.

2. For a superb view of this (from 1987) see Bonnie S. McDougall, "Breaking Through: Literature and the Arts in China, 1976–1986," in McDougall, *Fictional Authors, Imaginary Audiences*, pp. 171–204.

3. Chen Mo identifies *Red Sorghum* as a turning point in his "Xin shiqi dianying chuangzuo yu shichang guannian" (Filmmaking in the new age and conceptions of the market), *Dangdai dianying*, 1998, No. 6 (November), p. 22. Wang Yichuan also makes this point, in his "'Wu dai qi' Zhongguo dianying," pp. 20–27, especially pp. 23 and 26.

4. See Clark, *Chinese Cinema*, pp. 167–172.

5. The senior critic Shao Mujun made this point in a 1998 interview: "Cong shijie jiaodu kan Zhongguo dianying" (Chinese film from an international perspective), *Dangdai dianying*, 1998, No. 6 (November), pp. 58–59. Huang Jianxin acknowledged this in 1994: Chai Xiaofeng, *Dangdai dianying*, 1994, No. 2 (March), p. 39.

6. One commonly cited statistic saw the number of TV sets in China rising from about 10 million in 1980 to over 200 million by the early 1990s.

7. Ding Yaping, "Zhuanhuan yu weiyi: Xin shiqi di yi ge shi nian (1979–1989) dianying zonglun" (Transition and displacement: A summing up of the first ten years of the new age), *Dangdai dianying*, 1998, No. 6 (November), p. 11.

8. For audience changes in the twenty years after 1978, see Chen Mo, "Xin shiqi dianying chuangzuo yu shichang guannian" (Film making and the market idea), *Dangdai dianying*, 1998, No. 6 (November), pp. 19–24.

9. Ding Yaping argues that the concept of generations in Chinese filmmaking only made sense in the 1970s and 1980s: *Dangdai dianying*, 1998, No. 6 (November), p. 12.

10. Interview with Chen Kaige, Beijing, 21 November 1980.

11. This is a point made by Yang Yuanying, in the preface to a collection of articles on the fifth generation in the 1990s, published in 2000, and reprinted in *Dangdai dianying*, 2000, No. 4 (July), pp. 90–94.

Chinese Film Title List

—∭—

This list includes all Chinese films mentioned in this book, and one Japanese film made by a Chinese director.

Anonymous Phonecall, The	匿名电话
Anxious to Return	归心似箭
Army Nurse	女儿楼
At the Beach	海滩
Back Alley	小街
Behind the Movie Screen	在银幕后面
Big Parade, The	大阅兵
Black-Cannon Incident, The	黑炮事件
Black Mountain Road	黑山路
Bloody Morning	血色清晨
Blue Kite, The	蓝风筝
Blush	红粉
Boxers, The	拳击手
Breaking with Old Ideas	决裂
Camel Bell in the Desert, The	沙漠驼铃
Candidate, The	候补队员
Chen Huansheng Goes to Town	陈涣生上城
City of Sadness, A	悲情城市
Codename Cougar (a.k.a. The Puma Action)	代号「美洲豹」
Courtyard, The	小院
Crash Landing	紧急迫降
Crouching Tiger, Hidden Dragon	卧虎藏龙

Delamu	德拉姆
Desperation	最后的疯狂
Dislocation	错位
Dog to Kill, A	犬杀
Dove Tree	鸽子树
Drum-singers, The	鼓书艺人
Early Spring in February	早春二月
East is Red, The	东方红
Emperor and the Assassin, The	荆轲刺秦王
Evening Bell	晚钟
Family Scandal	家丑
Far from War	远离战争的年代
Farewell, My Concubine	霸王别姬
Fighting North and South	南征北战
For Fun	找乐
Forced Take-off	强行起飞
Four Apprentices	四个学徒工
Fragile Skiff, The	一叶小舟
Glorious Festival, The	盛大的节日
Goddess, The	神女
Good Woman, A	良家归女
Goodbye to Yesterday	向昨天告别
Great Waters, The	大水
Haixia	海霞
Happy Times	幸福时光
Herdsman, The	牧马人
Hero	英雄
Hero Zheng Chenggong, The	英雄郑成功
Heroic Sons and Daughters	英雄儿女
Hibiscus Town	芙蓉镇
Horse Thief	盗马贼
House of Flying Daggers	十面埋伏
How Steel is Made	钢铁是这样炼成的
Ice River	冰河生死线

Illegal Lives (a.k.a. Special Operating Room) 非法生命 (a.k.a. 特别手术室)
In the Wild Mountains 野山
In Their Prime 他们正年轻
Innocent Babbler 杂嘴子

Joyous Heroes, The 欢乐英雄
Judou 菊豆

Keep Cool 有话，好好说
Kidnapping von Karajan 绑架卡拉扬
King of Chess 棋王
King of the Children 孩子王

Last Camera Shot, The 最后的镜头
Last Day of Winter, The 最后一个冬日
Last Sunrise, The 最后的太阳
Li Lianying, the Imperial Eunuch 大太监李莲英
Li Shuangshuang 李双双
Liang Shanbo and Zhu Yingtai 梁山伯与祝英台
Liao Zhongkai 廖仲恺
Life on a String 边走边唱
Lights for Ten Thousand Homes 万家灯火
Lin Family Shop, The 林家铺子
Longing for Home 乡情

Magic Umbrella, The 可可的魔伞
Man at Forty, A 四十不惑
Manzan Benigaki 满山红柿
Marksman, The 无枪枪手
Marriage 结婚
Me and My Classmates 我和我的同学们
Merchant Shipping Tale, A 远洋轶事
Mill, The 大磨坊
Mine Warfare 地雷战
Mountains of the Sun 太阳山

Nanjing Massacre, The 南京大屠杀
National Anthem, The 国歌

Naval Battle of 1894, The	甲午风云
New Year's Sacrifice	祝福
Night Rain on the River	巴山夜雨
Not One Less	一个都不能少

Obsession	疯狂的代价
Old Well	老井
On the Beat	民警故事
On the Hunting Ground	猎场扎撒
Once Upon a Time in Shanghai	上海纪事
One and Eight	一个和八个
Our Corner	我们的角落
Our Fields	我们的田野

| Probationary Lawyer | 见习律师 |
| Promise, The | 无极 |

| Questions for the Living | 死者对生者的访问 |

Raise the Red Lantern	大红灯笼高高挂
Realm Between the Living and the Dead, The	阴阳界
Red Elephant, The	红象
Red Shores	红岸
Red Sorghum	红高粱
Rejoicing in Cold Creek Commune	欢腾的小凉河
Revolutionary Family, A	革命家庭
Rickshaw Boy	骆驼祥子
Road Home, The	我的父亲母亲
Rock 'n' Roll Kids	摇滚青年
Romance in Philately	邮缘

Sacrificed Youth	青春祭
Samsara (a.k.a. Transmigration)	轮回
San Mao Joins the Army	三毛从军记
Secret Decree	喋血黑谷
September	九月
Shangrao Concentration Camp	上饶集中营
Shanghai Triad	摇啊摇，摇到外婆桥

Sister	姐姐
So Close to Paradise (a.k.a. The Girl from Vietnam)	扁担姑娘 (a.k.a. 越南姑娘)
Song at Midnight, The	夜半歌声
Sound of Hoofbeats, The	马蹄声碎
Special Task (a.k.a. A Thousand Year Enterprise)	特殊任务 (a.k.a. 千秋业)
Spring in a Small Town	小城之春
Story of Qiuju, The	秋菊打官司
Summer Experience, A	夏天的经历
Sun Showers	太阳雨
Sun Yat-sen	孙中山
Swansong	绝响
Taking Tiger Mountain by Strategy	智取威虎山
Target, The (a.k.a. This Train's Last Stop)	目标 (a.k.a. 本次列车的终点)
Temptress Moon	风月
Terracotta Warrior, A	秦佣
Three-Family Alley	三家巷
Three Women	女人的故事
To Live	活着
Together	和你在一起
Tribulations of a Chinese Gentleman, The	少爷的磨难
Tunnel Warfare	地道战
Twenty-six Girls	二十六个姑娘
Under the Bridge	大桥下面
Unforgettable Battle, The	难忘的战斗
University in Exile	流亡大学
Unrequited Love	苦恋
Visions from a Jail Cell	魔窟中的幻想
We Are Still Young	我们还年轻
White-Coated Fighter	白衣战士
White-Haired Girl, The	白毛女

Xiao Hua	小花
Xu Mao and His Daughters	许毛和他的女儿们
Yellow Earth, The	黄土地
Yinyang Man	阴阳人
Yongzheng Emperor, The	雍正王朝

Suggested Reading

—ɯ—

Barmé, Geremie and Linda Jaivin, eds., *New Ghosts, Old Dreams: Chinese Rebel Voices*, New York: Times Books, 1992.

Barmé, Geremie and John Minford, eds., *Seeds of Fire: Chinese Voices of Conscience*, New York: The Noonday Press, 1989.

Berry, Chris, "Chinese New Women's Cinema," "Interview with Zhang Nuanxin," Interview with Hu Mei, *Camera Obscura*, No. 18 (1988), pp. 8–41.

——"Chinese Urban Cinema: Hyper-realism Versus Absurdism," *East-West Film Journal*, Vol. 3, No. 1 (1988), pp. 76–88.

——"Neither One Thing nor Another: Toward a Study of the Viewing Subject and Chinese Cinema in the 1980s," in Nick Browne et al., eds., *New Chinese Cinemas: Forms, Identities, Politics*, Cambridge: Cambridge University Press, 1994, pp. 88–115.

——ed., *Chinese Films in Focus: 25 New Takes*, London: British Film Institute, 2003.

——ed., *Perspectives on Chinese Cinema*, enlarged and revised edition, London: British Film Institute, 1991.

Berry, Chris and Mary Ann Farquhar, *Cinema and Nation, China on Screen*, New York: Columbia University Press, 2005.

——"Post-Socialist Strategies: An Analysis of *Yellow Earth* and *Black Cannon Incident*," in Linda C. Ehrlich and David Desser, eds., *Cinematic Landscapes: Observations on the Visual Arts and Cinema of China and Japan*, Austin: University of Texas Press, 1994, pp. 81–116.

Braester, Yomi, *Witness against History: Literature, Film, and Public Discourse in Twentieth-Century China*, Stanford: Stanford University Press, 2003.

Browne, Nick, Paul G. Pickowicz, Vivian Sobchack and Esther Yau, eds., *New Chinese Cinemas: Forms, Identities, Politics*, Cambridge: Cambridge University Press, 1994.

Chen, Kaige and Tony Rayns, *King of the Children & The New Chinese Cinema*, London: Faber and Faber, 1989.

Chow, Rey, *Primitive Passions: Visuality, Sexuality, Ethnography, and Contemporary Chinese Cinema*, New York: Columbia University Press, 1995.

Clark, Paul, "China: Reframing History," in Aruna Vasudev, Latika Padgaonkar and Rashmi Doraiswamy, eds., *Being & Becoming: The Cinemas of Asia*, New Delhi: Macmillan India, 2002, pp. 64–91.

——*Chinese Cinema: Culture and Politics since 1949*, Cambridge: Cambridge University Press, 1987.

——"Ethnic Minorities in Chinese Films: Cinema and the Exotic," *East-West Film Journal*, Vol. 1, No. 2 (1987), pp. 15–31.

——"Filmmaking in China: From the Cultural Revolution to 1981," *China Quarterly*, No. 94 (1983), pp. 304–322.

——"Reinventing China: The Fifth-Generation Filmmakers," *Modern Chinese Literature*, Vol. 5, No. 1 (1989), pp. 121–136.

——"The Sinification of Cinema: The Foreignness of Film in China," in Wimal Dissanayake, ed., *Cinema and Cultural Identity: Reflections on Films from Japan, India, and China*, Lanham: University Press of America, 1988, pp. 175–184.

Cornelius, Sheila with Ian Haydn Smith, *New Chinese Cinema: Challenging Representations*, London: Wallflower, 2002.

Cui, Shuqin, *Women through the Lens: Gender and Nation in a Century of Chinese Cinema*, Honolulu: University of Hawai'i Press, 2003.

Donald, Stephanie, *Public Secreto, Public Spaces: Cinma and Civility in China*, Lanham: Rowan & Littlefield, 2000.

Farquhar, Mary Ann, "The 'Hidden' Gender in *Yellow Earth*," *Screen*, Vol. 33, No. 2 (1992), pp. 154–164.

Gladney, Dru C., "Representing Nationality in China: Refiguring Majority/Minority Identity," *Journal of Asian Studies*, Vol. 53, No. 1 (1994), pp. 92–123.

——"Tian Zhuangzhuang, the Fifth Generation, and Minorities Films in China," *Public Culture*, Vol. 8, No. 1 (1995), pp. 161–175.

Kuoshu, Harry H., "*Beijing Bastard*, Sixth Generation Directors, and 'Generation X' in China," *Asian Cinema*, Vol. 10, No. 2 (1999), pp. 18–28 [and Correction, *Asian Cinema*, Vol. 12 (2001), p. 2].

——*Celluloid China: Cinematic Encounters with Culture and Society*, Carbondale: Southern Illinois University Press, 2002.

Lau, Jenny Kwok Wah, "*Farewell, My Concubine*: History, Melodrama and Ideology in Contemporary Pan-Chinese Cinema," *Film Quarterly*, Vol. 49, No. 1 (1995), pp. 16–27.

——"*Ju Dou*: A Hermeneutical Reading of Cross-Cultural Cinema," *Film Quarterly*, Vol. 45, No. 2 (1991–92), pp. 2–10.

——"*Ju Dou*: An Experiment in Color and Portraiture in Chinese Cinema," in Linda C. Ehrlich and David Desser, eds., *Cinematic Landscapes: Observations on the Visual Arts and Cinema of China and Japan*, Austin: University of Texas Press, 1994, pp. 127–145.

Li, H. C., "Color, Character, and Culture: On *Yellow Earth, Black Cannon Incident*, and *Red Sorghum*," *Modern Chinese Literature*, Vol. 5, No. 1 (1989), pp. 91–119.

Link, Perry, *The Uses of Literature: Life in the Socialist Chinese Literary System*, Princeton: Princeton University Press, 2000.

Lu, Sheldon Hsiao-peng, ed., *Transnational Chinese Cinemas: Identity, Nationhood, Gender*, Honolulu: University of Hawai'i Press, 1997.

Lu, Tonglin, *Confronting Modernity in the Cinemas of Taiwan and Mainland China*, Cambridge: Cambridge University Press, 2002.

McDougall, Bonnie S., *Fictional Authors, Imaginary Audiences: Modern Chinese Literature in the Twentieth Century*, Hong Kong: The Chinese University Press, 2003.

——*The Yellow Earth: A Film by Chen Kaige*, Hong Kong: The Chinese University Press, 1991.

McDougall, Bonnie S. and Kam Louie, *The Literature of China in the Twentieth Century*, New York: Columbia University Press, 1997.

Ni, Zhen, *Memoirs from the Beijing Film Academy: The Genesis of China's Fifth-Generation*, translated by Chris Berry, Durham: Duke University Press, 2002.

Pickowicz, Paul G., "Popular Cinema and Political Thought in Post-Mao China: Reflections on Official Pronoucements, Films and the Film Audience," in Perry Link et al., eds., *Unofficial China: Popular Culture and Thought in the People's Republic*, Boulder: Westview Press, 1989, pp. 37–53.

Rayns, Tony, "The Narrow Path: Chen Kaige in Conversation with Tony Rayns," in John Boorman and Walter Donohue, eds., *Projections 3: Filmmakers on Filmmaking*, London: Faber, 1994, pp. 47–58.

Semsel, George S., ed., *Chinese Film: The State of the Art in the People's Republic*, New York: Praeger, 1987.

——*Chinese Film Theory: A Guide to the New Era*, New York: Praeger, 1990.

——*Film in Contemporary China: Critical Debates, 1979–1989*, New York: Praeger, 1993.

Silbergeld, Jerome, *China in Film: Frames of Reference in Contemporary Chinese Cinema*, London: Reaktion, 1999.

Tam, Kwok-kan and Wimal Dissanayake, *New Chinese Cinema*, Hong Kong: Oxford University Press (China) Ltd., 1998.

Tang, Xiaobing, *Chinese Modern: The Heroic and the Quotidian*, Durham: Duke University Press, 2000.

——"Configuring the Modern Space: Cinematic Representation of Beijing and Its Politics," *East-West Film Journal*, Vol. 8, No. 2 (1994), pp. 47–69.

Wang, Jing, *High Culture Fever: Politics, Aesthetics, and Ideology in Deng's China*, Berkeley: University of California Press, 1996.

Wang, Jing and Tani Barlow, eds., *Cinema and Desire: Feminist Marxism and Cultural Politics in the Work of Dai Jinhua*, London: Verso, 2001.

Wang, Shujen, *Framing Piracy: Globalization and Film Distribution in Greater China*, Lanham: Rowman & Littlefield, 2003.

Widmer, Ellen and David Der-wei Wang, eds., *From May Fourth to June Fourth: Fiction and Film in Twentieth-Century China*, Cambridge, MA: Harvard University Press, 1993.

Zhang, Xudong, *Chinese Modernism in the Era of Reforms: Cultural Fever, Avant-garde Film, and the New Chinese Cinema*, Durham: Duke University Press, 1997.

Zhang, Yingjin, *Chinese National Cinema*, London: Routledge, 2004.

——"Ideology of the Body in *Red Sorghum*: National Allegory, National Roots, and Third Cinema," *East-West Film Journal*, 4 (1990) 2, pp. 38–53.

——*Screening China: Critical Interactions, Cinematic Reconfigurations and the Transnational Imaginary in Contemporary Chinese Cinema*, Ann Arbor: Center for Chinese Studies, 2002.

Zhang, Yingjin et al., eds., *Encyclopaedia of Chinese Film*, London: Routledge, 1998.

Zhu, Ying, *Chinese Cinema in the Era of Reform: The Ingenuity of the System*, Westport: Praeger, 2003.

Index

—⁓—